Caring Families

DATE DUE

NO 09 '05			
NO 07 '95			
AP 20 '96			
AP 22 '96			
AP 20 '98			
AP 13 '98			
AP 14 '00			
AP 21 '00			
MR 22 '04			
MR 31 '04			
AP 08 05			
FE 15 08			
MAY 0 1 '12			
APR 23 '12			

Caring Families

Supports and Interventions

Deborah S. Bass

NASW PRESS

National Association of Social Workers, Inc.
7981 Eastern Avenue
Silver Spring, MD 20910

Richard L. Edwards, *President*
Mark G. Battle, *Executive Director*

Library of Congress Cataloging-in-Publication Data

Bass, Deborah S.
  Caring families: Supports and interventions / Deborah S. Bass
    p.   cm.
  Includes bibliographical references and index.
  ISBN 0-87101-185-9
  1. Aged—Care—United States. 2. Parents, Aged—Home care—United
States. 3. Caregivers—United States. 4. Children—Care—United
States. 5. Mentally handicapped—Home care—United States.
I. National Association of Social Workers. II. Title.
HV1461.B36   1990
362.82—dc20   90-6277
                                         CIP

Printed in the United States of America
Cover design by
Janice Mauroschadt Design
Cover: Detail from *Ballet Scene;* Edgar Degas; National
Gallery of Art, Washington; Chester Dale Collection

This book is dedicated to my father, Ralph Bass, who cared for my grandparents more than 16 years before they died and gave us strength during his own illness and death.

Contents

Foreword

Most families do not desert family members who need care. Families take care of their own, even when it means totally reorganizing their lives to do so. In today's world, ongoing or periodic need for family caregiving often means a complete revamping of usual family activities because the task is increasingly complex and demanding. Caregivers, principally women, face the dual demands of the work world and the home. On the one hand, their continued employment is an even greater necessity because of the often astronomical medical costs; on the other, the time required to provide care can equal a full-time job. The problems are exacerbated when more than one family member—an elderly parent and a young child, for example, or more than one adult—needs care.

Clearly, these families need support. And social workers have been providing support to caregiving families since Mary Richmond began her work in Baltimore. Over the past 100 years, as the needs of caregiving families grew more complex, so did the needs of social workers who provide supports and interventions.

The products and services provided by the National Association of Social Workers (NASW) have evolved in an effort to meet these growing needs. Recent products that are very specific to family caregiving have been based on previous policy statements and materials that were broader in scope. For example, when NASW presented *A National Social Agenda for America's Families* to the presidential campaign committees in 1988, the document included a call for priority attention to and adequate federal funding for a number of caregiver support systems, such as family leave, respite care, caregiver income supports, child care, and so forth. In 1989, the NASW Commission on Family and Primary Associations began the work of building a consultation network based on a set of family support principles that address the needs of family caregivers and the professionals who assist them.

Each year, NASW conducts a major public education campaign on a social policy theme. Building on previous themes such as Aging Parents, Children in Poverty, AIDS, and Homelessness, the

Board of Directors approved a two-year campaign on Strengthening Families for 1990 and 1991. The family caregiving component of the public education campaign makes note of the profound changes in family structure that necessitate new services to families.

Publication of *Caring Families: Supports and Interventions* is a milestone in NASW's recognition of social work's continuing commitment to finding better ways to help families. Because NASW represents a practice profession, we are particularly pleased to publish this book that is directed toward practitioners and the families they support. Deborah Bass offers social workers and other professionals technology to facilitate their work; she provides families an empathic and well-informed description of the challenges they face. I recommend the entire book to both groups, with particular emphasis on the final chapter, which outlines future initiatives. As we work together, we can help forge a brighter vision for all families.

MARK G. BATTLE, ACSW
Executive Director
National Association of Social Workers

Introduction

Caring families are part of the history of the United States. They are the source of support for most people. So why is caregiving suddenly receiving attention? Are caregiving functions unlike those of the past? Caregiving always has included routine activities such as shopping or housecleaning and the intimate activities of bathing or toileting. Because families always have cared for relatives in these ways, what is now different about that care? For one, the number of people needing help is growing. Currently, 5 million older Americans living in communities (as opposed to institutions) need help with personal care such as bathing and dressing. By 2030, the number of older Americans requiring help with personal care will be 65 million (U.S. Department of Health and Human Services, 1986). In 1980, 65 percent of all 50-year-old women in the United States had living mothers, whereas in 1940, only 37 percent had living mothers (Wood, 1987). With increased age, there is greater risk of illness or impairment. Ninety percent of the nearly 4 million people with developmental disabilities live at home with their families. The number of chronically ill children is increasing as a result of advances in medical technology that keep those ill children alive when they certainly would have died in earlier years. Currently, between 10 and 15 percent of children under age 18 suffer from chronic illness (Patterson, 1988). Many more of the estimated 29 million Americans suffering from mental illness are living in their own homes and communities—therefore, more caregiving families exist.

What makes caregiving more difficult today is the need for many families to care for more than one person at a time for extended periods. Medical technology and drugs now keep elderly people and developmentally disabled people with severe problems alive, but in need of daily care. Before medical advances, these people would not have survived. The literature contains examples of families who not only provide routine care for their children but also care for frail elderly parents. Little has been written about families who care for more than one relative who suffers from serious illness or impairment. Because the number of people who need help is growing, more families will be providing such help, and to more people. Thus, families and professionals need to understand the normal responsibilities of most caregiving families, what the specific caregiving tasks are for people who suffer from different illnesses or impairments, and what types of services and supports are available to help caregiving families manage all their responsibilities.

Another difficulty with caregiving is that most caregivers are women employed outside the home. Until recently, primarily women provided free care, from shopping to personal care, for anyone in the family who needed help. Now, families must either purchase formal services (if the services are available) or the caregiver must juggle a work and caregiving schedule. Current family income, retirement income, and the health of the needy family member all may suffer. If the caregiver takes too much time off or is unable to travel, his or her career may suffer. If a caregiver quits work because services are unavailable, not only is the caregiver's immediate income affected, but he or she also may have a smaller retirement income. Researchers have found that employed caregiving daughters continue to devote time and energy to their families and elderly parents. However, these researchers also suggest that caregiving women work because they and their families need the income (Ince, 1987). If the caregiver quits work, the family may suffer not only from reduced income, but also possibly from increased medical and therapeutic costs associated with a dependent family member. If the caregiver does not quit work, the family member may have to wait until evenings or weekends to receive needed medical attention.

Another difficulty with current caregiving is that caregiving tasks affect the entire family—not just the primary caregiver—when one member requires special help. When a caregiver quits work or reduces the number of hours worked, the entire family has less money. If an individual juggles work and caregiving responsibilities, he or she has limited time for the rest of the family. If the person who needs help lives with the caregiver, other family members may need to give up a room; restrain some of their activities, such as having company; or even help with some caregiving responsibilities. Both the caregiver and the entire family feel physical and emotional stress.

Family conflict can result in a nonsupportive environment for everyone and even can contribute to the dissolution of the family. Marriages may dissolve. Children may run away from home or leave as soon as they are of age instead of pursuing college or vocational opportunities. Yet, if everyone maintains some individual freedom, the rewards of providing care for a needy family member are immense. The wisdom that results from an elder's life experiences or the innocence of a retarded child is refreshing. The unconditional love and concern of a family member is its own reward. Although the rewards may not be as great in caring for someone who no longer recognizes relatives or is sometimes belligerent, the caregiver feels better knowing that he or she is providing the type of care the caregiver wants the parent or child to have.

Even though chapters in this book address current problems associated with caregiving, they do not suggest that families do not want to provide care or that families do not benefit from the provision of care. The intent of this book is to identify problems and possible ways of dealing with them so that caregiving is a little easier. Rather than offering a compilation of current research, the goal of this book is to push beyond current approaches and research to find a better vision for future work on behalf of caregiving families. Researchers have tested some of the training and techniques discussed for caregivers of people with a particular illness or impairment. Now, practitioners must apply the results of those tests—what has been learned about supporting families who help a specific group—to all caregiving families. Practitioners need to support the family as a unit and help each family member achieve full potential even though the caregiving responsibilities take time and energy.

The time is right politically for the United States to address the problems faced by the millions of caregiving families. Introduction of the Pepper/Roybal bill (H.R. 2263, Long-Term Home Care Act of 1989), with 130 sponsors in Congress, showed a growing commitment to helping caregivers, although the bill did not pass. The bill proposed services for chronically ill seniors, disabled people, and children under age 18 years if a doctor certified that they needed significant help with normal daily activities. The time also is right for practitioners to broaden their areas of expertise. No longer do practitioners need to develop separate public benefits or worksite programs for elderly people and children, or developmentally disabled and mentally ill people. No longer do practitioners need to view clients as part of a separate system, even if they are from the same family. Practitioners have the opportunity to create a better vision for tomorrow.

This book is an effort to examine both the practical needs of families who provide care and the professional role. All sample questions in this book should be thoroughly tested before routine use. This book does not address questions of what public programs should pay for when people themselves are not able to pay, or whether third-party reimbursement should exist for the professional role. Rather, a clear description of family needs and the professional role and needs will allow policymakers and insurers to focus on the critical phases and tasks that each caregiving family must deal with and when professional or financial help will both help families and alleviate costs of more expensive and, perhaps, unnecessary care. Decisions about public support and third-party reimbursement must be made to alleviate the caregiving crisis and the skyrocketing health care costs now facing this country. The challenge to professionals as this debate continues is to develop norms for the type, duration, and frequency of care. The challenge also is to educate other professionals to perform the role most needed by the family—not only to help resolve the debate, but to ensure that caregiving families receive the help they need.

REFERENCES

Ince, S. E. (1987). Caregiving: The challenge of eldercare. In *Information and action manual* (pp. 1-11–1-13). Southwestern Bell Telephone.

Patterson, J. M. (1988). Chronic illness in children and the impact on families. In C. S. Chilman, E. W. Nunnally, & F. M. Cox (Eds.), *Chronic illness and disability* (pp. 69–107). Beverly Hills: Sage.

U.S. Department of Health and Human Services, Office of Human Development Services. (1986). *Family caregiving initiative.* (Fact Sheet). Washington, DC: U.S. Government Printing Office.

Wood, J. (1987). Labors of love. *Modern Maturity,* 29–34, 90–94.

1

Risks and Benefits of Caregiving

Everyone knows that caregivers do not have much free time and have to make sacrifices. However, many people do not consider other possible consequences of caregiving. They may consider caregiving just a normal part of life. What do caregivers face? Is their health likely to suffer? There does not seem to be a direct relationship between the caregiver's feelings of burden and the severity of the client's illness or impairment (Cutler, 1985). Yet, many people are aware that caregivers face much stress. Caregivers' abilities to cope with strains depend on facts such as whether other people help them or whether formal services are available when they need respite or other types of help. This chapter discusses the stresses caregivers and their families face. Other chapters identify ways to help caregivers cope with these problems. This chapter also describes how caregiving families benefit from their experiences. Caregiving families, themselves, identified some of the benefits. Few people think about the strengths that many of these families have. Yet, any effort to support caregivers and help them improve their coping abilities needs to build on their strengths.

Although other authors have described risks of caregiving, the intent of this chapter is to consolidate previous discussions of risks caregivers of different populations face and to show the similarity of the problems that most caregivers and caregiving families encounter. The intent also is to show the parallel problems other family members face. For practitioners to work effectively with caregivers and care receivers, they must understand the impact of the problems and potential solutions on the family as a whole.

INITIATION OF CAREGIVING

The *diagnostic process*—discovering that chronic illness or impairment exists—initiates the stressful caregiving role. Once the patient reports symptoms to a doctor, the doctor may order multiple and time-consuming tests to diagnose the problem. Symptoms range

1

from a child's failure to develop normally to an older person's chronic pain. For the person stepping into a caregiving role, this is the beginning of rearranging schedules to take the person to doctor appointments or hospital tests. The ill or impaired person may need help in traveling to appointments or may need support to deal with the fear of tests or the anxiety of not knowing what is wrong. The longer the diagnostic process takes and the more dangerous and painful the tests, the more anxious both the patient and the caregiver become. If a diagnosis cannot be made with certainty following testing, or if it is difficult to recommend a specific course of treatment, the anxiety increases.

Once a diagnosis is made, or accepted because tests ruled out other diagnoses, the physician projects the normal course of the disease or impairment, prescribes treatments or therapies, and discusses the work needed to provide care. However, the physician does not know how well the person will cope with treatments, therapies, or medicines. The doctor also is unaware of what accommodations the caregiving family will have to make because the doctor recommends one treatment over another (where there are options). Some patients will make choices based not only on their coping abilities but also in anticipation of the caregiver's or family's coping abilities (Corbin & Strauss, 1988).

RISKS TO THE CAREGIVERS

What kinds of physical strain do caregivers face? If the care involves helping someone with activities of daily living, such as bathing and dressing, the tasks may include lifting or providing support (Cutler, 1985). If the care recipient has Alzheimer's disease, the caregiver may need to be alert 24 hours as the disease progresses. Sleepless nights result in greater susceptibility to illness. Efforts to manage a hyperactive child or spastic teenager may require great physical exertion (Wikler, 1983). Yet, one of the few research studies on the well-being of people who were caring for memory-impaired adults suggested that the caregiver's physical health was not seriously affected. However, the caregiver's mental health and social participation deteriorated greatly: the study showed that the caregivers exhibited three times the stress symptoms of a comparison sample (George & Gwyther, 1986).

Literature on health prevention suggests that caregivers may control or reduce stress through regular physical exercise, appropriate nutrition, and relaxation techniques. Older people who regularly exercise report better stress tolerance, more energy, and relief from minor depression. Exercise helps to control weight and improve cardiovascular health—which lowers the risk of hypertension, stroke, and heart attack. Exercise also helps to prevent diabetes and to control arthritis (National Council on the Aging, 1986). Yet, caregivers may not take the time to care for themselves. Although stress is not directly a result of lack of physical exercise or poor nutrition, it is probably those deficiencies that contribute to the stress caregivers feel.

What types of problems are difficult for the caregiver to cope with emotionally? One problem is a loss of control over one's own time. The constant demands of meeting another person's daily needs, arranging for and transporting the person to medical and therapeutic appointments, maintaining employment, and other responsibilities leave little time for relaxation, socialization, or personal enjoyment through hobbies or other activities. Over a long period, these demands may lead to feelings of anger and frustration. The caregiver then may feel guilty, as though he or she is not being fair to the care receiver or other family members. Even if the person in need of care is hundreds of miles away, the caregiver may suffer. Travel back and forth and constant long-distance telephone calls to arrange needed care, if the care receiver does not want to move, are time-consuming for the caregiver. The caregiver must maintain or reschedule other responsibilities. When the caregiver participates in planning, from comprehensive care of an elder to individualized educational plans for handicapped or mentally impaired children, it takes more of the caregiver's time even though such planning is highly desirable. If the dependent family member is living with the caregiver, then the caregiver not only loses control over personal time, but also loses privacy if the care receiver is someone who has not recently lived with the caregiver.

Some people may assume that once a caregiver places a relative in a nursing home, intermediate care facility, or a residential arrangement for mentally ill people the caregiver role ends. Instead, most caregivers who live nearby visit often and monitor the care their relative receives. Although the caregiving role is not as draining physically, the emotional strain exists and visits still are time-consuming. Not only does the caregiver feel a loss of control over personal time, but also over the care of a loved one. Until the caregiver understands the nature of the disease or impairment and learns to provide care (when appropriate), he or she is totally dependent on the judgment of professionals. Even after becoming more knowledgeable, the caregiver must defer to the recommendations of medical professionals.

Added to the loss of control is constant or periodic grieving. The parents of a newborn child who is developmentally disabled are grieving for the normal child they expected. The families of mentally ill people and people with dementia grieve for the loss of the person they once knew. Families of mentally ill members grieve for the loss of potential they saw in that family member. Families of terminally ill members grieve as their loved one suffers and as they mourn the loss of that person. Grieving for a terminally ill person may result in feelings of guilt and depression because the person is still alive (Cole, Griffin, & Ruiz, 1986). The caregivers need permission to grieve even as they plan the care of their loved one.

Some caretakers add additional stress to their caregiving responsibilities by trying to protect other family members from the full impact of the disease on their loved one. By protecting family members, the family also is unaware of the difficulties that the caregiver is facing alone. Although the caregiver may have reasons for protecting young children from some of the negative aspects of the care receiver's condition, usually the professional should encourage the caregiver to communicate the full range of problems with other family members. One study on caregivers of memory-impaired adults showed that positive responses to measures of well-being were directly related to whether the caregiver had social support (George & Gwyther, 1986).

Other families add stress to their caregiving responsibilities when they fail to acknowledge relationship problems that will make it difficult for some family members to provide care for others, or fail to acknowledge the limitations of their abilities to cope with caregiving responsibilities. For example, if the nearest son or daughter never got along with the widowed elderly mother who now requires care, family expectations that the closest child assume primary responsibility are unrealistic. Constant arguments will not help the care receiver solve problems but will only add stress. If family members willingly provide care based on loving relationships, but do not recognize that there may be a point when they will not be able to fulfill all the caregiving responsibilities, they are setting themselves and the caregiver up for unnecessary guilt and anguish. Even the most loving families may find that they have to place a loved one in a nursing home or institution because they are unable to provide all the needed care.

When the family member suffers from a mental/dementia illness that makes his or her behavior unpredictable, traditional support from neighbors and friends becomes almost nonexistent even if the caregiver shares his or her caregiving problems with others (Hatfield, 1987). For example, new acquaintances are unlikely to invest the time and energy needed to become friends with someone who is continually providing care and is unable to participate in recreational activities. Old friends may feel uncomfortable around a care receiver whose behavior is unpredictable. Extended family even tends to drift away. If the care recipient has acquired immune deficiency syndrome (AIDS), then the caregiver's stress may be much worse than other stresses described. The caretaker and other family members may learn that their loved one, in the prime of life, is gay or is a drug user when they find out about the illness. They may experience two types of grief—(1) grief for the "normal" person they thought was part of the family and (2) grief over the impending deterioration and death of someone they love (Zlotnik, 1987). The stigma and fear of AIDS are even worse than those of mental illness. Complete isolation is likely. It also is difficult to find needed services because many service providers fear they will lose their other clients or patients if it becomes known that they serve a client with AIDS. Some providers worry about their own safety.

The degree of stress experienced with these problems may relate to the family's culture and values. If it is normal to care for a disabled or ill relative and everyone supports the primary caregiver, feelings of stress may be minimal. If the cultural expectations are that the primary caregiver assumes all responsibility with little or no support, the caregiver will experience extreme stress and guilt for any feelings of anger and frustration. If the family culture accepts different life-styles, caring for someone with AIDS will be much easier than in a culture where the family would no longer accept the person. One researcher asks a question about how practitioners determine who is coping effectively: Is the person who provides excellent care, but is stressed, coping more or less effectively than the person who does not spend much time with the care receiver, but is not so stressed? (Wasow, 1986).

Cultural differences and willingness to help also may relate to cultural perception of the illness or impairment. If the problems are viewed as fate, as in some countries, families may not be willing to help the care receiver achieve his or her maximum functional ability or help the caregiver if that is the caregiver's aim. However, in other countries, this cultural attitude means that people will tolerate the individual—even if his or her behavior is bizarre. Thus, if a mentally ill person is not held responsible for the affliction, expectations and alternative occupational choices are available and adapted to the individual's abilities (Lefley, 1987). If the cultural belief is that only health professionals can make decisions about care, family members will not assume control and will not become competent in the caregiving role. Thus, a caregiver's sense of burden may relate to the client's problems or to the caregiver's ability to cope with caregiving problems. In a New York study (Sherman & Ehly, 1985), when interviewers asked parents of developmentally disabled children about the most serious problem they face, they got mixed responses (Figure 1-1). When respondents discussed the impact of caregiving problems on family life, the responses revealed resulting problems with relationships and activities with other family members (Figure 1-2).

Sometimes, the caregiver is at risk of emotional or physical abuse by the care receiver. Those care receivers who cannot control their behavior also have trouble controlling emotions. They may lash out at the caregivers because they recognize and resent their dependence on the caregivers.

If caregivers manage to plan for their loved ones and achieve some balance in their own lives, crises still will occur. Elderly people may experience periodic acute health crises. People with AIDS will experience frequent serious illness. Parents of developmentally disabled children may experience emotional crises as their

Figure 1-1. Worst Problem Faced by Parents of Developmentally Disabled Children (Percentage of Parents Identifying)

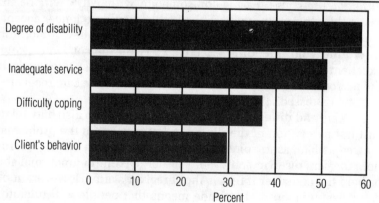

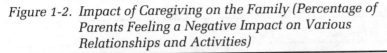

Figure 1-2. Impact of Caregiving on the Family (Percentage of Parents Feeling a Negative Impact on Various Relationships and Activities)

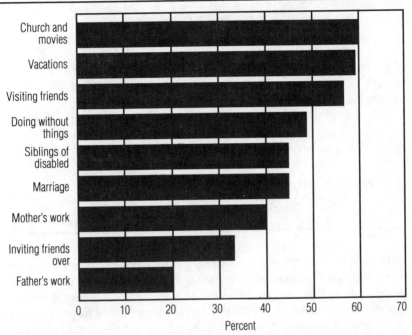

children fail to achieve the developmental milestones that "normal" children are achieving, such as walking and talking. A study of 100 families with children suffering from cystic fibrosis revealed that parental coping patterns fluctuated with changes in the child's health (McCubbin et al., 1983). Even though there is not a direct relationship between the caregiver's feelings of stress and the severity of the family member's illness or impairment, there may be a relationship between changes in the care receiver's health or functional ability and the degree of stress experienced by the caregiver.

These problems may affect the caregiver's outlook on the future. When the caregiver is unable to maintain a balanced perspective on life and look forward to events, he or she will experience the most stress and the caregiving role may be overwhelming (Rakowski & Clark, 1985). Indeed, the caregiver may experience a variety of stresses (Table 1-1).

To understand the caregiver's outlook and feelings of "stress," it is revealing to look at what the caregiver does when extended res-

Table 1-1. Caregiving Stressors

Stage of Process	Stress Factor
Diagnostic tests	Rearranging schedule Loss of time from work or responsibilities Fear of painful tests Anxiety pending results
Prognosis	Concern about treatments, therapies, medicines Patient depression
Ongoing care	Physical strain Poor health maintenance Loss of control over personal time Loss of control over care of loved one Grief Not sharing feelings Isolation Lack of social support Poor outlook on life Financial problems

pite is available. Ninety-nine family caregivers of disabled veterans who used an extended respite care service located in a Veterans Administration Hospital participated in a study (Osterkamp & Schafer, 1986). These caregivers used the service for up to 14 days and nights at a time once every 2 months. They also used the service for up to 28 days and nights once a year. Interviewers asked the caregivers why they used the extended respite programs (Figure 1-3). Although the sample was small and nonrepresentative of all caregivers, the choices made by the caregivers reinforce the preliminary research suggestions that caregivers most often experience emotional and mental health problems as a result of caregiving responsibilities. Most (81 percent) used respite for emotional rest. However, the need caregivers had for physical rest (77 percent) suggests that practitioners need to look more closely at the physical health impact of caregiving.

RISKS TO THE FAMILY

It is not only the caregiver who is likely to face many health and emotional problems. Other family members also are at risk. Although other family members are not as likely to suffer physically unless they participate in lifting the care receiver or in supervising

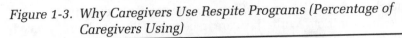

Figure 1-3. Why Caregivers Use Respite Programs (Percentage of Caregivers Using)

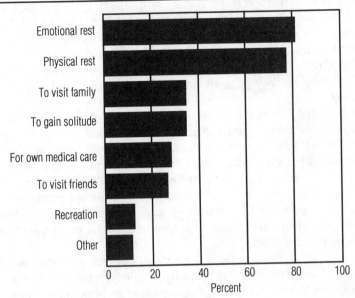

him or her at night (resulting in sleepless nights), the entire family may be in distress over the difficulties of providing care. For example, when an older person such as a grandparent is seriously ill, not only may that person's relationship with grandchildren change, the parents of those children may be so preoccupied with the older person's care that they do not pay enough attention to the developmental and continuing needs of the children. A seriously ill child may leave the caregiver insufficient time for other children or for elderly parents. Parents may expect a healthy child to assume some share of the caregiving responsibilities for a sibling or grandparent. If children do not get enough attention or must assume too much responsibility for their ages, they may become sick frequently or develop behavior problems, adding to family stress. Adolescent siblings of chronically ill youths may have trouble making the transition to independence—either leaving abruptly, or not leaving because of the probable impact on the family (Patterson, 1988). Some members of the family may not be able to cope with the new information about a family member with AIDS. The entire family may be torn apart by conflicting reactions and differences of opinion about whether to have the person move in. Such family distress may exacerbate any existing conflicts among family members and any previous conflicts with the care receiver. The family may need professional help to resolve these conflicts. Help becomes critical when the conflicts impair the caregiver's ability to care for the family member or when the family is unable to make decisions for a loved one who is no longer competent to make decisions. When it is not critical to resolve the conflict immediately, families can handle such conflicts while developing an action plan to meet caregiving responsibilities.

Besides chronic distress, the family, as a unit, loses control over personal time. Family activities may cease if someone must always be with the care receiver. Even if the care receiver does not need around-the-clock care, the family may curtail activities simply because the caregiver's time is more limited. If the person in need of care lives with or moves in with the family, the entire family has less privacy. Some family members may have to share rooms to allow an elderly person to move in or to accommodate the equipment needs of a severely disabled child.

The entire family feels the loss of control over the care of a dependent relative. However, family members may feel the loss of control over the well-being of the caregiver most acutely. They may not only see their relative as unhappy or suffering, but also may believe that the caregiver is emotionally distraught, more often ill, and unable to cope with normal family communication and activities. The family may be unaware of the types of communication and support the caregiver needs. Sometimes spouses and children may be angry or frustrated, leading to even more stress for the caregiver.

The entire family also experiences chronic grieving. Children may grieve the loss of a relationship with grandparents or with a sibling. Adults may grieve the loss of a parent. All family members grieve what they fear will be the loss of a normal family relationship. The stages of family members' grief may mirror that of the caregiver: denial, overinvolvement, anger, guilt, and acceptance. For the family, as a unit, to reach acceptance, however, may require some professional involvement or education and training for all family members so that they can give each other mutual support. Expert help is especially important when the family includes young children. Siblings of young children with life-threatening illnesses may feel responsible for the illness or feel such overwhelming fear the person will die that they cannot sleep or eat (Koch-Hattem, 1986). Rolland (1988) suggested that the family, as a unit, must create meaning for the illness that allows the family to integrate the past, the present, and the future despite the changing tasks and grief.

Social support is almost as important to the family as the individual caregiver. Yet, the entire family may feel stigmatized. Peers may ridicule teenagers with a retarded brother or sister. Parents may not allow children to visit and play with someone who has a mentally ill (and unpredictable) relative living in the house. Friends and neighbors might lose patience when the family cannot participate in planned activities because of chronic care needs or health crises of a relative. There is not much research on the impact of caregiving on the family unit, which experiences many stresses (Table 1-2). Some authors suggest that chronic distress can result in divorce. Now that experts are paying attention to the needs of caregivers, they must broaden their efforts to assess the needs of caregiving *families* and the impact of chronic distress and to develop methods for helping the family unit maintain its integrity.

RISKS TO THE FINANCIAL WELL-BEING OF THE CAREGIVER AND THE FAMILY

Everyone recognizes the added medical, therapeutic, and equipment costs of a chronic and incapacitating illness. Some people

Table 1-2. Family Stressors (Ongoing Care)

Family Need	Stressor
Time as a family	Loss of caregiver's time Fewer family activities
Emotional support	Exacerbated interpersonal conflicts Caregiver distraught, in poor health Grief Stigma
Personal time and privacy	Shared bedroom Loss of space to equipment
Financial security	Costs of doctors and therapy Costs of equipment and special food Poor insurance coverage Lost income and opportunity costs Lower expected pension

understand that insurance often does not cover these costs. Elderly people often are destitute after paying for care for a spouse. Families of developmentally disabled children may exhaust lifetime limits of health insurance coverage. They have to use up assets and apply for Medicaid coverage. Congress is debating the merits and costs of catastrophic health insurance coverage and long-term care coverage for some populations. Some states are looking at relative responsibility statutes to require people to pay for the care of a family member who is not part of their immediate family. On the other hand, some states allow tax credits or tax deductions for in-home caregivers. Others pay the family member who is giving care, which is important if the caregiver has had to reduce or terminate employment. Developmental disabilities professionals are leaders in obtaining public funding for caregiver support. A 1983–84 national survey of state family support programs for people with disabilities revealed that 9 states offered cash assistance programs; 33 states, supportive service programs; and 7 states, a combination of cash and support services (Bradley & Agosta, 1985). Only one state did not have any type of program. Most of these programs exclude people who have normal intelligence as well as those who are mentally ill. Many states now pay caregivers of the elderly who meet restrictive eligibility criteria (Abel, 1987).

These major costs of care are only part of the costs associated with chronic illness or impairment. Costs of special food or clothing and increased use of utilities (incontinence, for example, results in more frequent use of the washer and dryer) are hidden costs. When the caregivers are elderly people living on fixed incomes, these hidden costs become even more significant (Jennings, 1987). Added to the basic costs of caring for someone who is chronically ill or impaired are the lost opportunity costs of the primary caregiver's reduced or ended employment and reduced pension income because of unstable or periodic employment. Little research has been done on the extent of these costs. Estimating the total lost opportunity costs for caregivers is difficult, if not impossible. One major research project, a national survey of caregivers of functionally impaired elderly family members, revealed that the care responsibilities had a big impact on employment (U.S. Department of Labor, 1986) (Tables 1-3 and 1-4). This is not surprising when one realizes that one-fifth of all caregivers identified in the survey, one-fourth of the caregivers who were children of the impaired elder, and one-third of other caregivers reported having children under the age of 18 in their households.

Table 1-3. Employment Status of Caregivers (Percentage)

Status	Primary Caregiver Only (n = 722)	Primary Caregiver with Informal Help (n = 630)	Primary Caregiver with Formal Help (n = 212)
Working	15.0	30.8	27.2
Not working	73.2	58.7	64.6
Never worked	10.6	9.5	8.2

Table 1-4. Work Arrangements to Accommodate Caregiving (n = 1,023,000)

Arrangement	Percentage
Worked fewer hours	21.0
Rearranged schedule	29.0
Took time off without pay	18.6

When poor insurance coverage is a problem besides reduced or ended employment, the finances of a family are bleak. Little or no mental health coverage is common (many federal health insurance plans pay only $20 out of $85 or $90 per visit). Catastrophic coverage and insurance coverage of long-term care costs generally are not available. A survey of 68 corporations conducted by retirement advisers showed that only 16 percent had health coverage for eldercare and 13.2 percent offered long-term care insurance (Creedon, 1987). Insurance coverage of supportive services is almost nonexistent. The survey of 68 corporations found that 8.8 percent had insurance coverage of home/adult day care. Families that are already poor because of the costs of caring for a loved one are not likely to have money to pay for supportive services when insurance coverage is unavailable.

Publicly funded coverage of home care services that help caregiving families probably will not expand dramatically in the near future because it is costly. Coverage of home health care alone has escalated tremendously since the enactment of Medicare and Medicaid. In 1969, Medicare covered 8,500 home health visits, reimbursing them at $78.1 million (U.S. Department of Health and Human Services, 1987). In 1982, Medicare covered 30,800 visits, reimbursing them at $1.1 billion. The number of Medicaid recipients who received home health care rose from 109,900 in 1973 at a payment level of $25.4 million to 421,800 in 1983 at a payment level of $597.2 million (U.S. Department of Health and Human Services, 1987).

BENEFITS OF CAREGIVING

The benefits of caregiving are not obvious when so much attention focuses on the risks and burdens of providing care. However, millions of people would not provide care if they did not benefit. From the person who provides care to fulfill an obligation to the individual who wants to be with the care receiver and give the best care possible, caregivers feel some satisfaction. Both the caregiver and the entire family benefit from the caregiving experience, but in different ways.

The caregiver benefits by caring for the loved one in the way that he or she wishes, thereby eliminating worry about the type of care other people are providing. Caregivers believe they are contributing to the quality of the care receiver's life because most people prefer home care to care in a residential facility, nursing home, or hospital. Caregivers feel satisfied that they have proved their love or returned the type of care that they received at an earlier time from the care receiver. If the caregiver is aiding an older person who still is cognitive of his or her environment, earlier unresolved feelings or issues may resolve themselves as the caregiver listens to the care receiver review his or her life. When caregivers receive training in communication and problem-solving skills, these skills will help them in their relationships with other family members and friends. Caregivers experience pride in doing a good job of providing care. Many parents of developmentally disabled children believe they became stronger people as a result of their caregiving experience (Wikler, Wasow, & Hatfield, 1983). Just as parents of normal children experience pride and joy in their children's accomplishments, caregivers experience those feelings when a chronically ill or impaired family member is able to maintain a level of functioning for some time and participate in family interactions.

Other family members benefit from the caregiving experience by feeling secure in a strong kinship system. They know that they, too, can depend on other family members for help. If they receive training or respond to the caregiver's new communication skills, they gain a better understanding of each other's needs. If extended families live together (multiple generations), they learn from each other and gain a greater tolerance for other people's problems. Older people can benefit from watching the joy of children's new discoveries and experiences whether they are disabled or nondisabled children. Young people can benefit from the wisdom of older people and enjoy the stories they retell as part of the review of their lives.

When interviewers in a 1980 long-term care survey asked caregivers of elderly people how they benefit from the caregiving role, almost three-fourths said that caregiving makes them feel useful (Subcommittee on Human Services, 1987). If the caregiver is elderly, this role may compensate somewhat for the loss of roles older people experience. Many respondents appreciated the company of the care recipient and experienced other benefits (Figure 1-4).

When all family members feel self-reliant and cohesive as a family unit, each individual member is more likely to remain independent, productive, and more satisfied with life (Bradley & Agosta, 1985). The key to achieving this family relationship is for each family member to have self-esteem, feel adequate in their roles in the family and the larger community, and feel pride in their abilities to manage all their roles and responsibilities (Patterson, 1988). How do practitioners help people enjoy the caregiving role they have chosen? Chapter 2 discusses the caregiver's training needs.

Figure 1-4. Percentage of Caregivers Benefiting from the Care Receiver and the Benefits They Receive

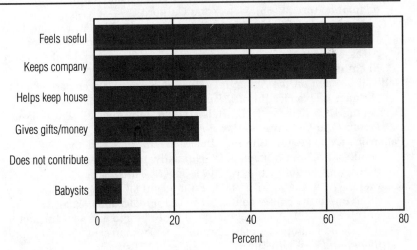

REFERENCES

Abel, E. (1987). *Love is not enough: Family care of the frail elderly.* Washington, DC: American Public Health Association.

Bradley, V. J., & Agosta, J. M. (1985). Keeping your child at home: The case for family support. *The Exceptional Parent,* 10–22.

Cole, L., Griffin, K. , & Ruiz, B. (1986). Comprehensive approach to working with families of Alzheimer's patients. In R. Dobrof (Ed.). *Social work and Alzheimer's disease* (pp. 27–39). New York: Haworth.

Corbin, J. M., & Strauss, A. (1988). The onset and diagnosis of chronic illness: A new life course begins. In *Unending work and care: Managing chronic illness at home* (pp. 22–32). San Francisco: Jossey-Bass.

Creedon, M. A. (Ed.). (1987). *Issues for an aging America: Employees and eldercare (A briefing book).* Bridgeport, CT: University of Bridgeport, Center for the Study of Aging.

Cutler, L. (1985). Counseling caregivers. *Generations, 10,* 53–57. San Francisco: American Society on Aging.

George, L. K., & Gwyther, L. P. (1986). Caregiver well-being: A multidimensional examination of family caregivers of demented adults. *The Gerontologist, 26,* 253–259.

Hatfield, A. (1987). Social support and family coping. In A. Hatfield & H. P. Lefley (Eds.). *Families of the mentally ill: Coping and adaptation* (pp. 191–207). New York: Guilford.

Jennings, J. (1987). Elderly parents as caregivers for their adult dependent children. *Social Work, 32,* 430–433.

Koch-Hattem, A. (1986). Siblings experience of pediatric cancer: Interviews with children. *Health and Social Work, 11,* 107–117.

Lefley, H. P. (1987). Culture and mental illness: The family role. In A. B. Hatfield & H. P. Lefley (Eds.), *Families of the mentally ill: Coping and adaptation* (pp. 30–55). New York: Guilford.

McCubbin, H. I., McCubbin, M. A., Patterson, J., Cauble, A., Wilson, L., & Warwick, W. (1983, May). CHIP—Coping Health Inventory for Parents: An assessment of parental coping patterns in the care of the chronically ill child. *Journal of Marriage and the Family,* 359–370.

National Council on the Aging, Inc. (1986, November/December). The importance of exercise [Insert]. *Perspective on Aging, 15.*

Osterkamp, L., & Schafer, D. E. (Eds.). (1986, July/August). [Entire Issue]. *Parent Care Resources to Assist Family Caregivers.*

Patterson, J. M. (1988). Chronic illness in children and the impact on families. In C. S. Chilman, E. W. Nunnally, & F. M. Cox (Eds.). *Chronic illness and disability* (pp. 69–107). Beverly Hills: Sage.

Rakowski, W., & Clark, M. (1985). Future outlook, caregiving and care-receiving in the family context. *The Gerontologist, 25,* 618–623.

Rolland, J. S. (1988). A conceptual model of chronic and life-threatening illness and its impact on families. In C. S. Chilman et al. (Eds.), *Chronic illness and disability* (pp. 17–68). Beverly Hills: Sage.

Sherman, B., & Ehly, C. (1985). Critical factors affecting families' decisions to place developmentally disabled family members. Unpublished report to the New York State Council on Children and Families.

Subcommittee on Human Services of the Select Committee on Aging, House of Representatives, One Hundredth Congress. (1987). *Exploding the myths: Caregiving in America* (Report No. 99-611). Washington, DC: U.S. Government Printing Office.

U.S. Department of Health and Human Services, Health Care Financing Administration, Office of Research and Demonstrations. (1987). *Health care financing program statistics: Medicare and Medicaid Data Book, 1986* (HCFA Pub. No. 03247). Washington, DC: U.S. Government Printing Office.

U.S. Department of Labor, Women's Bureau. (1986). Facts on U.S. working women (Fact Sheet No. 86-4). Washington, DC: U.S. Government Printing Office.

Wasow, M. (1986). Support groups for family caregivers of patients with Alzheimer's disease. *Social Work, 31,* 93–97.

Wikler, L. (1983). Chronic stresses of families of mentally retarded children. In L. Wikler & M. P. Keenan (Eds.), *Developmental disabilities: No longer a private tragedy* (pp. 102–110). Silver Spring, MD: National Association of Social Workers.

Wikler, L., Wasow, M., & Hatfield, E. (1983). Seeking strengths in families of developmentally disabled children. In L. Wikler & M. P. Keenan (Eds.), *Developmental disabilities: No longer a private tragedy* (pp. 111–114). Silver Spring, MD: National Association of Social Workers.

Zlotnik, J. L. (1987). *AIDS: Helping families cope/recommendations for meeting the psychosocial needs of persons with AIDS and their families* (Report to the National Institute of Mental Health). Silver Spring, MD: National Association of Social Workers.

2

Training Families to Meet Current Needs

What types of problems do caregivers experience besides a lack of personal time? Many caregivers do not know what behavior or problems are "normal" for any particular illness or impairment or what type of aid their relative needs. Thus, they feel anxious or guilty if they assert their own needs. Or, caregivers may be angry if they think the family member is deliberately acting helpless. Often caregivers are unaware of available training. However, training can help caregivers understand

- the normal course of the disease or impairment
- what the family member is experiencing and how he or she feels
- how to communicate with a loved one so everyone feels good about interactions and decisions
- how they feel about providing care to care receivers
- how to act as case managers to obtain and supervise needed services
- how to feel confident in providing "medical" services, such as catheterization, through training and supervision
- how to care for themselves and solve problems in a systematic way

This chapter explores the techniques and training available to caregivers and their families—both to meet current and anticipated needs. The recommended way to help caregivers is to help them develop an action plan that meets client needs and gives them education and training.

FEELING COMFORTABLE THAT NEEDS ARE UNDERSTOOD

Just as many men and women are not knowledgeable about changes that result from the normal aging process, most do not know what to expect when impairment or illness strikes. Yet, there are

18

ways to compensate for the sensory loss associated with aging. Techniques and technology help caregivers compensate for or help people cope with the loss of control resulting from illness or impairment. A coping inventory developed in 1983 (McCubbin et al., 1983), based on a sample of 100 parents of children with cystic fibrosis, revealed that caregivers can adjust to illness or impairment if three aspects of knowledge and support are available: (1) continued family integration, (2) an understanding of the medical problems and prognosis, and (3) maintenance of a social support network.

Often education classes are available for family members. If not, successful programs exist elsewhere and often are repeated. For example, a structured educational program developed in 1983 teaches families about the perceptions of a mentally ill person when he or she is suffering from a psychotic episode (Ferris & Marshall, 1987). Caregivers learn how distortions of mood and feeling associated with mental illness can result in behavior that is uncomfortable for the family. Families also are taught how to manage the behavior through appropriate communication. For developmentally disabled children, parental training might include learning about the developmental stages of childhood. Parents need to learn what stage their child is in and how the child is likely to progress. Once again, understanding the type of communication that simplifies learning and behavioral management is important (Wikler & Keenan, 1983).

For elderly people and others suffering from impairment and sensory loss, it is possible for caregivers to experience the changes care receivers are feeling. For example, caregivers can use ear plugs while conversing, use plastic wrap over glasses or goggles when taking a walk, or use plastic gloves when touching someone. These exercises can allow both professionals and caregivers to experience the effects of decreased senses (Springer & Brubaker, 1985). A creative professional can help caregivers simulate some of the losses family members are experiencing either because of functional loss or an inability to develop functionally as peers are developing. As a caregiver simulates the loss, how does he or she feel? Defining the range of emotions may provide insight into how the care receiver feels and why his or her behavior and moods change. What would the caregiver change in the environment or in the way other people respond to the difficulties that the caregiver is experiencing? What tools would be useful?

Caregivers also can try exercises to simulate feelings of those who cannot control their physical movements (Bane & Halpest, 1986). For example, to simulate experiences of a person who had a stroke, the caregiver must complete a form requesting name, address, social security number, occupation, and hobbies. However, the caregiver must fill out the form using the hand opposite the one normally used and must move the leg opposite the hand he or she is using in a counterclockwise motion. This exercise demonstrates interference in the message between the brain and the hand.

To add the experience of mild mental limitation to the physical loss exercise, a professional could try the following exercise in a group of caregivers. Pass out questions to subgroups of participating caregivers. Ask one set of questions in such a way that only a simple answer is likely. Ask other questions in a way that encourages creativity. Participants with the simple-answer questions can discuss how they felt when others gave more complex responses. Examples of questions are

> Simple: What color is (an object)?
>
> Complex: What color is (an object)? How many other objects in the room have a similar color? How would you describe the different color shades of each identified object? How does this color make you feel?

When asking for the responses, the professional might say, "Tell me about the color of this [object]" and then ask the participants with the question designed to elicit the simplistic answer how they felt. The professional might then ask participants with the most complex questions how they reacted to the first group's answers.

DECIDING ON CARE AND SUPPORT

Thinking about the types of care a person needs and whether the caregiver can meet those needs is quite complicated. Every individual perceives things differently. Therefore, each family member may think the care receiver needs a different type or amount of care. Perceptions of the care receiver may differ from those of other family members. Each person's ability to cope with illness or impairment varies as does individual effort to overcome problems and remain independent. Thus, an assessment of needed care should be done individually, not in a group. The professional might use a checklist for the family member's care that includes all activities of daily living. The professional can change this checklist after an initial interview to discuss individual circumstances, demands, and resources of the person. The checklist then can more accurately capture the amount of time spent on certain activities. If possible, it also would be helpful to have both the care receiver and the caregiver identify the care receiver's needs as each of them perceives the needs. This exercise may reveal that the caregiver was unaware of certain needs or that the caregiver may be providing some care that the receiver does not feel is necessary. If the family member is incapable of providing this information, it may be useful to compare the caregiver's assessment of need with the recommendations of other health, mental health, and social services personnel the family member has seen. Care receivers and caregivers can use a checklist to help assess care needs. To compare the caregiver, the care receiver, and the professional assessment of the care receiver's needs, the professional also can use a checklist (Table 2-1).

Once an expert identifies the differences, the caregiver and the professional can ask several questions to help them focus realistically on essential care. What do you think are reasons for the perceived differences? Why do you think the differences exist? Through discussions with everyone individually, or with family members as a group, can the professional help everyone understand

Table 2-1. Checklist to Assess Care Needs

Amount of Help Needed by Family Member (Care Receiver or Caregiver Report)

Type of Care	Hours Spent Daily	Hours Spent Weekly
Personal care	___	___
Meals	___	___
Housekeeping	___	___
Shopping	___	___
Transportation	___	___
Home repair	___	___
Total time needed	___	___

Differences in Perceived Needs of Family Members by Hours of Service Needed Weekly

Type of Care	Care Receiver	Caregiver	Professional
Personal care	___	___	___
Meals	___	___	___
Housekeeping	___	___	___
Shopping	___	___	___
Transportation	___	___	___
Home repair	___	___	___

the different perspectives and come to agreement on what is most needed and helpful to the family member? Can you determine whether the care receiver needs encouragement through behavior modification or better communication to be more independent? Once the caregiver has looked at the time needed by a loved one, the caregiver needs to see how he or she is dividing available time. Perhaps the time required by others precludes the caregiver from meeting this family member's needs. Perhaps the caregiver's expectations of himself or herself are unrealistic given other demands on time. If the family member is able to fill out a form that describes the caregiver's use of time and one that describes personal needs, it could sensitize the family member to the caregiver's needs just as training sensitizes the caregiver to the care receiver's needs (Table 2-2). A comparison of checklists on the family member's needs and the caregiver's available time will show whether anyone is aware that the care recipient has unmet needs and whether the caregiver has any time for himself or herself. If either unmet needs or a lack of personal time is a problem, the caregiver may be able to eliminate or consolidate activities, such as making multiple meals at one time and freezing some food for a later time. Or, other people may be available to provide care.

Table 2-2. How the Caregiver Divides Time

Activity	Hours Spent Daily	Hours Spent Weekly
Sleeping	—	—
Preparing meals for own household	—	—
Preparing meals for other household	—	—
Eating	—	—
Housekeeping (own)	—	—
Housekeeping (other)	—	—
Shopping (own)	—	—
Shopping (other)	—	—
Employment	—	—
Own transportation	—	—
Transportation of others	—	—
Personal care		
Of spouse	—	—
Of children	—	—
Of parent	—	—
Of other	—	—
Personal care for self	—	—
Leisure time	—	—
Total time used	—	—

At this point, relationship problems may become obvious as anger surfaces if the caregiver or care receiver believes the other person could do more or if it is felt that caregiving responsibilities are excessively burdensome to the primary caregiver. This is also the point at which the caregiver needs to describe the help or activities that are important to his or her sense of well-being (Table 2-3). The caregiver and care receiver also need to describe their feelings about their relationship. The caregiver should describe what he or she needs to help with caregiving responsibilities if these roles and responsibilities are part of a mutually satisfying relationship (Table 2-4). If a poor relationship precludes problem resolution, the professional needs to help family members decide whether they can develop a caregiving relationship or whether they should look for alternative ways to manage care needs. The professional may find that angry or guilty feelings or poor communication patterns among family members make a particular task seem difficult or burdensome. However, the professional can use a checklist to help simplify the identification of burdensome caregiving problems (Table 2-5).

If items identified by the professional result in serious problems, then the caregiver may benefit from group sessions or individual counseling to help him or her develop what is sometimes referred to as a "self-change plan" (Couper, 1987). A self-change plan would

Table 2-3. *Assessing Activities That Are Important to the Caregiver's Well-being*

Why Do You Need Time? (Hours Per Week)

Need	Hours Wanted
No additional time needed	___
Relaxation	___
Socializing with friends	___
Meals alone	___
Uninterrupted sleep	___
Exercise	___

What Would Be Helpful? (Hours Per Week)

Service	Hours Needed
Housecleaning help	___
Repair service	___
Respite	___
Day care for family member	___
Homemaker/home health care	___

Table 2-4. Assessing Perceptions of the Relationships

Relationship as Perceived by Care Receiver

How do you feel about [family member's name] doing/providing [service] for you?
     Comfortable ___   Uncomfortable ___

Is there anyone else you would rather have help from?   Yes ___   No ___

If yes, specify: _____

What do you like most about your relationship with [family member's name]?

_____

What would you like to change in your relationship with [family member's name]?

_____

Relationship as Perceived by Caregiver

How do you feel about doing/providing [service] for [name of care receiver]?
     Comfortable ___   Uncomfortable ___

Do you think any other family member would be more comfortable providing this care?
     Yes ___   No ___

If yes, specify: _____

What do you like most about your relationship with [name of care receiver]?

_____

What would you like to change in your relationship with [name of care receiver]?

_____

become part of a total action plan, which includes identifying and obtaining help from other relatives and friends (informal sources) and purchasing formal services. The self-change portion of the plan includes finding ways to minimize unpleasant tasks, building in extra time for satisfying activities, and gaining control over feelings by exerting greater control over activities that are important to the caregiver. A self-change plan may be easier to develop once the caregiver understands both the loved one's needs and feelings and the caregiver's own needs and feelings.

At the same time that the caregiver is developing a self-change plan, the practitioner can begin to look at family dynamics and needs. Chapter 1 showed that other family members living with the caregiver may feel neglected. Because these feelings can result in negative reactions of family members and impede the development of the caregiver's self-change plan and a plan for the routine manage-

Table 2-5. What Is Burdensome?

Burdensome Item	Checklist
Providing services	——
Lack of time for self	——
Inadequate financial aid	——
Lack of time for family	——
Other. Please describe:_____	
_____	
_____	

Why is it so difficult? _____
_____
_____
_____

ment of caregiving tasks, it is important to identify what the family members need from the caregiver. Asking each family member individually to complete a checklist will show how that family member believes the caregiver should divide his or her time (Table 2-6). If more than one family member identifies the same need to change the caregiver's use of time, it is a problem for the family as

Table 2-6. How the Caregiver Should Divide Time, as Perceived by Other Family Members

Activity	Hours Spent Daily	Preferred Hours Spent
Sleeping	——	——
Preparing meals for own household	——	——
Preparing meals for other household	——	——
Eating	——	——
Housekeeping (own)	——	——
Housekeeping (other)	——	——
Shopping (own)	——	——
Shopping (other)	——	——
Employment	——	——
Own transportation	——	——
Transportation of others	——	——
Personal care		
Of spouse	——	——
Of children	——	——
Of parent	——	——
Of other	——	——
Personal care for self	——	——
Leisure time	——	——

Comments: _____

a whole, not just one member. Another way to assess family needs is to ask each person what needs are not being met by the caregiver (Table 2-7).

After family members identify the specific needs that are not met, their general anxiety or anger may dissipate. They also may be ready to discuss what they can do to relieve the caregiver either by providing help directly to the care receiver or providing support to the caregiver, so they can have more of the caregiver's time (Table 2-8). If the family is able financially, family members may decide to purchase some of the needed services. For example, if the care receiver maintains a separate household, family members might purchase housecleaning for the care receiver. Or, if the care receiver is afraid to let a stranger into the house, he or she might purchase this service from someone known. If money is not a problem, the caregiver might purchase the service for both the caregiver and care receiver households.

Once immediate family members decide how they are willing to help, it is time to find out if other relatives and friends (informal sources of support) can assist with responsibilities. Many family members live great distances from each other; however, many other families still have sisters, brothers, aunts, uncles, and cousins who live nearby and are willing to help. In other cases, close friends or neighbors are willing to help each other because they also may require a support system. The practitioner should help the caregiver identify people the caregiver believes would offer some help and also identify the types of aid these people can provide (Table 2-9). After

Table 2-7. *Needs Not Met by Caregiver, as Described by Other Family Members*

Activity	Needed Daily Hours (Respondent)
Meals	
Housekeeping	___
Time to eat together	___
Shopping	___
Transportation	___
Personal care	___
Leisure time together	___
Help with homework/work	___
Time to talk with each other	___
Family activities	___

Name and relationship of respondent _____

Table 2-8. Helping the Caregiver Have More Time

How the Respondent Is Willing to Help

Activity for Care Receiver	Weekly Hours of Respondent's Time	Activity for Caregiver	Weekly Hours of Respondent's Time
Prepare meals	____	Prepare meals	____
Housecleaning	____	Housecleaning	____
Shopping	____	Shopping	____
Transportation	____	Transportation	____
Personal care	____	Yardwork	____
Yardwork	____	Home repairs	____
Home repairs	____	Babysitting	____
Companionship	____	Emotional support	____

Respondent: _____

Other Ways to Meet Family Needs

Activity	High Priority	Low Priority
Pay for housecleaning	____	____
Ready-made meals	____	____
Drive caregiver to spend time together	____	____
Purchase equipment	____	____
Develop neighborhood cooperative to exchange caregiving	____	____
Other (list):		

Respondent: _____

identifying potential sources of help, the reality of the help depends on whether the caregiver asks for it. In part, this depends on the caregiver's ability to approach relatives and friends. If the caregiver's emotional state precludes him or her from requesting help directly, it may be useful for the caregiver merely to ask that all identified informal supports meet with the professional in group sessions. (It probably is more realistic to ask family members to participate in such sessions, rather than neighbors or friends.)

Making informal care a reality also depends on barriers or problems that other relatives or friends are experiencing. People providing the informal support also may be caring for young children or someone else with chronic problems and working as well, leaving them with little free time. If transportation or scheduling of help are problems, the professional or the caregiver can help the relative or friend make necessary arrangements. The care receiver may react negatively to the new informal caregiver, perhaps because he or she prefers the primary caregiver. Thus, the caregiver or the professional

Table 2-9. Description of Potential Informal Support: A Checklist
          for Possible Sources of Help

Person	Respite	House-cleaning	Repairs	Financial	Social
Mother	___	___	___	___	___
Father	___	___	___	___	___
Sister	___	___	___	___	___
Brother	___	___	___	___	___
Aunt	___	___	___	___	___
Uncle	___	___	___	___	___
Cousin	___	___	___	___	___
Friend	___	___	___	___	___
Neighbor	___	___	___	___	___
Other	___	___	___	___	___

Comments: _____

needs to prepare both the care receiver and the informal caregiver in advance. The relative or friend who agrees to help needs to understand that the help is as much for the caregiver as for the care receiver. If the caregiver shows appreciation, the friend or relative may continue to help even if the care receiver behaves badly. If the care receiver and the person who could help have never had a good relationship, the caregiver might ask for some help that does not involve much contact with the care receiver (such as shopping).

The Honolulu Gerontology Program of the Honolulu Medical Group goes beyond group sessions for families and helps families acquire informal sources of support. When family members other than the primary caregiver are far away and are not helping in any way, members of the program ask permission from the caregiver to contact other family members. Letters then are sent to the rest of the family, asking them to contribute money if they are unable to provide other types of aid. Any money then is used to purchase needed services. Even a small amount of money from several family members often is enough to purchase services or to provide the portion of funding needed to seek additional foundation monies. When the care receiver has needed services and is more satisfied, the caregiver is able to focus on some of his or her own needs as well. (See Chapter 3 for a more detailed discussion of this program.)

When informal support does not meet all the care receiver's or caregiver's needs, formal services become important. Unfortunately, the availability of formal services is idiosyncratic to the local community. If services are scarce in a community, an information and referral system probably will not exist. In communities with many services, multiple information and referral services probably do exist. Separate information systems may exist for elderly, developmentally disabled, and mentally ill people. The caregiver may contact agencies such as area agencies on aging, developmental disabilities planning councils, and community mental health centers to find information and referral services or to identify individual service providers. If an individual has a dual diagnosis or if two people (different populations) in the same family need care, the caregiver will need to access two systems.

Working with staff from two information and referral systems is easy if the staff are professionals who check the appropriateness of agencies on the basis of what the caregiver wants and then follow up to ensure that the information and referral agencies do not refer the caregiver from one agency to another. However, if the staff merely lists agencies that offer a variety of services, the caregiver may give up in frustration after several phone calls or visits to agencies. In the midst of caregiving responsibilities, professional help in identifying and discussing the usefulness of different providers is appreciated. It is one less activity for the caregiver to coordinate when he or she already is coordinating medical and therapeutic appointments and, perhaps, juggling the schedules of an older relative, children, and his or her own employment.

In a General Accounting Office (GAO) (1989) survey of 892 parents contacted through 14 hospitals in 11 states and the District of Columbia, parents reported that three elements accounted for most of their problems in obtaining support services: (1) lack of health insurance coverage, (2) limited information on services available, and (3) lack of a central focal point they could contact when they needed help with home care. Two out of these three elements result from the caregiving families' need for professional help, possibly a case manager, and their need for access to services. More than one-half (56 percent) of the parents surveyed by GAO who needed support services had trouble getting them. A professional social worker should be able to provide case management and help the parents access supportive services.

To help caregivers develop a complete action plan, any effective professional must know what formal services are available, their cost, duration, frequency, eligibility requirements, and geographic coverage. The professional also needs to know which agencies have sliding fee scales and what other financial assistance is available to pay for services. Agencies might include voluntary services organized through more formal institutions such as churches or synagogues. It is helpful to maintain a registry of available community services (Table 2-10).

SUPPORT GROUPS AND EMPOWERMENT

Most caregivers seem to benefit from support groups, which can be *informal* (voluntary and led by another caregiver) or *formal* (arranged and led by a professional). The most important aspect of support groups is that they offer caregivers empowerment—the sense that they are once again in control. Some support groups initially are run by professionals who educate and train participants. Most groups, if not all, evolve into peer-led groups that provide emotional support, bringing participants to an "equal" level with the professional.

Many people join support groups to obtain more information about their relatives' needs and to learn how other people manage the work involved in caregiving. This is the first step in regaining control. Some of the topics discussed in these groups include

- knowledge of the disease process/impairment and any likely complications
- legal issues in caregiving
- how to be assertive with medical providers

Table 2-10. *Sample Registry of Community Services by Eligible Category*

Service	Agency Name, Address, Phone Number	Cost/ Unit of Service	Frequency	Duration	Will Agency Help Secure Financial Aid?
Respite	Family Service, 100 Main, 555-1000	$5/hour	Once per week	2 Hours	No
Homemaker	Home Helpers, 200 Fifth, 555-2000	$7/hour	Twice per week	4 Hours	Yes

Services are provided through federal, state, or local program funding.

- how to find and use community resources
- how to deal with stress (Lidoff, 1985)

Support groups may be set up for spouses, children, or all relatives. Some groups are only for relatives of people with a particular illness or disability such as stroke or cancer. Long-distance caregivers who are arranging services and providing financial and emotional support may even participate in support groups.

Support groups may offer families a sense of community with other families who are experiencing similar problems. Thus, families may become more confident about the management of caregiving tasks. Within this community, there is no stigma (Biegel, Shore, & Gordon, 1984). According to professionals who lead support groups, family members say that one of their greatest needs is to share feelings and experiences with other people who are experiencing similar problems (Simank & Strickland, 1986). Their sense of isolation, and sometimes stigma, makes this sharing critical to the caregivers' abilities to cope with stress. In support groups, caregivers express feelings of anger, frustration, and guilt without fear that the listeners will judge them and think that they do not care about their loved one. This is an important type of social interaction that caregivers often do not have outside the group.

Older people may use the support group to help them decide how to plan for the care of their adult dependent children after their deaths. Parents of developmentally disabled or chronically ill children may find that support groups for siblings of the disabled child are as important to the family unit as their own support group. Some groups develop a system in which members call on one another during a crisis. These activities are a form of empowerment, of returning control to the caregiver as he or she deals with multiple demands and feels powerless to control demands on his or her time. Some groups move beyond the continued emotional support to produce newsletters that offer current information or organize and advocate for needed services, living arrangements, and acceptance (to decrease stigma). This is empowerment! Empowerment allows caregivers to become leaders, representing the needs of many caregivers in their communities. It allows participants an outlook that enables them to achieve goals.

Research on the impact of support groups is inconclusive. Researchers have not been able to prove that support groups alleviate caregiver stress. However, because most caregivers believe that they benefit from support groups, experts not only should inform new caregivers about the groups, but should encourage them to try the groups. So many facts influence caregiver well-being (the caregiver's own physical health, financial resources, and the number and frequency of health crises he or she experiences) that the impact of support groups alone will be difficult to identify. However, if the caregivers believe the groups help them regain control or make them feel better, then the groups are providing needed support.

SKILLS FOR THE CAREGIVING FAMILY

Just as caregivers (and their families) may not understand their loved one's needs or be aware of their own needs, once they understand the problems, they may not know what to do about them. If the family member needs specific health services, such as catheterization, caregivers expect training. When caregivers need to use specific types of communication or behavior management skills, they often do not know that training for these skills is available. Besides training in health care techniques, caregivers may need training in communications skills, problem solving, and training and supervision.

Communications Skills

Understanding the perceptions and emotions of the care receiver may help to eliminate negative reactions to questions, demands, and forgetfulness. The caregiver is less likely to show negativism through gestures, facial expressions, or tone of voice. However, understanding does not teach the caregiver special communication techniques that help someone who is suffering from Alzheimer's disease or teach behavioral management approaches that work with an individual who is suffering from mental illness or retardation.

One project, designed to evaluate behavioral intervention for mentally and physically impaired elderly and their caregivers, has shown potential for increasing the client's self-care and cognitive abilities and for decreasing negative interactions between client and caregiver (Pinkston & Linsk, 1984). Behavioral management can involve using learning principles, such as reinforcement of desired behavior; learning ways to decrease anxiety (because anxiety can impair learning); and learning ways to improve cognition (for example, the use of labels for people with Alzheimer's disease) (Wikler &

Keenan, 1983). Improvement of "problem behaviors" helps the caregiver feel better and eases communications among family members.

One manual on seminars for caregiving families recommends training for the entire family in "active listening" (Montgomery, 1984). When a person is actively listening, he or she does not respond to someone else with personal reactions. Instead, the listener reflects back the thoughts of the speaker. Active listening can be effective not only with the care receiver, but also with the caregiver and frustrated or upset family members.

Problem-Solving Skills

One of the most basic reasons that the practitioner works with the entire family, rather than just the client or the caregiver, is to help the family members learn to work together to solve a problem. One method of encouraging family problem solving is to help members develop family meetings (Zarit, Orr, & Zarit, 1983). The degree of burden experienced by caregivers varies according to the amount of support and help they receive from relatives and friends. During family meetings, members share information so that everyone knows about the illness or impairment, its prognosis, the needs of the care receiver, and the needs of the primary caregiver. Most important, the meeting includes a discussion of the types of support each person can give the client and the caregiver. Many professionals believe that psychotherapy is necessary when family meetings reveal long-standing conflicts. However, even when families need to resolve conflicts, it should be possible to focus initially on the conflicts related to the illness or impairment, agree on short-term goals for providing support, and agree on each person's role in achieving that short-term support with the aid of a professional.

Another method for working with the caregiver individually to enhance his or her problem-solving and coping abilities seems to offer promise. The Palo Alto Veterans Administration Medical Center, Center for the Study of Psychotherapy and Aging, tested this approach (Gallagher, 1985). The program offers respite care so that caregivers can attend. Its purpose is to help caregivers improve their ability to manage the personal problems they face in their caregiving role. The center offers a life satisfaction class in which participants are taught to track their moods and to determine how their feelings change with specific activities. Participants develop contracts to do activities that make them feel better and to reward themselves. An example of a contract is scheduling a 15-minute walk each day or calling a friend on the phone when feeling overwhelmed. The center also offers a class in problem solving. This class teaches caregivers to approach problems systematically so that problems do not become overwhelming. Caregivers learn how to identify the "real" problem, how to develop an array of potential solutions, how to assess the solutions and choose one, and how to reevaluate and modify solutions as necessary.

Both the family-oriented problem solving and the caregiver education to increase coping and life satisfaction seem to be necessary for any long-term solution to caregiver "burden" and the associated risks to the integrity of the family. If the rest of the family does not help at all, it is possible that no amount of caregiver coping may be sufficient to overcome the excessive demands on the caregiver both physically and emotionally. If the family does help, but the caregiver cannot break a cycle of feeling that every problem is insurmountable, the caregiver still will feel burdened.

Training and Supervision Skills

Skill development includes both training and supervising the caregiver so that he or she feels competent doing necessary tasks and teaching the caregiver to supervise the provision of services by formal agencies.

The caregiver will need training and supervision when he or she must perform medical procedures, transfer a paralyzed individual, or follow regimens ordered by the doctor. A one-time training session is not enough. Helping the family member put on special prostheses, changing tracheotomy tubes, learning to transfer a paralyzed person from bed to wheelchair, or performing a multitude of other specialized tasks requires supervision until the caregiver perfects the tasks. Otherwise, the care receiver is at risk and the caregiver will be anxious.

Equally as important as the medical tasks, but often overlooked, is the need for health maintenance. Diet; exercise or muscle manipulation; preventive dental, eye, and other checkups; and regular social interaction promote improved physical and emotional functioning and can inhibit further deterioration in some degenerative or chronic diseases. These health maintenance activities can help the family member become more independent. Health maintenance also is important in helping the caregiver to prevent health deterioration as a result of the constant stress of caring for someone else. Also, if the caregiver feels better, he or she will be better able to cope with the caregiving stresses. One manual (Couper, 1987) recommends following a "Healthy Lifestyle Checkup for Caregivers"; a checklist helps assess, for example, whether the caregiver exercises and eats properly. It also assesses whether the person feels guilty saying no or worries excessively. Any checklist that assesses personal time, nutrition, medical checkups, exercise, and social support can be used (Table 2-11).

When the caregiver is unable to meet all the needs of the care receiver and needs to purchase services, a different type of education

Table 2-11. Checklist for Caregivers: Do You Take Care of Yourself?

Do you exercise regularly? If so, how often? _____	Yes ___	No ___
Do you have a job or regular volunteer activity that is gratifying?	Yes ___	No ___
Do you have a hobby or another leisure time activity that you enjoy regularly? If so, how often? _____	Yes ___	No ___
Do you smoke or drink alcoholic beverages? If so, how many packs/drinks per day, and has it increased in recent months? _____	Yes ___	No ___
Have you gained or lost 10 pounds or more in recent months?	Yes ___	No ___
Do you eat balanced meals three times each day? If not, how often do you eat balanced meals? _____	Yes ___	No ___
Do you often experience sleeplessness or anxiety? If so, what are you doing about it? _____	Yes ___	No ___
Do you have a close relative or friend with whom you discuss problems and successes? If not, do you talk with a professional or someone of your religious faith?	Yes ___ Yes ___	No ___ No ___
Do you make, and keep, preventive and necessary medical and dental appointments? If not, what would help you do so? _____	Yes ___	No ___
What are your goals and what are you doing to achieve them?		

_____
_____
_____
_____

is necessary. The caregiver needs to learn how to access services (that is, learn how to identify potential service providers and determine, based on eligibility requirements, types and amounts of services offered, and when to meet with appropriate agencies); gain the care receiver's acceptance of the service(s); develop a plan or schedule for coordinating needed services; and monitor the services (Montgomery, 1984). The caregiver must learn to act as a case manager, unless case management is one of the purchased services. These functions become much more complicated when the family has limited financial resources. Then the caregiver also must learn about agencies that may offer financial aid or purchase services for the client. Finally, the caregiver should be aware of the normal frequency, duration, and functions of each service. Then the family can evaluate the appropriateness of the purchased services.

ELEMENTS OF AN EFFECTIVE ACTION PLAN

Families traditionally have functioned as care providers and case managers. If they sought help, service providers assumed that they only needed guidance on what the client needed. More recently, service providers have realized that primary caregivers also need respite and emotional support. In individual communities, some service providers and professionals even provide education and training for caregiving families. Access to such training now needs to become available across all communities and should become a standard part of each professional's work with caregiving families.

One of the best ways to ensure that families are aware of, and have an opportunity to participate in, needed training is to build training into a complete action plan. The action plan should help the caregiving family members meet the client's needs and their own. It should include

- an assessment of the client's needs
- an assessment of primary caregiver time and ability to help
- an assessment of the caregiver's needs (education and training, counseling, respite, and help in giving care)
- encouragement and arrangements for entry into a support group
- arrangements for a schedule of caregiver training and service needs
- development of a self-change plan

- identification of sources of informal help for the family member
- a schedule and methods for coordinating informal assistance
- identification of gaps where formal services are needed
- identification of agencies or service providers appropriate to meet the care receiver's needs
- a schedule and methods for coordinating formal services
- development of criteria and a plan for evaluating services regularly

The action plan will specify the caregiver's and the professional's role in each part of the plan. The action plan is necessarily so complex that it does not include a developmental perspective for each family member or the family unit as a whole. Because future outlook and goals are critical to each person's coping ability, showing people how to create a developmental plan should be the next step as professionals continue to learn how to help caregiving families. Chapter 4 discusses a developmental perspective for caregivers and the benefits of such an approach.

REFERENCES

Bane, S. D., & Halpest, B. P. (1986). *Information for caregivers of the elderly.* Kansas City: University of Missouri, Center on Aging Studies.

Biegel, D. E., Shore, B. K., & Gordon, E. (1984). *Building support networks for the elderly: Theory and applications.* Bevery Hills: Sage.

Couper, D. P. (1987). *Aging and our families: Handbook for family caregivers.* Hartford: The Travelers Center on Aging, University of Connecticut and the State of Connecticut, Department on Aging.

Ferris, P. A., & Marshall, C. A. (1987). A model project for families of the chronically mentally ill. *Social Work, 32,* 110–114.

Gallagher, D. (1985, November). *Coping with caregiving: Two psychoeducational approaches.* Paper presented at the annual meeting of AABT, Houston, TX.

General Accounting Office. (1989). *Health care: Home care experiences of families with chronically ill children.* Report to the Chairman, Committee on Finance, U.S. Senate. (Report No. GAO/HRD 89-73). Washington, DC: U.S. Government Printing Office.

Lidoff, L. (1985). *Supports for family caregivers of the elderly: Highlights of a national symposium.* Washington, DC: The National Council on the Aging.

McCubbin, H. I., McCubbin, M. A., Patterson, J., Cauble, A., Wilson, L., & Warwick, W. (1983). CHIP—Coping Health Inventory for Parents: An assessment of parental coping patterns in the care of the chronically ill child. *Journal of Marriage and the Family,* 359–370.

Montgomery, R. (1984). *Family seminars for caregiving.* Washington, DC: Department of Health and Human Services, Office of Human Development Services, Administration on Aging.

Pinkston, E. M., & Linsk, N. L. (1984). Behavioral family intervention with the impaired elderly. *The Gerontologist, 24,* 576–583.

Simank, M. H., & Strickland, K. J. (1986). Assisting families in coping with Alzheimer's and other related dementias with the establishment of a mutual support group. In R. Dobrof (Ed.), *Social work and Alzheimer's disease* (pp. 49–58). New York: Haworth.

Springer, D., & Brubaker, T. H. (1985). *Family caregivers and dependent elderly: Minimizing stress and maximizing independence.* Beverly Hills: Sage.

Wikler, L., & Keenan, M. P. (Eds.). (1983). *Developmental disabilities: No longer a private tragedy.* Silver Spring, MD: National Association of Social Workers.

Zarit, S. H., Orr, N. K., & Zarit, J. M. (1983). *Working with families of dementia victims: A treatment manual.* (Publication No. OHDS 84-20816). Washington, DC: Department of Health and Human Services.

3
Case Study of a Caregiver Support Program

Most of the comprehensive caregiver support programs are relatively new. Evaluations of their success are incomplete. From a research perspective, no one knows which programs are most effective. However, program staff do know which programs participants prefer and whether participants believe a particular program makes a difference in their lives. One particular caregiver support program, the Honolulu Gerontology Program of Child and Family Service, offers comprehensive support for caregiving families. It provides services both to care receivers and caregivers. Within the program, health maintenance groups help frail, disabled, and depressed elderly care receivers build and maintain physical and mental health. Groups, which meet twice a week, offer physical exercise, education, discussion, and socialization. Clients learn to cope with their limitations by working with peers in the group, which becomes an effective support group. All participants receive case management services, including an assessment, development of a care plan, arrangements of needed services, and counseling for the individual and the family. Every participant must have physician approval to participate in the program.

The health maintenance group itself can be of considerable support to caregivers. It provides caregivers a few hours of respite twice a week. For some caregivers, this is all the respite they need. Other caregivers report that they not only benefit from respite but that those they care for also improve in mood and become more self-sufficient as a result of group participation. The care receivers may model themselves after the most well-adjusted members of the group or simply may look around and find comfort in knowing they are not alone. As care receivers increase their independence and minimize self-pity and depression, the caregiver's job becomes more tolerable and pleasant. Still other caregivers who accompany their care receivers to the health maintenance group informally talk with other caregivers on the fringes of the group activity. Group leaders encourage this informal networking among caregivers.

In 1980, the Honolulu Gerontology Program provided linkages between companion-aides and elderly people who could not live alone. This program was expanded in 1988 to offer respite for caregivers who did not work outside the home. The caregiver support portion of the Honolulu Gerontology Program began in 1985 with groups designed to both educate and offer support. In 1988, the program instituted an annual eight-lecture educational series for caregivers in addition to providing the support groups, thus integrating services to the care receiver and the caregiver. Before discussing the program in more detail, however, it is important to understand who the caregivers are and why they participate in the caregiver support activities.

CAREGIVER CHARACTERISTICS

The Honolulu Gerontology Program is typical of most caregiver programs in that most of its caregiver participants are women. It is atypical in terms of the diversity of ethnic backgrounds and the combination of people caring for those with mental disorders and people caring for those with physical impairments. In the caregiver group (n = 48), the ratio of women to men is 38:10 (Brown & Csordas, 1988). Although the largest single ethnic population in the caregiver group is Caucasian (n = 19), a significant number of members are Japanese (n = 10) or Chinese (n = 10) (Table 3-1). A few caregivers are Portuguese or Hawaiian. The diversity of care receiver diagnoses also is remarkable. Primary diagnoses for care receivers whose caregivers participate in the caregiver group are dementia and stroke (Table 3-2). However, a variety of other diagnosed care receiver illnesses

Table 3-1. Ethnicity of Participating Caregivers

| Ethnicity | Initial Group | | Those Who Continued in the Group | |
	Members (n = 48)	Members (%)	Members (n = 18)	Members (%)[a]
Caucasian	19	40	7	39
Japanese	10	21	4	22
Chinese	10	21	2	11
Portuguese	4	8	3	17
Part Hawaiian	3	6	1	6
Other	2	4	1	6

[a]Total does not equal 100 percent because of rounding.

Table 3-2. Diagnosis of Care Receiver as Reported by Caregiver

Primary Diagnosis	Initial Group		Caregivers Who Continued in the Group	
	Clients (n = 48)	Clients (%)[a]	Clients (n = 18)	Clients (%)[a]
Dementia	12	25	6	33
Stroke	10	21	4	22
Depression	3	6	1	6
Arthritis	3	6	1	6
Psychiatric problem	2	4	0	0
Hearing impairment	2	4	2	11
Heart problem	2	4	1	6
Parkinson's disease	2	4	1	6
Quadriplegia	2	4	1	6
Vision impairment	2	4	0	0
Back problem	1	2	0	0
Amyotrophic lateral sclerosis	1	2	0	0
Diabetes	1	2	0	0
Unknown	5	10	1	6

[a]Total may not equal 100 percent because of rounding.

also result in caregiver problems. Differences in care receiver diagnoses do not seem to have a negative impact on the usefulness of the group to the participants. Although many people (n = 25) attended the group only once or twice, they were people in a crisis. Once they resolved the crisis or arranged for individual help, they no longer felt the need for a support group.

Out of the 48 people who participated in caregiver support groups, 18 continued to attend the group for 2 or 3 years (Brown & Csordas, 1988). Those who continued to attend were similar in ethnic backgrounds to those who began initially. Thus, ethnicity does not seem to be a deciding factor in whether a caregiver continues to seek support (Table 3-1). For those who continued to participate, the diagnoses of the people for whom they cared were similar to the diagnoses of care receivers in the initial group, except that those caring for dementia victims were more heavily represented and the percent of participants caring for people with hearing impairment was somewhat greater (Table 3-2). Continued participation by such a diverse group may be, in part, the result of individual meetings with caregivers who needed extra help apart from the group sessions. (Leaders will meet individually either after the meetings or by special appointment.) Because more has been written about groups of caregivers dealing with similar illnesses or impairments, the success of the Honolulu program presents fertile ground for further research.

RISKS TO THE CAREGIVER IDENTIFIED
DURING GROUP PARTICIPATION

Originally, the Honolulu Gerontology Program expected to reach some caregivers who had become, or were at risk of becoming, abusive to care receivers (Brown & Csordas, 1988; M. Ramsey, personal communication, February 14, 1989). Much to the staff's surprise, they found that many of the caregivers are victims of abuse—either physical or mental—perpetrated by the care receiver. Abuse of caregivers takes many forms, although the care receiver diagnosis does not seem to be associated with abuse. Abuse often is perpetrated by the care receiver but also by siblings, children, or other family members. One of the most common forms of abuse reported by caregivers is the care receiver who demands that only the caregiver provide the care. The care receiver will not allow any other family member, friend, or agency to help, and makes the caregiver feel guilty about taking any time off for his or her own health or pleasure. A spouse also may become jealously possessive, for example, accusing their caregiving mate of infidelity every time he or she is away from the spouse.

Some abuse results from long-standing family conflicts that intensify or recur when family members move in together after years of physical separation. Mother–daughter conflicts are especially evident. Two of the mother–daughter relationships discussed in the caregiver group were so hostile and debilitating to the daughters that group leaders recommended psychiatric counseling outside the group. Family jealousy and fights to control money surfaced, especially among sibling groups, during group discussions. In one case, the mother of a caregiver gave money and favor to the child who did not help while she abused her caregiver daughter even though the daughter cared for her mother 24 hours a day. In another case, a granddaughter provided full-time care for her grandmother, with whom she always had shared a special, loving relationship. The grateful grandmother willed her estate to the granddaughter, who then had to fend off relatives' constant efforts to undermine the granddaughter's relationship with the grandmother.

Some caregivers also reported verbal and physical aggression. Caregivers of male stroke victims, in particular, reported that the stroke victims were perpetrators of such abuse—these care receivers might swear at or strike the caregiver with a limb or a cane. Female caregivers reported that their male care receivers were not able to accept the role reversal that came with the physical and mental limitations imposed by their illness. Statistics were not kept on the percentages of caregiver group members abused by those for whom they cared, but the staff estimated that nearly one-third of the 48 group members were abused. It is undoubtedly significant that the caregiver group's educational session on "Managing Demanding and Manipulative Behavior" had twice the number of attendees as any of the other sessions in the educational series. The caregivers apparently recognize the abuse or manipulative behavior, but do not know how to handle it without feeling guilty. Although the educational session on optimizing health did not include a discussion of risks of caregiving, group leaders and participants discussed these problems and possible sources of help in regular monthly group sessions.

Group support is particularly effective for abused caregivers. Through education and support of other members, caregivers are able to develop more assertive behavior and self-confidence and to better understand and manage the care receiver's abusive behavior. They learn that it is not only right, but necessary, to take time for themselves, and they learn ways to reach out to other family members and agencies to get supportive help.

SELF-IDENTIFIED RISKS

Most of the problems identified by caregivers in the Honolulu program correspond with those discussed in the literature on caregiving. Problems described by caregivers in the Honolulu program included depression; isolation and loneliness; lack of control (for example, experiencing the pain of watching the physical or mental deterioration of a loved one); uncertainty about the care receiver's capability to function independently; lack of privacy (feeling suffocated); feeling guilty about respite; physical fatigue from constancy of care; physically demanding care; lack of sleep; and difficulties dealing with role reversals. Furthermore, the caregivers also identified risks that are not well described in the literature. Abuse by the care receiver is one such risk. Other caregivers suffered memory lapses and weight loss because of demanding caregiving responsibilities and stresses and having to care for too many people—one caregiver, for example, cared for a mother who had a stroke, a father who is an amputee, and a 6-year-old son (Brown & Csordas, 1988).

DESCRIPTION OF THE PROGRAM

Caregiver Respite Project

The Honolulu Gerontology Program identifies companion-aides to give in-home relief to informal caregivers, providing referrals and matching aides to caregiver needs. The caregiver must check references, develop an agreement for services the aide will provide, and hire the aide at a set rate of $6 per hour. The caregiver also must maintain household insurance that covers the aide if he or she has an accident or is injured. The program provides a sample agreement form and monitors services that the aide provides.

Program staff screen out caregivers who want an aide so they can work—the program provides services under a specifically funded respite project for 4 to 16 hours per week, not full time. (The program does apply to private foundations for the care receivers to pay for aides to enable the caregivers to remain employed, but not as part of this respite project.) Once the staff determine that a client's care needs meet the criteria for acceptance into the respite project, they may assign a specially trained senior adviser (that is, a retired professional volunteer) to complete a comprehensive in-home assessment of client and caregiver needs. This assessment includes gathering information on the care receiver's social situation, finances, mental health, physical health, and activities of daily living. Sometimes, however, it is apparent that respite help is clearly the only need present. In those instances, the program's respite worker begins immediately to link the client with an appropriate companion-aide. (M. Ramsey, personal communication, September 29, 1988).

Program staff select an aide who can provide needed services to the care receiver and give the aide's name and phone number to the caregiver. Before the caregiver interviews the aide, the staff decide how much reimbursement will be made to the caregiver (that is, the share of the aide's $6 per hour). Program staff also send the caregiver a packet that contains a guide about what services he or she can expect the aide to provide and how to form a contract for those services, an expense sheet to submit for reimbursement after the caregiver pays the aide, and a caregiver stress quiz that is self-administered and serves as a pretest.

Once the caregiver understands the services and requirements of the program, he or she interviews the aide, checks references, and develops the contract for services. Expectations for aides typically include bathing, changing linens, dressing the client, using the bedpan/toileting, making simple transfers, and preparing light meals. The caregiver pays the aide directly an amount that equals the program portion and the care receiver portion. The program then reimburses the caregiver. The sliding scale used to determine the caregiver share of the cost of an aide takes into account funds needed to purchase or rent special equipment, diets, and transportation expenses, before assessing the caregiver's ability to pay (Table 3-3). Program staff monitor services provided by the aide either through visits or by telephone. Staff, in most cases, use telephone monitoring because a shortage in staff and resources does not allow them to visit clients at home regularly.

Program staff administer the caregiver stress quiz 6 months after an aide begins working for a family to identify any differences in stress levels. Caregivers may be informed about the caregiver group when they are first accepted into the program and their names will be placed on the group's mailing list. In other cases, the respite worker discusses the caregiver group with the caregiver at the point he or she is assigned the case and makes contact with the family. A memorandum describing the caregiver group is included in the

Table 3-3. Subsidy after Allowed Expenses in the Honolulu Gerontology Aide Program

Basic and Reasonable Expenses (Monthly)

Acceptable Expenditures	Amount ($)
Housing	500
Food	150
Utilities	90
Telephone	25
Clothing	20
Transportation	50
Medical insurance	55
Medical expenses (medications, diapers, bedpads)	No limit
Miscellaneous	30
Outstanding bills	50

Amount of Subsidy (Per Hour of Aide Time)

Money Left after Expenses ($)	Subsidy ($)
300	None
200	2 per hour
100	4 per hour
No remainder	6 per hour

packet of information the caregivers receive along with an attached referral form for caregivers to complete and return to program staff if they are interested in participating in group sessions.

Caregiver Groups

The caregiver education and support groups began as monthly, 75-minute sessions in 1985. The groups spent about 30 minutes of the sessions discussing educational issues; the remainder of the time was devoted to encouraging participants to share their experiences (both positive and negative) and concerns. When these sessions began, they had a formal 7-month agenda. Initially, these groups were open to families with members who were participating in the health maintenance program or receiving case management from the program. The groups expanded and included those involved in the program's respite project and any other caregivers in the community.

In 1988, the program obtained funds to provide an annual, intensive 8-week educational series. Basic information is consolidated into this educational component. The eight session topics are Overview of the Aging Process; Stressful Emotional Situations and How to Cope; Optimizing Your Health While Caregiving; Managing Demanding and Manipulative Behavior; Legal Issues; Long-Term Care Insurance; Acute Care, Care Homes, and Nursing Homes; and Community Resources for Caregivers. These support groups teach a basic understanding of the aging process, communication skills, and skills for finding community resources and financial help. The educational series portion of the groups is on videotape so group leaders can use them again and so other programs can borrow them.

The 30-minute educational component at the beginning of the monthly group sessions may reiterate and reinforce some of the material covered in the 8-week sessions. For example, the monthly session may expand the discussion on stress. The caregivers then will have a chance to verbalize their concerns and frustrations in these monthly meetings. Regarding the topic of community resources, the monthly sessions may focus on only one or two resources in-depth at a time, such as home care or various types of respite options.

Periodically, group leaders ask participants what type of information they would like to learn through the group. (Many of the issues on the "established" topics list began at the request of previous caregiver group members.) Participants primarily have asked for more information on available community services and ways to pay for the cost of care, such as Medicaid, long-term care insurance, and personal care homes and nursing homes. Participants, when surveyed by group leaders, also requested information on home care services, managing memory loss, coping with the emotional stress of caregiving, respite options, nutrition, and how to hire help in the home. Group leaders also use a caregiver quiz as a teaching/discussion tool. (The quiz is not the same test as used in the respite program.) Problem solving is a component of the support group proceedings. Supervision of aides is taught individually outside the group sessions, either by case managers or the respite project worker.

Members of the caregiver groups include those with and without aides. Although no specific stress tests have been given to caregiver group members, their comments during group discussions are clear indicators that respite help has made a significant difference in their lives, both to the caregivers who receive respite on a regular weekly basis and those who hire an aide once a year for several weeks, thus allowing them an opportunity to take a vacation. Group members who have not hired in-home help often become less resistant to the notion of hiring an aide after hearing about the experiences of others. Caregivers who feel less stress as a result of the respite inject a positive note into group discussions and often add humor to the discussions because they are able to handle their own difficult situations with a new perspective. However, these caregiver groups have not moved toward peer leadership. Initially the social worker co-leaders presented and fostered this idea, but most of the caregivers are too overwhelmed with their own needs to take on a leadership role. There has been internal leadership shown in particular group sessions, however.

The Honolulu Gerontology Program includes all the elements of an action plan as described in Chapter 2 (Table 3-4). The program is quite comprehensive. Grants allowed different parts of the program to develop, but required separate treatment of clients for purposes of the demonstrations. Thus, not all client/caregiver families receive all services available through the program. However, once the demonstrations end, and if the program secures continued funding, families could receive the full range of program activities.

SELF-IDENTIFIED CAREGIVER CHANGES

The effect of the program and its parts (that is, aide, respite, and support group) have not been thoroughly evaluated. However, as the program has progressed, caregivers have shared the solutions and

Table 3-4. Action Plan Components

Action Plan	Honolulu Gerontology Program
Make client assessment	By senior adviser (who gives the information to the case manager)
Make caregiver assessment	By senior adviser
Evaluate assessments	By case manager
Encourage and schedule caregiver training and services	Arrange aide (respite) support group
Develop self-change plans	Discuss techniques and provide individual help on request
Identify sources of informal help	Convene family meeting and write letters to distant members
Schedule and coordinate informal help	Caregiver responsibility with case manager consultation
Identify need for formal services	Handled through assessment
Identify community resources	Assessment care plan or through support group
Coordinate formal services	Caregiver responsibility with case manager consultation
Evaluate services	By phone/follow-up home visit

case management techniques they were developing. Without an evaluation, it is impossible to determine whether caregivers would have tried particular case management techniques if they had not been involved in the program, yet members of the group who benefited by learning from other caregivers believed that they did so directly as a result of their participation in the group. Some of the personal behavior changes caregivers reported included managing feelings better; thinking ahead and planning; encouraging the independence of the care receiver; practicing assertive behavior; enjoying respite; setting short-term goals (for example, taking a trip); and asking relatives for help.

GROUP LEADER EVALUATION OF SUCCESS

The group leaders believe that the caregiver groups are meeting a definite need for education and support among caregivers who feel a need and are able to get to the meetings. The groups seem to work best for long-term caregivers who may experience burnout and even caregiver breakdown or illness. Many of the caregivers in the group have been filling demanding caregiving roles for 5 or 10 years with no relief in sight. Peer support in such a situation is valuable, as is the professional encouragement to take one's own needs seriously and to reach out, even over the care receiver's protests, to get outside help. The open-ended model seems to have the flexibility to meet variable caregiver needs.

PLANS FOR CONTINUED CAREGIVER SUPPORT

The program intends to continue its present format for the caregiver groups. Staff will maintain the monthly education and support meetings and the annual 8-week education series. Various locations on the island of Oahu need such groups to make caregiver support more readily accessible outside the Honolulu area. This outreach will be possible only if expanded funding becomes available.

The health maintenance group program has expanded over the past 8 years from one central Honolulu location to the present seven sites, thus providing this service to the entire island population. The need for caregiver support likewise exists in all areas. Program staff recognize the research opportunities inherent in their multiethnic and multidiagnostic caregiver group. However, funding limitations prevent research from becoming a reality.

INDIVIDUAL CASE STUDIES

Caregiver needs and the ways in which the program helps are illustrated best through the following case studies.

Roy and Louise

Roy and Louise retired from their careers in their fifties to enjoy the "good life" while they were still young. They moved from the East Coast to Hawaii where they could enjoy the year-round golf and tennis they loved so well. After just a year in Hawaii, Louise suffered a stroke resulting in left hemiplegia. Their retirement plans were abruptly and permanently altered. Louise recovered well, however, and improved physically and mentally with the help of her husband and the program's health maintenance group. Unfortunately, in another year, Louise suffered two more debilitating strokes, became depressed and reclusive, and demanded Roy's full-time attention. Roy came to the caregiver group seeking support because he had overwhelming feelings of anger and depression. He was trapped by Louise's increasing demands. Her balance was poor—he was afraid to let her walk. Her poor balance made Louise weaker and more fearful, and the couple was becoming caught in a spiral of decline. In the caregiver group, Roy learned that others experience feelings similar to his, his needs are important, and services are available to help Louise regain some independence and learn new interests while giving Roy some time to himself. Adult day care for Louise was the solution. Program staff obtained funds from a local foundation to help Roy pay for Louise's care. Day care enabled Roy to take up part-time work and to pursue his golf. Roy, genuinely grateful for the group's help, has continued to attend the group, where he has become a catalyst by encouraging others to seek and find solutions.

Violet

Violet recalls planning with her husband more than 28 years ago for their retirement. Before they could fulfill such plans, he died suddenly of a heart attack. One year later, Violet took her mother into her home and began caring for her. She continued this care over the years—Violet was 76 years old; her mother, Rose, 97 years old. Rose had multiple problems including arthritis, incontinence, severe memory loss, and extreme stubbornness. Two years later, Violet's son, age 52, developed cancer and died. She was, for the second time, overwhelmed with grief, yet had to continue to manage the care of her mother. The day-to-day responsibility soon began to overwhelm Violet—emotionally, she became angry and frustrated; physically, she developed high blood pressure and frequent nose bleeds.

About that time she began attending the caregiver group where she readily vented her feelings of futility about the seemingly never-ending and difficult, stubborn behavior her mother constantly presented. Violet received help in two ways from the group—(1) support that she was not alone in her circumstances and (2) education regarding the causes of difficult behavior and memory loss. As a result, she was able to distance herself emotionally from her mother. She shared with the group that she had finally stopped trying to change her mother. Because Violet's attitude changed, her mother became less agitated and easier to handle.

Violet also took advantage of the respite project to hire a temporary live-in companion-aide, which enabled her to take a badly needed 3-week vacation to visit one of her grandchildren on the mainland.

The program has successfully helped both families illustrated in the case studies because the needs of caregivers and care receivers were met. Caregivers were encouraged to become empowered, that is, to assume responsibility for meeting their own needs (Table 3-5). Care receivers had the services they needed, yet were forced to accept some independence from the caregiver.

Table 3-5. Caregiver Empowerment (Case Studies)

Name	Services for Caregiver	Services for Care Receiver	Empowerment for Caregiver
Roy	Caregiver group	Health maintenance group	Roy became group catalyst, encouraging others to seek and find solutions
	Funds and help obtaining care for Louise	Adult day care	
Violet	Caregiver group Support Education Respite (live-in companion aide)	Aide and multiple medical services	Violet was able to leave her mother for a 3-week vacation with her grandchild

REFERENCE

Brown, A., & Csordas, B. (1988, October). *Group work with caregivers.* Paper presented at the Hawaii Pacific Gerontological Society Conference.

For further information about the Honolulu Gerontology Program, which is part of Child and Family Service, contact Mildred Ramsey, Program Director, the Honolulu Gerontology Program, 550 South Beretania Street, Honolulu, HI 96813.

4

Stages of Caregiving: A New Approach for Professionals and Caregivers

Although social work professionals are aware of the developmental stages that chronically ill or impaired people go through from infancy to old age and the support that they need (Lapham & Shevlin, 1986), often neither their families nor the professionals helping them focus on the corresponding developmental stages of the caregiving family and each of the other family members. Information materials on care of chronically ill or impaired people describe the difficulties and the associated health and mental health risks (discussed in Chapter 1) that caregivers face. Relief and personal time for the caregiver always are recommended—both through respite and the use of formal services. Current professional practice includes an assessment of the family's ability to cope with the emotional and physical stress of caregiving and a review of resources available to supplement family care. (Social workers often make these assessments because, traditionally, they understand that the entire family unit needs support.) However, even improved family-focused plans, which include the training components described in Chapter 2, do not include a developmental plan for the caregiver or other family members, nor do they suggest how a developmental approach can improve family relationships.

The developmental stages of caregiving relate more to the care receiver's age, developmental stage, and the nature and course of the disease or impairment, than to the caregiver's own age if he or she is in good health. The developmental stages of caregiving also relate to the circumstances of the caregiving family. For example, when both parents must work and must care for other children, they may spend less time visiting a chronically ill infant or child who is in the hospital. The lack of bonding or parental involvement may affect both the development of the person who is hospitalized and the patient's parents.

A developmental perspective assumes that the developmental stage of caregiving and the developmental stage of the family and each of its members must be considered. The developmental stages of caregiving begin with a crisis that is either sudden or long term.

Gradually, symptoms may increase or a sudden illness or accident may create a crisis. Family stress may increase when an infant is born with immediately obvious problems. Family stress may begin with noticeable symptoms (for older children and adults), or with a diagnosis. Once the family recognizes the crisis, they experience shock, denial, and grief. The family may regress to an earlier stage of development such as nurturing an adult child who becomes chronically ill instead of moving into a period of greater independence. Eventually, the family moves to a stage of acceptance and adaptation. This stage may be a calm, long-term approach to coping with a chronic problem, or it may require periodic changes in adaptation to accommodate acute health crises or progression of a disease. Movement from the crisis to the adaptation stage also may be affected by the developmental stages of the family and its individual members (Chilman, Nunnally, & Cox, 1988). This chapter discusses the interaction of family members with a chronically ill member, the ages of family members, and the stages they go through. Once the family reaches the adaptation stage appropriate for its members, it is possible for the family and all family members to have a future-oriented outlook, with goals of their own.

A developmental plan for the family may help even families with difficult caregiving situations in which the person is unlikely to get better, to stop being belligerent, or to recognize the environment or family. Although professionals need to continue helping people meet immediate and short-range needs, they also need to help them plan to accomplish greater goals over the long term. Short-term help includes helping people understand and accept the prognosis of their loved one's illness or impairment and the tasks involved in providing care, and encouraging caregivers to take care of themselves by admitting their feelings, getting appropriate nutrition and exercise, maintaining social contacts, and setting reasonable expectations for the amount of help that can be given. Aside from a training component, such action plans also include needed education for the caregiver and the family. A developmental plan, however, could help caregivers look ahead. Goals and achievements will result in happier and more stable family relationships. Emerging research shows that caregivers who work scored better when screened for psychiatric symptoms (Brody, Kleban, Johnsen, Hoffman, & Schoonover, 1987). This is probably because they have established and attained some career goals. This is not to say that caregivers do not have a difficult time watching loved ones suffer. Rather, as families help to the best of their abilities, there will come an appropriate time to think of themselves and their own potential and needs. Caregivers probably will want to participate in developmental planning at similar times in the stages of the caregiving process. However, because client populations differ, discussion about this planning is by age group (Lapham & Shevlin, 1986).

INFANCY AND EARLY CHILDHOOD

Problems of infancy range from conditions that are disfiguring, but not life threatening, such as anencephaly, to those that threaten life, such as severe respiratory distress syndrome where the infant needs a ventilator to survive. The conditions that require intensive care have the most immediate impact on the infant and the family. Separation of the infant and mother inhibits bonding and increases stress on a family already drained by the normal stress of pregnancy. Constant stimulation, pain, and chaotic care in a hospital prevent the infant from learning that each experience has a meaning. The infant does not learn to trust a caregiver. Between the two extremes of conditions that are and are not life threatening are chronic conditions that will affect the newborn into childhood, and affect the family (Eisenberg, Sutkin, & Jansen, 1984). Some of the chronic childhood illnesses include epilepsy, leukemia, congenital heart disease, diabetes, and asthma. Also, an increasing number of children have acquired immune deficiency syndrome (AIDS). A growing number of children are developmentally disabled or remain dependent for several years on technology that keeps them alive. Children suffering from developmental disabilities include the mentally retarded, hearing impaired, and visually impaired; those suffering from severe emotional disturbances; and those with physical handicaps.

What are the developmental stages for parental caregivers? Shock, disbelief, and anxiety are likely to be part of the first or discovery stage. Parents may feel guilty, as though they could have prevented the disability. There is no point in discussing goals until parents accept their child's problems to the extent that they can and learn how to care for the child. Some researchers believe the grieving period for an infant or child with a handicapping condition or illness extends beyond the normal mourning process for someone who died or who is terminally ill. Grief for a terminally ill member may continue longer, but the mourner can accomplish the final stages of grieving when death does occur. The normal grieving period for someone who died is 6 months to a year. However, the constant presence of the infant or child and the multitude of emotions, including guilt if the problem is genetic or caused by the mother's diabetes or other illness, may preclude final mourning. Some mourning then may continue throughout infancy or childhood (Eisenberg et al., 1984). During this phase, parents need constant reassurance and help in dealing with medical personnel and treatments for the child. If the parents are young or have not successfully completed their own development, they may need special help learning and adjusting to the nurturing skills they will need. They need to understand the child's fear of pain, anxiety about hospital procedures, and needs for security. Parents may need help finding programs that offer financial aid and help with the care of other children.

Financing may be especially difficult to arrange. Insurance companies are not eager to assume the risks of paying for different care settings for technology-dependent children.

> Because the cost of home care depends so heavily on social and environmental, rather than medical, factors, it is not possible to identify a specific group of technology-dependent children based on clinical criteria alone for whom home care will be cost saving to third-party payers. However, if a child is medically stable, the home has a good potential for being a less expensive setting of care. (Kaslow, 1986, p. 55)

Parents may need help in responding emotionally to the developmental needs of other children so they do not become totally preoccupied with the ill or impaired child.

The second stage for caregivers is acceptance and adaptation. Parents learn to care for the infant or young child and learn to differentiate between normal, routine needs and the needs resulting from the illness or condition. As they gain confidence, they make a clear decision to care for the child at home. Sometimes arrangements are made to remain at a hospital with the child or work out a frequent visitation schedule at the hospital or nursing facility. The parents adjust and receive training in how to meet the needs of the child. When children are dependent on mechanical ventilators, tube feeding, or respiratory support, or when they need catheters or colostomy bags, training is more intensive and parents require more supervision. (The specialized needs of the child are not discussed here in detail because the focus is on the caregiver.)

Adaptation may take much longer because parents may be afraid that they could make a mistake. Parents also may be upset if the child is not developing appropriately—as is likely with frequent or continued hospitalization. The best time to begin to think about respite, support groups, and other activities may be when the parents work through their fears. It also may be appropriate to discuss a return to work. However, a caregiver may need both encouragement and help finding needed services, such as day care for children with special needs.

Thus, many of the caregivers who must leave an infant or young child in the hospital may need all the education and training before they take their children home. Training may include help with communication skills. For example, parents of a blind infant need to learn how to watch the baby's hands to understand how the baby feels. The necessary medical and social supports also must be arranged before discharge (Eisenberg et al., 1984). This need for training and supportive services places a greater responsibility on hospital staff and increases the need for interdisciplinary teams. Both the need for training and for emotional support suggest that support groups sponsored by hospitals are useful to help families progress to a stage of adaptation. Groups could be conducted by staff or experts brought in for specific sessions.

The third stage begins either when the problem resolves itself or the caregiving family makes permanent adaptations to accommodate the chronic, lifelong disability and associated needs for care. The problem may resolve itself if the patient stabilizes, goes into remission, or dies. This is the point where a developmental plan can be thoughtfully constructed (unless the patient dies—then a grieving period may have to come first). Career goals, leisure time goals (for example, playing a musical instrument or sports), desired living arrangements, and life-style all could be part of this plan. Where there are other siblings, it is important that this family process carefully consider their needs as well. The caregiver's ability to achieve some of these goals may be heavily dependent on the availability of community services. (See Chapter 5 for a discussion of these services.)

The stages vary depending on the age a child succumbs to illness or impairment, how a disease progresses, and how supportive existing family relationships are. If the problem occurs at birth, the initial grieving period and adaptation should occur before the infant progresses to other developmental stages. Thus, the caregiver and other family members could have a developmental plan in place by that time if the disability is permanent. If the problem is an illness in which remissions, progressions, and changes in functional ability occur periodically, the patient and the caregiver may go in and out of stages, making permanent adaptation and planning much more difficult for the entire family. The family may face constant or periodic financial pressures, transportation needs, or needs for help in dealing with emotional stresses (including feelings of guilt or fear among siblings). These pressures will affect the development and achievement of personal goals.

SCHOOL AGE

If chronic illness or impairment occurs when a child is already in school, both the child and the family face more difficult adjustment problems. The child may regress developmentally in response to the problems. Parents may react initially by viewing the child as permanently handicapped rather than as a person who needs special services to achieve full potential in school (Office of Technology Assessment, 1987). Even when a child has had a problem for some time, that the child is of school age complicates any adjustments that already have been made. When a student misses school because of illness, medical appointments, or therapy, and cannot participate in physical education or sports, he or she risks not being promoted to the next grade level and may experience peer ridicule (Adams, 1985). If all children in the family are school age, the primary caregiver also is likely to be committed to more activities and to be working. The care of a chronically ill child will add additional stress to family responsibilities that already are difficult to accomplish. Families with busy schedules have little time together as a family. Both parents may be working to improve finances. A single parent has no alternative to a full-time job in addition to other responsibilities. Yet, the caregiver still needs to meet medical appointments and negotiate arrangements with the school.

The developmental stages may take longer to work through when the child is of school age. The discovery of a problem may be more of a shock because the child may have been completely normal for some time. Parents may become overprotective, complicating the child's ability to develop competence in areas where he or she still has control and to develop new areas of competence to compensate for skills lost to an illness or handicapping condition. Parental regression to an earlier stage of care for the child may complicate relationships between spouses and between parents and other children, creating more anxiety for the child in need of special care. This is not the same type of stress a family faces when the child is young and there are other siblings. The caregiver may have fewer options and supports, for example, less control over job-related activities (there is no maternity leave to care for a sick child). This lack of control over other critical aspects of one's life when already one cannot control the illness or impairment and needed treatment regimens can lead to even greater stress. Adaptation may be much more difficult—arranging time off from work, finding someone to care for other siblings, and working out home study or other arrangements with the child's school so the child does not fall too far behind in his or her schoolwork. If the ill child responds to the illness by regressing in behavior and social functioning, or by becoming restless and depressed with difficulty sleeping, or by becoming dependent on a parent for everything, the impact on parental and family functioning is even more dramatic.

Parents can obtain some help according to provisions of the Special Education Law, P.L. 94-142. This law requires that each "handicapped" child have an individualized educational program (IEP) designed to meet his or her special needs. The IEP must be developed based on diagnostic information and information from classroom teachers and from parents. The development of an IEP at least assures parents that school personnel will help arrange to meet the child's educational needs. In states where public education begins at age 4 years, the child is eligible to receive free services beginning at that age. Available services should include audiology, counseling, medical services, psychological services, recreation, school health, social work services, speech pathology, and transportation (Adams, 1985).

Planning for a child with a chronic illness that does not result in a serious disability (such as epilepsy) may be as difficult as planning for a child with serious disabilities. The child is not "normal" in that the child must remember to take his or her medication. However, because no obvious disability exists, the child does not receive support or special consideration from others. Some researchers suggest these children may need more psychosocial help than their chronically ill peers (Eisenberg et al., 1984). If parents use the services available through P.L. 94-142, they may alleviate some of their anxiety and feel that they have an adequate plan for the child. However, they still will not have a plan for the rest of the family. Family members still will need training. When parents and professionals finalize the plan for the child, and parents receive training, parents may be ready to begin developmental planning.

The process of arriving at a developmental plan may help the caregiver and family find community resources and adapt to what may be permanently changed needs and responsibilities. If the caregiver is already involved in many activities, including work, the plan may be a confirmation or extension of already established goals. If the individual does not have these goals, this process could be similar to the process of establishing an initial plan for a family with a young child who is seriously ill. However, as a child progresses through school age, it is more likely that the child's parents will have older parents who need help as well as their ill or impaired child. If this is the case, the family may need intensive help for a lengthy period before members can finally adapt and begin to focus on their own developmental needs.

ADOLESCENCE

Just as school age brings certain unique problems to a family's ability to cope with chronic illness or handicaps, so does adolescence. An adolescent is forming career goals and becoming independent. Parents may be looking forward to their children developing mature relationships and could be planning their own activities in anticipation of their greater independence. They may be expecting to have reduced responsibility.

Peer pressure and the need for acceptance by peers dominates the adolescent's life. Thus, the sudden onset of disease, impairment, or any permanent condition compromises the most important aspect of life: peer relationships. Besides the shock of discovering the problem and the need for acceptance of and adaptation to a chronic condition, the age of the child may result in problems such as unwillingness to comply with treatment regimens, conflict with close family members, regression, or an inability to plan for career goals and independence (Driscoll, 1986; Karlin, 1986). Even if the child and family have been coping with a chronic condition for a long time, adolescent pressures still may result in similar problems. However, by that time the caregiver is no longer coping with the initial shock of discovering the problem, so, with the help of social workers or other professionals, the parent should know about what to expect and how to cope with changed behaviors.

At this stage, parents, as caregivers of normal children, experience adjustment problems. They are accustomed to providing care and exercising judgment about their child's activities. However, normal adolescents want to assume greater responsibility for themselves more rapidly than their parents may feel is appropriate.

Parents may find it difficult to relinquish responsibility. When chronic disease or impairment complicates this normal developmental stage, regression is probable. The child's relationships with family and friends will suffer and caregivers are likely not only to have difficulty relinquishing some control, but they may have a real fear of the consequences if the child does not follow medical regimens. Yet, if parents do not give an adolescent some control or independence, the adolescent is more likely to rebel by refusing treatment or refusing to obey rules or comply with scheduled appointments (Eisenberg et al., 1984).

The adolescent also may experience developmental problems, particularly if he or she is suffering from cancer or loss of a limb (whether from cancer, another disease, or an accident). Apart from fear of peer ridicule, which may decrease the youth's willingness to participate in social activities, the adolescent may believe that independence is impossible. In these cases, caregivers must find ways to help the adolescent achieve maximum independence. One of the best ways to encourage independence is to expect a return to school. Because being a student is the adolescent's primary role, a return to this role reaffirms competence and independence (Eisenberg et al., 1984). Thus, it is important from the time of initial diagnosis that parents and the youth expect this return to school.

Professional counseling may help family members negotiate the ups and downs of shifting control until the family members establish mutual respect and support. It will be difficult for family members to move beyond their anxiety to create a developmental plan before they establish this relationship. For the family to fully control their anxiety, not only will the relationships need to improve, but the adolescent will need to begin to establish future goals within the context of his or her new reality. It is important to gain control over family anxiety—research shows that chronically ill adolescents can maintain their self-esteem and control their anxiety even when the prognosis is uncertain (Eisenberg et al., 1984).

The process of helping an adolescent think through goals may help other family members begin developmental planning. Because the youth may have to alter goals and give careful thought to how to achieve the goals within the constraints of disease or handicaps, the process will be instructive to other family members if the teenager is successful. Family members will realize that a person can be happy with more than one set of goals and that a person can achieve those goals in a variety of ways.

If the prognosis is poor, and the teenager might die, intervention at the time of diagnosis is critical if the family wants to make the fullest use of the remaining time. Family members may need to overcome relationship problems to support each other. One study showed that in families that did not develop appropriate coping mechanisms, 95 percent of the survivors reported health problems and 43 percent of the surviving siblings and 51 percent of the surviving adults reported problems fulfilling their major responsibilities (Eisenberg et al., 1984). Education and training (communication and problem solving) are the most immediate needs besides medical and supportive services. Developmental planning may have to wait until the youth's death, and subsequent mourning period, are over.

If chronic mental illness strikes, such as schizophrenia, which usually appears during late adolescence or young adulthood (Hatfield, 1987), the developmental process will be more difficult. Although American society has begun to accept that physically handicapped or retarded people may offer a certain level of productivity, society has not defined an acceptable level of productivity from those people who are mentally ill, but intelligent and physically normal. The family and the mentally ill person will have to come to terms with their own goals and measures of productivity. Mental health support groups may help.

ADULTHOOD

When people reach adulthood, society expects them to be financially and socially self-sufficient. Society also expects adults to be able to make personal sacrifices when necessary to help close relatives and friends. During adulthood, as one progresses from young adulthood to the stage before old age, each person has to deal with physical and emotional changes. Living arrangements may change many times (Adderly & Levine, 1986). An adult must cope with changes and remain independent.

If a young adult who has not started a family suddenly is faced with chronic illness or handicapping conditions, he or she may have trouble maintaining independence and self-esteem. If family members are not honest about the person's capabilities or performance, or if the care receiver must return to the parents' home for care without accommodating changes in roles and relationships that reflect family acceptance of that person's adulthood, the young adult may lose trust and have trouble developing intimate relationships. For the young adult without a family, ultimately aging parents may become his or her caregiver. This particularly seems to be the case when an adult child has AIDS.

If the chronic problems occur when an adult is responsible for a family, feelings of guilt, inadequacy, and concern about the family may complicate the person's ability to accept and adapt to changed abilities and care needs. The caregiver may be torn between the spouse's needs, the needs of any children, and efforts of the care receivers' parents to assume control over treatment decisions or the selection of health care professionals. Or, parents may assume financial responsibility for the adult child's new family because chronic illness or disability affects employment and employability. Excessive stress from multiple demands may leave the primary caregiver unable to meet all needs or to be supportive. This stressful and anxiety-ridden situation is worse when the person has a life-threatening illness such as cancer.

Family takes on a much broader meaning for the young adult. *Family* means his or her family of origin and the new family to whom a commitment has been made. To effectively share information and resolve control issues, all of these family members may need to meet with a professional at the time of diagnosis. This meeting probably will have to occur even before arranging education and training for all family members. Developmental planning cannot occur until the roles and relationships for every family member are clear.

If the adult is developmentally disabled or has a history of mental illness, entry to adulthood is a time marked by transition— transition to a sheltered workshop or to employment and transition to greater independence. This transition is especially difficult for caregivers who never believed that it would be possible for their developmentally disabled child to become even semi-independent. They continue to worry about whether someone will take advantage of the developmentally disabled person.

For the older caregiver of an adult, if that adult remains in or returns to the family of origin, or is placed in a special residential facility, developmental planning may be easier if it is done simultaneously with lifecare planning. *Lifecare planning* is planning to meet the caregiver's own needs should the caregiver become incapacitated and planning to meet the needs of a dependent family member when the primary caregiver dies (Bass, 1986). This planning includes thinking about the preferred type of services, environment, and caregiver. Developmental planning allows adult caregivers to determine what they want to accomplish during their lifetime. If it is done in conjunction with lifecare planning, caregivers will realize that eventually they may face incapacity themselves. Getting caregivers to recognize their own vulnerability and to believe that they can help themselves may be the most difficult task a professional faces. Case study after case study shows how serious this problem is for caregivers. For example, one case study of a man suffering from a severely disabling stroke showed an extreme impact on the caregiver, his wife. The financial cost of his care meant that his 65-year-old wife had to continue to work. However, she was unable to control her blood pressure because of the dual responsibility of work and caregiving. She retired. Her blood pressure still would not drop because she still worried about her husband, their finances, and her own health. One year after retirement, she suffered a massive stroke (Sommers & Shields, 1987, pp. 56–57). If caregivers can understand and accept their own vulnerability and needs, definable achievements apart from their caregiving responsibilities become much more important. They want to take action on their own behalf. Hopefully, the entire family can come to understand that this type of planning is a lifelong process.

Developmental planning for the family as a whole (family of origin and new family) is dependent upon the care receiver's ability to maintain self-esteem by adjusting to the impact of chronic illness or handicapping conditions on the major activity—work. Although some buildings still are inaccessible to people in wheelchairs, and the person may have fewer job choices because of the problems the care receiver faces, technology and training make it possible for most people to work at some type of job. The care receiver's adjustment and acceptance of vocational goals and discovery of an appropriate job opportunity may be a lengthy process and he or she may need extensive support. Developmental planning for the family as a whole also is dependent upon satisfactory resolution of roles and responsibilities among members of the family of origin and the new family. Although this resolution of roles may be a bigger problem for young adults, it may be an issue as long as the parents of the care receiver are living.

If chronic illness or a handicapping condition strikes when the care receiver is middle aged, the spouse and the caregiver may need to redefine their well-established relationship. If the husband is incapacitated, his wife, if she had worked within the home, may need to seek work outside the home. If the wife is incapacitated, the husband may have to assume responsibility for household chores that perhaps he has never performed before (Eisenberg et al., 1984). If teenage children still live at home when a middle-aged parent is incapacitated, they may have to assume more responsibility for household chores and caregiving. They may find it difficult to proceed with vocational plans and plans for greater independence. Resolution of appropriate roles and responsibilities is essential to their development.

ELDERLY

Although a growing number of people with lifelong illnesses or disabilities reach old age, the majority of older people who need help have not had lifelong disabilities but have experienced a recent decline or have suffered from chronic or debilitating illness. The older people facing recent problems must make adjustments that those with lifelong problems already have made. Those with lifelong problems may experience additional problems. All senses diminish as people age. Eyes need more light and some colors become hard to distinguish. Elderly people often suffer from some loss of hearing. Taste buds decline and the ability to taste sugar and salt diminishes. Smell declines. Older people may not be able to tolerate extreme temperatures (Springer & Brubaker, 1985). Even without serious changes that require the provision of care by someone else, close relationships are likely to change. As the older relative's senses change, he or she experiences reduced coordination, balance, and dexterity. He or she may be more prone to falls and may be unable to drive at night. The person may experience more difficulty in communicating because of a hearing loss. Unless relatives understand the sensory loss, they may believe that the older person is suffering from cognitive impairment. They also may jump to the conclusion that the older person is unable to live alone or make decisions.

When an older person develops a chronic or terminal illness, the problems and adaptations associated with the normal aging process seem minor. O'Donnell and Grosser (1986) described the impact on the family:

> Family members find their normal roles are disrupted. Even though the patient experiences the most change, financial support, time, and a change of social status may affect all family members. All members need time to express their feelings and help to learn how to cope with the changes. (p. 125)

With social support networks dwindling (after retirement there is no support from worksite colleagues, friends die, and children live in independent households—sometimes far away), older people may need more help adapting. They and their families need to understand that rehabilitation often is possible when illness robs them of some functional abilities and that treatment for other problems is available. They do not have to suffer because they are aging. Family at this stage of life means children, and often brothers or sisters who again develop a closer relationship.

When a spouse is the caregiver of an older person, the couple is likely to reach a point, after adapting, where they begin planning for the care of the disabled spouse should the caretaker die. They also try to plan for their financial integrity. However, they often do not have a positive future outlook unless they are anticipating a special event such as a child's wedding or the birth of a grandchild. As more attention focuses on older people returning to college and changing careers, a positive outlook may become easier to achieve. For older people to establish developmental plans (including leisure time goals), and for their families to establish goals rather than temporarily putting their own goals aside to care for the person, a positive attitude is essential.

SUMMARY OF DEVELOPMENTAL STAGES

Caregiving families should expect a lifelong series of adjustments to new problems, remissions, progressions, and regressions (Lapham & Ehrhart, 1986). Although each family member may go through these changes at different times when faced with major life events or crises, each member should expect these adjustments. The family as a whole should learn to expect and plan for changes in responsibilities and goals as a family unit. Caregiving throughout the life cycle goes through the stages of problem discovery, acceptance and adaptation, problem resolution, developmental planning, life review, and lifecare planning (Figure 4-1).

Problem Discovery

For the client, this stage involves recognizing the limitations and changes in appearance that result from the illness or impairment. For the caregiver and the family, it means recognizing the

Figure 4-1. Developmental Planning throughout the Life Cycle

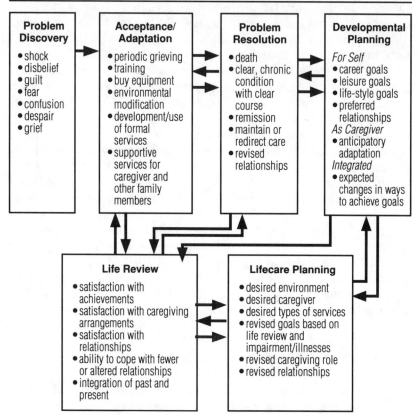

Problem Discovery	**Acceptance/ Adaptation**	**Problem Resolution**	**Developmental Planning**
• shock • disbelief • guilt • fear • confusion • despair • grief	• periodic grieving • training • buy equipment • environmental modification • development/use of formal services • supportive services for caregiver and other family members	• death • clear, chronic condition with clear course • remission • maintain or redirect care • revised relationships	*For Self* • career goals • leisure goals • life-style goals • preferred relationships *As Caregiver* • anticipatory adaptation *Integrated* • expected changes in ways to achieve goals

Life Review	**Lifecare Planning**
• satisfaction with achievements • satisfaction with caregiving arrangements • satisfaction with relationships • ability to cope with fewer or altered relationships • integration of past and present	• desired environment • desired caregiver • desired types of services • revised goals based on life review and impairment/illnesses • revised caregiving role • revised relationships

limitations that the illness or impairment places on their interactions with the client. As suggested earlier, besides shock, confusion, grief, and many other emotions, the caregiver may experience guilt—as though he or she should have been able to prevent the problem. Diagnostic difficulties prolong this phase. The confusion and fear continue. The family may become dysfunctional. Eventually, however, the need to develop a routine may help the family emerge from this phase. The caregiver and the family need to recognize that the amount and type of chores that one person handles will change. The types of family activities may need to change so the client and the primary caregiver can continue to participate.

Acceptance and Adaptation

At this stage, the caregiver responds to the client's acceptance of limitations or willingness to use special technology or to allow other family members to help and the willingness of other family members to help. However, the client may refuse to recognize symptoms, accept the diagnosis, accept the recommended treatment, or cope with limitations. If the client pretends that the illness or impairment does not create limitations, the caregiver and family may play along, harmlessly allowing the client to do easy tasks, usually done by others. Sometimes the reaction is not harmless, however. If a client refuses to acknowledge that he or she needs constant help, the caregiver may not want to upset the client. The result is that the caregiver becomes socially isolated, serving as the only constant companion. The caregiver may not purchase needed equipment, resulting in increasing strain for the family. As the stress increases, the caregiving family may feel resentful—and then guilty. Training may help the caregiver and the family provide appropriate care *and* cope with the client's problems of acceptance. (See Chapter 5 for a discussion of training.)

When the client, caregiver, and family do accept the limitations and prognosis, they adapt. This does not mean they are happy or that the acceptance is permanent (Corbin & Strauss, 1988). In fact, some denial may be useful—such as hoping that doctors will discover a cure for a disease. It does mean, however, that they reallocate household work and the work associated with caregiving. They decide which family activities they can continue and choose new ways to enjoy each other and strengthen their relationships. If the client's symptoms (for example, pain management), functional limitations, or prognosis change, everyone may have to work through this phase again. For acceptance and adaptation to occur, some control over the illness, functional limitations, or treatment is mandatory.

Problem Resolution

The problem resolves itself when a chronic condition is stable or the patient goes into remission and the family adapts. The family purchases needed equipment. Relationships and responsibilities are clear. If the illness trajectory changes, or the care receiver moves into another stage in his or her life cycle (such as childhood to adolescence or adolescence to adulthood), then the problem resolves itself at least temporarily, when the family redirects the care and establishes new roles for family members. Caregiving problems also end if the patient dies. The social and emotional reactions do not end, however. Until the caregiver and the family understand and accept their feelings, they may not be ready to move on to developmental planning.

Chilman, Nunnally, and Cox (1988) suggested that mastery of the transitions between phases is as important as working through each developmental phase. Families who meet and work together intensely during a crisis or problem discovery stage can distribute tasks effectively. However, it would not be helpful to continue that intense approach when the family is trying to adapt to the management responsibilities of a long-term chronic condition. If the dependent family member is unstable, the family must deal with periods of crisis that then require a new adaptation. These periodic transitions may be easier if the family does some anticipatory planning.

Developmental Planning

For the client, developmental planning may mean redirecting planned directions and goals. These changes result from a realistic integration of still intact skills with abilities that have been newly developed to compensate for limitations. For the caregiver, developmental planning means integrating personal goals with the goals and responsibilities of the caregiving role. The caregiver can develop and maintain career goals, sports, hobbies, and life-style if he or she focuses on personal goals, realistically sets aside some time, and anticipates what will be needed to fulfill caregiving responsibilities so that goals can be met.

Life Review

Corbin and Strauss (1988) suggested that a chronically ill or impaired individual goes through many types of review. First is a *symptom review,* in which the person reviews the initial symptoms and their progression based on current knowledge of their real meaning. Next is *treatment review,* in which the client assesses the value and risks of possible treatments. The client may make a *comeback review,* assessing the amount of recovery already experienced and how much remains. Some people may experience a *stable trajectory review,* projecting how much longer the illness will remain stable. Fears of people whose health is declining may result in a *downward trajectory review* where people worry about how much worse the illness and its symptoms may become. Many people will go through a *life review,* where they assess their accomplishments and satisfaction with their lives. It generally is believed that *terminally* ill people go through the life review. However, *chronically* ill or impaired people may well review their lives against what they would like to be able to accomplish and the types of relationships they wish they could have with other people.

The caregiver often goes through parallel reviews. During a symptom review, the caregiver may question why he or she did not notice the symptoms sooner, encourage the care receiver to get medical attention, or seek medical help for the care receiver. During a treatment review, the caregiver may be uncertain about what advice to offer and who to involve in discussions about any treatment options. If the client is going through a comeback review or a stable trajectory review, the caregiver, while wondering what to expect, may feel enough relief to begin looking ahead. The caregiver may foresee a lessening of caregiving responsibilities (even if it is temporary) and start focusing on his or her own needs and goals. The client's downward trajectory review, however, may send the caregiver back to a stage of acceptance and adaptation because the caretaker not only has to resume the caregiving role if the client was stable or had improved before, but the caregiving tasks may become increasingly difficult and time-consuming. The caregiver may go through a life review at several points during the course of his or her caregiving role. When the care receiver improves or stabilizes, the caregiver may think seriously about what he or she wants to accomplish—partly out of fear of becoming at risk of serious illness or impairment. Or, if the care receiver, during life review, expresses dissatisfaction, the caregiver may want to achieve greater satisfaction from his or her life. When the client experiences a downward trajectory review, the caregiver may be thrown into life review wondering if he or she will ever achieve personal goals. Ultimately, the caregiver must integrate past relationships with the care receiver and past goals with present realities and newly developed goals. Once this occurs, developmental planning is more likely to proceed even when caregiving responsibilities intensify.

Lifecare Planning

Caregiving families are more likely than other families to be sensitive to the need to plan for possible incapacity. If elderly parents are caring for a developmentally disabled or emotionally disturbed adult child or an adult child suffering from chronic illness or injury from trauma, then they will want to make provisions for that person's care after their deaths. All people who have been primary caregivers or part of a caregiving family likely will want to make provisions for their own care in the event they become incapacitated. By seeing first-hand the problems experienced by the client and the caregiver, members of the caregiving family will want to prevent such problems for themselves. As they begin to develop lifecare plans for themselves, they may become more acutely aware of what they want to accomplish and go through life review simultaneously. They also may find that they want to do more developmental planning both for themselves and the person for whom they are caring. This type of planning may help family members come to terms with their feelings about the caregiving experience.

When should a caregiving family seek help in this process and what type of help should the professional offer? Help probably should be available and offered as soon as the family discovers the problem and from that point on. According to Rosemary Regan-Gavin (1988), who suffers from systemic lupus erythematosus, the professional needs to help the patient, or train the family to help the patient, to redirect some of the negative energy that accompanies chronic illness into positive activities that build self-esteem and feelings of achievement. Gavin believes strongly that equally important is the professional's ability to help other family members cope with the illness: "Family members may also react negatively to the patient's unpredictable behavior. Social workers also could make an effort to help the family cope with the illness; by doing so they will be helping the patient" (p. 19). One way to cope is for family members to rechannel their feelings of anxiety to focus on their goals and accomplishments through developmental planning and through a process where they jointly plan, review their lifetime accomplishments, and develop lifecare plans for themselves (Figure 4-2).

The professional role does not begin until a doctor diagnoses the problem (Figure 4-2). Ideally, a professional would be brought in during conversations between the person, the family, and the doctor or therapist. However, until the initial shock passes, the patient and family may not really hear what the doctor says about the diagnosis,

Figure 4-2. Professional Help in Developmental Planning

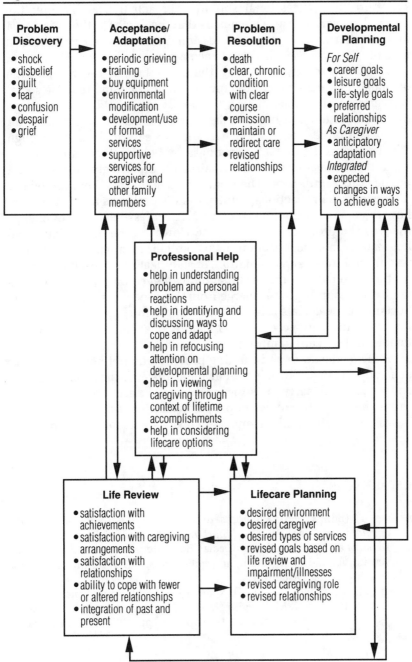

prognosis, and likely course of the illness, impairment, or recovery. Therefore, the professional should approach the family after the initial discovery phase. This means that the doctor or therapist must make a referral so that the professional knows when to contact a patient. Eisenberg et al. (1984) recommended that the doctor and social worker jointly meet with the entire family to give them the diagnosis and recommend treatment. They suggested that the social worker contact the patient and the family the next day, again, to go over information and begin to assess their needs.

The professional social worker can ease movement through the acceptance and adaptation phase by helping the family understand the disease process or impairment, the caregiving tasks, and the need for equipment. The social worker also can help the family understand their reactions to the patient's problems and teach them how to cope with the grief they feel. A professional cannot change the way the problem resolves itself. However, the professional can help family members begin to focus on their own needs and goals if resolution is recovery, adaptation, or stabilization. If resolution is the death of the patient, the professional can encourage a new focus as family members begin to emerge from the grief of losing a loved one. Social workers can also simplify the integration of past, present, and future as the caregiver or other family members go through life review and lifecare planning.

The education and training provided do not help a caregiver or family create a developmental plan. Instead, they help families cope with and solve existing problems. Education and training cannot help families to develop a positive future. In Chapter 5, ways in which to train family members to take a developmental approach are discussed.

REFERENCES

Adams, T. (Ed.). (1985). *Programs to support families of children with special needs for use in Head Start and public school.* Washington, DC: Department of Education's Special Education Programs, the Administration for Children, Youth, and Families, and the Administration for Developmental Disabilities.

Adderly, I., & Levine, J. B. (1986). Maturity: Guiding future generations. In E. V. Lapham & K. M. Shevlin (Eds.), *The impact of chronic illness on psychosocial stages of human development* (pp. 105–113). Washington,

DC: Georgetown University Hospital and Medical Center, Department of Social Work.

Bass, D. (1986, April). *Planning to meet lifecare needs* [occasional paper]. Silver Spring, MD: National Association of Social Workers.

Brody, E. M., Kleban, M., Johnsen, P., Hoffman, C., & Schoonover, C. (1987). Work status and parent care: A comparison of four groups of women. *The Gerontologist, 27,* 201–208.

Chilman, C. S., Nunnally, E. W., & Cox, F. M. (1988). *Chronic illness and disability.* Beverly Hills: Sage.

Corbin, J. M., & Strauss, A. (1988). *Unending work and care: Managing chronic illness at home.* San Francisco: Jossey–Bass.

Driscoll, P. T. (1986). Early adolescence: Identity formation. In E. V. Lapham & K. M. Shevlin (Eds.), *The impact of chronic illness on psychosocial stages of human development* (pp. 67–75). Washington, DC: Georgetown University Hospital and Medical Center, Department of Social Work.

Eisenberg, M. G., Sutkin, L. C., & Jansen, M. A. (Eds.). (1984). *Chronic illness and disability through the life span.* New York: Springer.

Hatfield, A. B. (1987). Coping and adaptation: A conceptual framework for understanding families. In A. B. Hatfield & H. P. Lefley (Eds.), *Families of the mentally ill: Coping and adaptation* (pp. 60–84). New York: Guilford.

Karlin, V. (1986). Late adolescence: Identity formation. In E. V. Lapham & K. M. Shevlin (Eds.), *The impact of chronic illness on psychosocial stages of human development* (pp. 79–87). Washington, DC: Georgetown University Hospital and Medical Center, Department of Social Work.

Kaslow, L. (1986). School age: Making, doing, achieving. In E. V. Lapham & K. M. Shevlin (Eds.), *The impact of chronic illness on psychosocial stages of human development* (pp. 55–64). Washington, DC: Georgetown University Hospital and Medical Center, Department of Social Work.

Lapham, E. V., & Ehrhart, L. S. (1986). Young adulthood: Establishing intimacy. In E. V. Lapham & K. M. Shevlin (Eds.), *The impact of chronic illness on psychosocial stages of human development* (pp. 91–101). Washington, DC: Georgetown University Hospital and Medical Center, Department of Social Work.

Lapham, E. V., & Shevlin, K. M. (Eds.). (1986). *The impact of chronic illness on psychosocial stages of human development.* Washington, DC: Georgetown University Hospital and Medical Center, Department of Social Work.

O'Donnell, P., & Grosser, F. (1986). Retirement age: Maintaining integrity. In E. V. Lapham & K. M. Shevlin (Eds.), *The impact of chronic illness on psychosocial stages of human development* (pp. 117–131). Washington,

DC: Georgetown University Hospital and Medical Center, Department of Social Work.

Office of Technology Assessment. (1987). *Technology-dependent children: Hospital v. home care: A technical memorandum.* Washington, DC: Congress of the United States.

Regan-Gavin, R. (1988). The war within: A personal account of coping with systemic lupus erythematosus. *Health and Social Work, 13,* 11–19.

Sommers, T., & Shields, L. (1987). *Women take care.* Gainesville, FL: Triad.

Springer, D., & Brubaker, T. H. (1985). *Family caregivers and dependent elderly: Minimizing stress and maximizing independence.* Beverly Hills: Sage.

5
Training for Developmental Planning

The most important aspect of training for a new idea or approach is to create a greater awareness and acceptance of the approach. It is no small task for professionals to try to get caregiving families with whom they work to accept a developmental approach. Caregiving families already are overwhelmed with emotion, the search for new knowledge and understanding about the disease process or impairment, and the need to make and carry out action plans to meet immediate needs. However, a skilled social worker can help family members look beyond immediate needs when they (collectively) reach an appropriate developmental stage.

As suggested in Chapter 4, ideally, professional involvement should begin when the family discovers a problem. Professionals can help family members understand their reactions, cope with their grief, and receive training in communications skills, management of medical regimens, and problem solving and personal coping skills. Professionals also can help family members achieve a more positive outlook and create developmental plans for themselves individually and as a family unit.

If the professional already uses the training techniques identified in Chapter 2, then this chapter will help him or her to encourage a positive approach for problem resolution and find ways to target appropriate stages of caregiving to help family members begin developmental planning. Some elements of this approach are

- sensitizing doctors and other medical personnel to the emotional needs of patients and their families so they will make referrals to social work professionals while they diagnose a problem
- creating a family-centered intervention approach as a standard for social workers, which emphasizes and maximizes positive family attributes, strengths, and skills
- helping families develop and nurture a positive outlook through special efforts such as home visits rather than office sessions, working with employee assistance programs, and initially or occasionally transporting the primary caregiver to arrange for needed services

- objectively observing interactions in the home, developing special plans for training family members individually and as a group—this element involves coaching family members to reduce behaviors that result in poor communication or conflict and to increase behaviors that improve communication and outlook
- creating developmental plans for individual family members and the family as a whole
- creating support groups (when appropriate groups do not exist) for clients, caregivers, and family members who are in similar stages of the caregiving experience
- stimulating peer leaders, through developmental planning, to encourage other caregiving families and to maintain the peer leader's developmental focus

SENSITIZING MEDICAL PERSONNEL

Sensitizing medical personnel is not the same as increasing general public awareness about how professional social work help benefits caregiving families (as will be discussed in Chapter 7). Medical professionals control access to medical services and all support services that are reimbursable by public funds or health insurance. They usually are the first point of contact for the client and the family. When the medical professional, the family's first contact with support systems, focuses on physically therapeutic or rehabilitative services, the family loses the opportunity for immediate emotional support. If the prognosis is poor, the family will focus on caregiving tasks, client deterioration, family conflict, and grief. The most important step for social workers in creating a developmental approach is the process of sensitizing medical personnel and establishing continuing communications with them. Even if a person has chronic symptoms that are not yet diagnosed, the doctor or other medical staff need to understand the confusion and disruption that the symptoms and diagnostic testing can cause. Professional help during diagnostic testing can prevent poor communication when other family members do not understand the potential care receiver's problems or believe the lack of diagnosis suggests there is no problem. Professional assistance also can help the family cope with the emotional stress of a drawn-out and sometimes painful diagnostic process. When a diagnosis is made, a sensitive medical gatekeeper immediately will refer the family to a helping professional. By meeting the family immediately, the professional can provide support at a time of despair.

This developmental approach may require some restructuring of roles and responsibilities in medical settings. It also may be necessary to place social workers on site. However, helping professions usually do not train family practitioners to work in many medical settings. One author suggested that psychiatrists deal with mental health problems, psychologists test patients and give them psychotherapy, and social workers help the family find community resources (Doherty, 1988). Each professional provides services as needed. If family-oriented practitioners cannot work effectively in a hospital setting, doctors' offices and clinics might be appropriate environments for these professionals. Hospital discharge planning units that expand their services also might be an effective environment in which practitioners can work with the entire family. Doherty (1988) suggested that doctors and families alike may feel most comfortable with professionals located in the primary care setting such as the office or clinic. The physician will feel more comfortable referring patients to a helping professional in house, where he or she might notice any problems. The patient and the family are accustomed to going to the office or clinic for services and, therefore, are more likely to keep appointments with a helping professional and follow through because of their relationship with the doctor.

When a physician refers a patient and family to a social worker in private practice or in a separate mental health setting, the helping professional often does not get the entire picture of what the family is going through. The practitioner will know the diagnosis and the reason for referral, but not how other family members might have influenced that referral. Doherty (1988) cited a case in which a 21-year-old woman with Chron's disease (chronic bowel disorder) was hospitalized repeatedly because she did not comply with diet and treatment regimens. The doctor referred the woman to an outside family therapist. The therapist discovered that, unknown to the doctor, the parents had made excuses for their daughter and did not demand that she be responsible for her own care. As a result of improved communications between the doctor and the therapist, the doctor learned that when the 21-year-old woman complained that she received poor therapy from the family therapist, she was complaining about the therapist trying to change family behavior problems. The doctor became supportive of the therapist's recommendations. The pattern of behavior and family functioning improved.

Although the doctor in the previous example might have made better use of an in-house professional, it is not impossible to make a referral early in the treatment process to an outside helping professional, especially as doctors and other medical personnel begin to understand the value of family practitioners. To sensitize medical personnel and maintain their interest in referring patients to family practitioners, the helping professional needs to develop a relationship (especially with the doctor) and establish clear expectations. When the doctor makes a referral, the practitioner needs to clarify with the doctor why the doctor has certain expectations and what those expectations are, requiring that the doctor understand that disruptive family behaviors will not change immediately. The practitioner initially may find joint sessions with the doctor and the family helpful. Continuing communication with the doctor and other medical personnel is essential to maintaining trust with them and with the family, and to understanding the current phase of the disease or handicapping condition (Doherty, 1988).

Communication also is essential to the social worker's ability to bridge the gap between the patient's developmental stage and the developmental stages of the family and individual family members. Particularly when the patient is in the hospital, time moves slowly and he or she only thinks about existing discomforts, testing, and uncertainty. Although the patient may be "stuck" in a developmental phase for some time, the family may review the past and begin to develop action plans (Power, Dell Orto, & Gibbons, 1988). The immediate support of family-oriented professionals can make the difference between a family that continues to despair and one that learns to cope with chronic illness or impairment and to modify goals or expectations so that accomplishments are possible. The next sections discuss the best way to initiate positive thinking.

CREATING A FAMILY-CENTERED INTERVENTION APPROACH

Many researchers allege that the mental health professions added stress to caregiving families in their efforts to deinstitutionalize, or prevent the institutionalization of, mental patients, elderly, and developmentally disabled people (Hatfield, 1987). These researchers maintained that professionals blamed families for causing problems of mental illness, and for being unwilling to provide care or for providing care in a way that was ineffective for the ill or impaired elderly and developmentally disabled people.

Clearly, cause and culpability are not the issues. Stress and management of caregiving tasks are problems faced by every caregiving family and every professional trying to help the family. Thus, social work and the mental health professions must focus first on how to help the family alleviate the stresses resulting from caregiving responsibilities, divide tasks among family members, and learn how to use formal services to supplement family care. Resolution of earlier or emerging conflicts between family members must be secondary. A task-centered approach that makes use of each family member's strengths may even alleviate some conflicts as family members work together to achieve the agreed-upon goals. The emphasis must be on helping families become effective caregivers while recognizing the strengths and needs of each individual family member.

It is especially important for mental health professionals to recognize the relationship between physical and emotional stress. Just as medical professionals do not always recognize emotional needs, mental health professionals sometimes ignore the physical stresses resulting from lifting, bathing, and dressing another person, or controlling physical outbursts. Formal help with some of the physical tasks can alleviate stress. Physical exercise and relaxation are as important as relief from emotional stresses.

HELPING FAMILIES DEVELOP AND NURTURE
A POSITIVE OUTLOOK

Adequate training and preparation sets the stage for a comfortable and positive caregiving relationship. This training may be as simple as learning to supervise the intake of medications or as complex as managing a tracheostomy. A program developed by the Children's Memorial Hospital in Chicago (the Ventilator-Dependent Discharge Program) in collaboration with the Division of Services for Crippled Children and the Illinois Department of Public Aid provides an excellent example of the type of training needed by families of ventilator-dependent children. Families are eligible for the program if they meet four criteria: (1) the child's condition is medically stable, (2) the patient and the family fully understand and accept the requirements for home ventilator care and consent in writing, (3) each child has a complete home care program approved in advance by the hospital, and (4) the family makes arrangements to pay for health care costs in advance. In the hospital, family members first are taught basic personal care, and then medical skills. Medical skills include tracheostomy care, suctioning, and bronchial drainage. Parents then learn how to use equipment, including the ventilator. Parents receive a checklist to use in adapting their home to providing care before a home visit is made to assess home readiness. Ventilator-Dependent Discharge Program staff recommend 24-hour-per-day nursing care for at least 1 month so that the family can become more comfortable and more than one person is enabled to learn needed caregiving skills.

The family then begins to assume more and more of the daily responsibilities. If the hospital team—comprising medical director, program coordinator, respiratory care discharge coordinator, social work coordinator, unit charge nurse, director of patient affairs, clinic services worker, and agency coordinators for the Division of Services for Crippled Children and the Department of Public Aid—does not know whether the family is ready to provide care, it then may provide care in the hospital under the supervision of staff so that the family receives continual feedback. At the end of an agreed upon period, parents and team decide whether home discharge is in the best interests of the child and the family. The family receives additional training after discharge to reinforce their prior training. Hospital staff use a predischarge quality assurance checklist to be certain the family learned the basic essential skills. The professional also could use a modified version of this checklist to assess a family's readiness to provide care for other types of patients as well (Goldberg et al., 1987) (Table 5-1).

Monitoring continues after the hospital discharges the child. Routine physician care and medication changes are done at home under the supervision of the primary care physician, using consulting physicians. Although the Ventilator-Dependent Discharge Program does not provide case management, the hospital must ensure that someone is responsible for this role. If the child is publicly funded through the Division of Services for Crippled Children, then that division assigns a case manager until the child is age 21 years. Then, the Illinois Division of Rehabilitative Services takes over the case. This extensive training and follow-up help caregivers build confidence and develop a positive outlook based on the knowledge that appropriate professional help is available when needed (Goldberg et al., 1987).

Although the example was of trust that developed when professionals trained parents in the provision of medical care, any professional providing a variety of services to caregiving families must establish a relationship built on trust with the caregiving family. The best way for the social workers to begin developing that relationship is through discussions with the family in their own home. A visit to

Table 5-1. Family Readiness for Caregiving

Professional Completing Form: _____

Family Name: _____

Agency Name: _____

Initial Date of Contact: _____   Date of this Assessment: _____

- All family members have been trained in emergency care
  (if appropriate)   Yes ____   No ____
- All family members understand procedures for contacting medical
  personnel in emergency   Yes ____   No ____
- All family members understand the diagnosis and prognosis   Yes ____   No ____
- All family members have reasonable expectations of the patient   Yes ____   No ____
- Primary caregiver(s) understands how and when to order
  supplies/equipment   Yes ____   No ____
- Primary caregiver(s) understands when to contact a doctor   Yes ____   No ____
- Primary caregiver(s) understands when to contact a social worker
  or other professional   Yes ____   No ____
- Primary caregiver(s) understands how to access, monitor, and
  evaluate needed community services   Yes ____   No ____
- All family members understand appropriate communication,
  problem solving, and behavior management   Yes ____   No ____
- All family members feel ready to accept caregiving responsibilities   Yes ____   No ____

Comments: _____

_____

_____

_____

_____

the home shows the family that the professional wants to see the problems they face, not just hear about those problems in a comfortable office. The visit shows a willingness to help without adding to the family's burden by forcing them to make alternative arrangements for the care receiver or requiring them to travel. For a family with strained financial resources, a home visit can determine whether a family can continue services. Offering help and making the help convenient is the first step in helping families achieve a more positive outlook. The caregiver and other family members can look forward to the help without extensive planning.

If the professional first meets the patient and family while the patient is in the hospital, then initial meetings may have to be held at the hospital. However, the social worker should visit the home to assess family readiness for caregiving responsibilities before the hospital discharges the patient. Although observation of family interactions with the patient is impossible until the patient returns home, the social worker can observe other family interaction patterns and discussions about the patient's problems during the initial meetings.

The next step in helping families nurture positive thinking is to continue home visits, training, and outreach for needed services. As family members relax in familiar surroundings, the professional will observe normal patterns of interaction, including strengths and weaknesses in behavior and communication patterns. Observing patterns of interaction also may reveal differences in family member beliefs about the illness and the family's ability to manage the illness. In some ethnic groups, ill members and their caretakers openly discuss all symptoms and problems. Other ethnic groups try to hide their difficulties (Rolland, 1988). Differences also exist in terms of whether the family prefers care at home or in another setting. If some family members have different beliefs, then conflict may impede progress in care management and the developmental stages of caregiving. Observation also will reveal whether family members view any improvement in the care receiver's functioning as positive, or whether they still measure the care receiver's performance against the functioning of people who have no illness or impairment. Home observation also will show whether family members reward themselves and each other for the help they provide and for their own accomplishments.

The professional should assess family interactions (Table 5-2). This assessment is important initially to identify the types of training that would benefit individual family members. The assessment is useful after training to measure the changes and to determine whether inadequate training was the only problem or whether underlying family conflict inhibited the formation of satisfactory caregiving arrangements. Training to help families overcome behavior that results in conflict or training to improve communications should build on family strengths (Bonjean, 1988) (Table 5-3). By discussing successful ways the family dealt with past crises, the professional may be able to elicit solutions from family members that are developmentally appropriate for the family at that point and at that stage of the care receiver's disease or impairment.

The continued home visits also will reveal any task overload and a poor division of labor. If someone has too much responsibility, he or she will be angry and frustrated. The professional can assess whether the care receiver can take on or resume responsibility for more tasks even if the care receiver needs technological aids to simplify tasks or vocational training or retraining. If the social worker already assessed family strengths, it may be possible to recommend a redivision of labor based on those strengths, particularly if the observed division of tasks is different from the division

Table 5-2. Family Training Needs: Assessing Family Interactions

Do caregiver interactions with the care receiver demonstrate realistic
expectations based on disease/impairment limitations?   Yes ___   No ___

Do family member interactions demonstrate realistic expectations
based on disease/impairment limitations?
     Family member names: _____   Yes ___   No ___
                 _____   Yes ___   No ___

If not, what specific incidents suggest unrealistic expectations?
     Family member names: _____   Incidents: _____
                 _____   _____

Are family behaviors helpful to problem resolution?   Yes ___   No ___

If yes, what behaviors are most helpful?
     Family member names: _____   Behaviors: _____
                 _____   _____

If no, what behaviors are a problem?
     Family member names: _____   Behaviors: _____
                 _____   _____

Do caregiver/care receiver and other family communications help to
resolve problems and divide caregiving tasks?   Yes ___   No ___

If yes, identify communication skills.
     Family member names: _____   Behaviors: _____
                 _____   _____

If no, identify communication problems.
     Family member names: _____   Behaviors: _____
                 _____   _____

What kinds of training (for example, behavior modification, communication skills) would be
helpful? _____
_____
_____

Table 5-3. Assessing Family Strengths

Can you identify a crisis your family experienced in the past?
How did your family cope with this crisis?
What helped you most to get through this crisis?
How is this crisis different?
Do you see any way you can use some of the approaches used in past crises to help with this
    problem?
How have other family members helped during this crisis?
How could you move from the types of help that family members currently are giving to the
    approaches that worked for you in the past?
What differences would make you feel that you have been successful?

identified by the caregiver or other family members (Table 5-4). For example, if one family member likes to maintain records, he or she may be the appropriate person to pay bills, even if that person previously did not have responsibility for that task. The professional can encourage positive reinforcement or rewards for each family member's contribution.

The amount of formal support or training available either for specific responsibilities or to help the entire family cope with

Table 5-4. Positive Distribution of Tasks for Each Family Member

Do the tasks done by each family member build
  on the strengths of that person?   Yes ___ No ___

If not, identify the person who seems to be
  doing a task inappropriately.

Name	Relationship	Task
_____	_____	_____
_____	_____	_____
_____	_____	_____

Does anyone else in the family seem to enjoy or
  be skilled at doing the task another member
  is doing inappropriately?   Yes ___ No ___

If yes, who and for what task?

Name	Relationship	Task
_____	_____	_____
_____	_____	_____

Is the family member receptive to doing the task
  that is more appropriate if overall tasks are
  redistributed?

Name	Relationship	
_____	_____	Yes ___ No ___
_____	_____	Yes ___ No ___
_____	_____	Yes ___ No ___

What is the newly agreed upon configuration of
  tasks?

Name	Relationship	Task
_____	_____	_____
_____	_____	_____
_____	_____	_____

responsibilities affects each family member's willingness to take on caregiving tasks. Another way for a social worker to show support and nurture a positive attitude is to transport the primary caregiver to arrange for some of the needed services. The caregiver can learn from the social worker how to approach providers and what to ask (for example, the number of visits per week that the caregiver can expect and the duration of service for each visit).

Training the family to act as case manager with social work support reinforces a positive family approach to caregiving. A good example of a supportive program is the Family Centered Community Care for the Elderly program developed by the Jewish Family and Children's Service of Greater Boston, Boston's Beth Israel Hospital, and Boston University School of Social Work. The program requires that the family member take responsibility for at least one case management task, the family member and the social worker develop a case management plan jointly and identify the case management tasks for which each is responsible, families receive comprehensive information about available community resources and entitlements, and the social worker maintain contact with the family to provide training (Seltzer & Mayer, 1988). This approach empowers the family to act as case manager, giving family members more control over the care of a loved one. However, the program does not offer a "sink or swim" approach. Families do not have to assume responsibility for *all* caregiving tasks, nor do they have to function as case manager without the continued advice or support of a professional when they feel they need such advice. Instead, the program allows the family to assume as much responsibility as they are able to and to ask for as much support as they need, depending on the developmental stage of the primary caregiver or the family.

Another program uses a family therapy perspective to help families who are caring for elderly relatives (U.S. Department of Health and Human Services, 1988). The program emphasis is on pragmatic solutions for the caregivers, not resolution of chronic problems or conflicts such as depression or alcoholism. Counselors (university students from counseling and guidance programs, social work, and nursing) may recommend a variety of supportive services such as transportation, nutrition counseling, home care, occupational therapy, home-sharing, or other social services. Counselors also recommend in-home therapy to treat family stress if they believe the family may be unable to cope with the changed condition of their elderly family member. A common problem is that older parents believe that their children tire of helping them and that children fear responsibility for managing caregiving tasks because they think that their parents want to retain control. Family discussions with the help of the counselor can result in a satisfactory distribution of responsibility and improved communications.

Another way to create a more positive attitude initially is to work with an employee assistance program (EAP), if available, at the caregiver's worksite or worksites of other family members. EAPs can give the caregiving employee help during a crisis and can help to arrange flexible hours or benefits with management. The involvement of an EAP provides the social worker with the benefit of another professional judgment about how the family member is coping and functioning. This information is important in creating training plans and developmental plans. EAPs also can help the care receiver who can still work to obtain needed training. Although it is important for family members to understand the care receiver's feelings and the likely course of the disease, and to assess essential tasks and to learn communication and problem-solving skills, equally important is continued help after the initial training.

One method of working with an EAP is for the social worker who is the initial contact person for the family to legitimize the feelings of the caregiver and other family members so they know that their feelings of anger, guilt, or frustration are normal. The social worker also can legitimize individual needs. The professional from the EAP can build on this positive beginning by offering ways to meet needs already identified as part of services offered to many employees. The professional also can help the family member assess short-term, and then long-term, career goals.

If family members make choices about services offered by worksite programs, learn how to negotiate the formal service system from the social worker, and work on short-term career goals, then they are empowered to act on their own behalf. Because they are not in control of the disease or impairment and its impact on their loved one, it is critical for them to have this sense of control in order to have a more positive outlook. When family members feel better, communications with each other will improve. If family members receive training in communication and problem solving, then besides feeling in greater control, they will feel empowered to act on their own behalf and for the care receiver when the care receiver is unable to act on his or her own behalf. Involvement of an EAP is especially important for women, because caregiving affects the employment of so many women. When an empowered family assumes more of the case management tasks inherent in caregiving, the professional no longer feels intense responsibility for the family's well-being, thus reducing the potential for professional burnout.

OBJECTIVE OBSERVATION AND COACHING

After the initial assessment, training, and implementation of activities designed to increase client empowerment, home visits and family observations can have a new focus. The social worker can observe continuing family interactions that do not change (Table 5-5).

Table 5-5. Continued In-Home Support after Training

Do caregiver interactions with the care receiver demonstrate improved
expectations based on the disease or impairment?   Yes ___   No ___

Do family member interactions demonstrate improved expectations
based on disease/impairment?
    Family member names: _____   Yes ___   No ___
                                _____   Yes ___   No ___
                                _____   Yes ___   No ___

If not, what incidents still show unrealistic expectations?
    Family member name: _____   Incident: _____
    Family member name: _____   Incident: _____

Are new family behaviors helpful to problem resolution?   Yes ___   No ___

What new behaviors are most helpful?
    Family member name: _____   Helpful behavior: _____
    Family member name: _____   Helpful behavior: _____

If behaviors still are not helpful, what are the problems?
    Family member name: _____   Problem behavior: _____
    Family member name: _____   Problem behavior: _____

Do caregiver or care receiver and other family communications now
help to resolve problems and divide caregiving tasks?   Yes ___   No ___

What new kinds of communication are most helpful?
    Family member name: _____   Good communication: _____
    Family member name: _____   Good communication: _____

What kinds of communication still are not helpful?
    Family member name: _____   Poor communication: _____
    Family member name: _____   Poor communication: _____

What other kinds of training (for example, behavior modification,
communication skills) would you recommend?

When the social worker observes repetitious and ineffective communications or behaviors, he or she can suggest alternative approaches (Osterkamp & Schafer, 1986). If the family starts discussions that will reopen areas of conflict, then the social worker can help the family focus on solutions to current problems and ways to accomplish caregiving tasks. Once again, the family becomes empowered if the social worker can help the family to identify solutions.

Once the caregiver and other family members accept their feelings and become empowered, then they probably are ready to create a developmental plan. However, if the care receiver is mentally competent but has not worked through his or her own developmental needs, then the caregiver's progress may be intermittent. Although the progress of the caregiver affects the care receiver's progress and vice versa, the progress may not be simultaneous. The other family members' progress also depends on the progress of the care receiver and caregiver. Each family member may go through developmental stages at a different time. However, it is important to understand the impact of the care receiver's and caregiver's developmental stages to assess their effects on other family members (Table 5-6).

Education in health promotion ideas will encourage the care receiver's belief in the worth of working to regain or maintain functioning, and the caregiver's belief that caregiving tasks associated with maximizing the care receiver's functioning and time management required to sustain one's own physical and mental health are worthwhile. Although an emphasis on nutrition and exercise also is helpful, health education is more focused. The individual, caregiver,

Table 5-6. Developmental Planning Built on Positive Outlook

For Care Receiver	For Caregiver
Continued belief that loss is worth regaining and desire to work for it	Integration of care receiver's belief in the importance of tasks with caregiver's own beliefs
Crystallization of tasks and remobilization of resources	Belief that all aspects of own life have worth
Development of realistic goals	Crystallization of tasks and remobilization of resources
Periodic indicators of progress	Development of realistic goals
	Periodic indicators of progress

and family learn how to mitigate problems resulting from the diagnosed illness, including the judicious use of medication and the benefits of specific diet and exercise. The caregiver's belief that his or her own life is important also depends on whether the care-receiver and caregiver accept the amount of necessary client dependence and work toward maximum care receiver independence. This belief also may relate to whether the caregiver receives and integrates health education ideas, such as stress reduction, diet, and exercise, into his or her own life as well. One way to arrange for health education is through support groups.

Training and positive support should result in an attitude that each family can achieve a meaningful life within the existing constraints—both for the care receiver and the caregiving family. This positive support sets the stage for the creation of a developmental plan based on achievable goals that provide life satisfaction. Even the terminally ill person and caregiving family can find satisfaction when the person decides what achievements are possible and desirable in the remaining time. If the care receiver never is able to develop a positive outlook and work toward improved or sustained functioning, then the caregiver and the family will find it more difficult to develop and maintain a positive developmental plan. However, doing so is not impossible. The caregiving family can derive satisfaction from knowing that their loved one receives loving and appropriate care and that they are doing as well as other caregiving families.

The social worker who continues home visits may observe some obvious needs and desires of the primary caregiver and other family members. If individual family members continue to complain about the same problems, such as their inability to do some things that they want to do because of caregiving responsibilities, then, initially, the social worker might help the family focus on that problem and develop goals. Then, the social worker would help family members identify the specific tasks and resources associated with achieving those goals along with ways to distribute tasks and access resources. Thus, family members might create a developmental plan in stages (Table 5-7). Once the family or individual family members identify and achieve goals (or make progress toward goal achievement), they may begin to identify other goals without prompting from the social worker.

The family, as a unit, may have to go through a similar process of setting developmental goals. If the family wants to spend time together engaging in recreational activities, then they may plan

Table 5-7. Achieving Developmental Goals

Goal	Tasks	Resources
Finish college	Secure financial assistance	Get more financial help from other family members for caregiving costs
	Get care for family member while gone	Get family to redistribute tasks
		Go to night school when other family members are home
	Gain cooperation of care receiver	Find ways to ask for care receiver's help

Progress indicator: Complete one course

activities or locations around the care receiver so he or she can participate. If the care receiver is too incapacitated or mentally incompetent to join in, then planning may require alternative activities or that someone stay with the care receiver while other family members periodically enjoy recreation together. One of the most important ways to reinforce these positive developmental approaches is to identify short-term accomplishments and rewards. For an addict, one day without succumbing to the habit is an accomplishment. The family can identify similar accomplishments for the client, caregiver, and other family members.

The critical elements of developmental planning are goals that build and maintain the self-esteem of the care receiver, primary caregiver, and other family members, and progress indicators that allow each person to increase or show his or her competence. Competence is a key part of self-esteem. As defined by Hatfield and Lefley (1987), after they surveyed the mental health literature of the past three decades, competence includes selecting relevant information, planning necessary action, and then taking the action to achieve goals and objectives. Competence is based on an individual's ability to perform all major social roles and to select the information, plan, and take action in all of these roles (p. 64).

SUPPORT GROUPS: MOVING FROM GROUP EMPOWERMENT TO INDIVIDUAL COMPETENCE

As suggested in Chapter 2, social workers should encourage all families of chronically ill people to join appropriate support groups. Support groups offer a sense of community and understanding that professionals who have not experienced the problem cannot offer. If the group moves into an advocacy role for the people for whom its participants are caring, then the group as a whole becomes empowered. However, empowerment and competence do not have to depend on a group's advocacy role. Because the goal is to allow each family member to build and increase his or her competence, support groups can, and sometimes do, offer each participant individual opportunities. When a motivated participant shares caregiving approaches and solutions, he or she is competent in the eyes of other participants. Support groups help build self-esteem and help the members of the caregiving family see themselves as competent. If the support group participant not only shares experiences, but serves as a resource to other participants or becomes a peer leader in the group, he or she is empowered and other participants perceive the leader as an expert—a person who not only is competent in coping with personal problems, but who also is competent in helping others cope as well.

The professional role in helping support groups get started should be to make participation and peer leadership a normative expectation among caregiving families. Social workers need to find out whether existing support groups help to create and sustain individual empowerment before recommending them to families. Because support groups often begin with professional help, but almost always evolve into peer leadership, this professional role leads to a "team" approach between professionals and caregivers.

EDUCATING PROFESSIONALS

Sensitizing professionals to families' needs is only possible through continuing education and curriculum development. Social workers need to be taught to view family coping mechanisms as normative responses to difficult problems. They need to learn, perhaps through role playing, how they can use their own words and body movements to convey support. Professionals need to stress the benefits of in-home consultation with students and with agency managers when the managers participate in continuing education activities. Case assessments need to focus on breaking down the caregiving roles into distinct tasks and identifying existing and preferred responsibilities for tasks. Professionals then would be taught that the action plan would include not only general training in understanding the problem and general skill development in communications and problem solving, but also would include training specifically tailored to the tasks for which an individual family member is responsible. A self-change plan for family members would involve not only a contract for needed time and respite, but a developmental plan for growth in terms of competence and empowerment. A developmental approach is not completely different from a standard action plan, but rather builds on the standard action plan (Table 5-8). Developmental planning allows each family member to learn to ask the right questions of all professionals, evaluate the answers, and make decisions based on his or her own developmental needs and the needs of the care receiver.

The standard action plan, alone, requires curriculum and continuing education changes. Professionals need to learn about emotional and physical stress reduction techniques and prevention activities, such as diet and exercise and special support group activities, to avoid social isolation and caregiver health problems. Professionals need to learn techniques for educating and coaching members in communication, problem solving, and behavior management skills. One way to train professionals may be to videotape practice sessions with mock families. According to Hatfield and Lefley (1987), professionals must learn to teach (p. 78). Developmental

Table 5-8. *Action Plan Versus Positive Developmental Approach: A Comparison of the Old Approach and the New*

Standard Action Plan	Positive Developmental Plan
Assesses client's needs, primary caregiver time and ability to help, and caregiver needs	Assesses tasks inherent in client self-care when possible and tasks involved in each of the caregiving roles assumed by various family members
Encourages general division of labor in caregiving	Encourages specialization of responsibilities based on competence
Arranges and schedules general training and skill development	Provides general and specific training and skill development based on individual task responsibility
Makes referrals to support groups	Creates or makes referrals to support groups designed to increase competence and empowerment
Coordinates informal and formal help; teaches family to function as case manager	Empowers family to coordinate formal and informal help and to serve as case manager by providing only support needed

planning requires knowledge about age-appropriate and developmentally appropriate behaviors of caregivers and care receivers. This means, for example, that the needs of a middle-aged couple whose children are grown, but who have one mentally ill child still at home, would differ from those of a young couple with a developmentally disabled toddler.

Although the emotional stresses and support needs of caregiving families are similar, the developmental needs, such as career and leisure time, differ. Knowledge of these needs will allow the professional to focus on individual strengths and help each family member build competence in areas that are developmentally appropriate. Videotapes may be useful in training families and professionals. Families may improve their communications skills by observing the importance of listening skills and appropriate interaction—that is, the expression of positive and negative feelings. Families can enhance their problem-solving skills by learning to identify and define the problems and develop alternative ways to resolve them. Behavioral management skills may increase when family members observe the impact of limit setting and a reward system.

The role that professionals must learn for a positive developmental approach begins with the provision of information and training, then moves on to the support that continues as long as they work with a family, and then to consultation in developmental planning (Figure 5-1). Thus, the professional needs to learn technical information and skills, approaches for educating families, supportive techniques that help caregivers enhance their coping abilities, and activities that stimulate family members to think about their future and begin to plan. Additionally, attitudes about appropriate social work roles need to change. Therapist and case manager are not the only desirable roles. A role of sharing information, training, supporting the family, or acting as consultant to the family and to individual members may be most important to the family.

Schools of social work need to develop specialized courses in chronic illness and impairment and in caregiving because the amount of information that professionals need to learn is extensive. The courses should include literature in the areas of social work, nursing, psychology, sociology, and marriage and family therapy to train professionals about the

- etiology of different types of disease and impairment
- likely caregiving demands and technological aids that correspond to the etiology

*Figure 5-1. Professional Role for a Positive Developmental
            Approach*

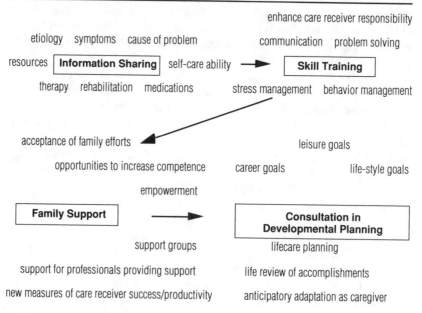

• impact of different cultures and belief systems on a family's approach to caregiving and ability to work with professionals, and appropriate methods for working with families from other cultures

• different approaches to the management of caregiving tasks, including ways to maximize caregiver self-sufficiency

• professional role of information sharing, skill training, family support, and consultation

Research and demonstrations should continue to increase the social work knowledge base, but curricula can be drawn from current knowledge. Joint development of some curricula with schools of medicine, nursing, psychology, and sociology is desirable. For example, schools of social work might develop curricula on the etiology of different diseases and conditions with schools of medicine and nursing.

With a variety of agencies developing their own approaches to supporting caregiving families, a "learn as you go" approach is no longer preferable. Basic knowledge and skills should be taught in graduate school and through continuing education series.

REFERENCES

Bonjean, M. J. (1988). Psychotherapy with families caring for a mentally impaired elderly member. In C. S. Chilman, E. W. Nunnally, & F. M. Cox (Eds.), *Chronic illness and disability* (pp. 141–155). Beverly Hills: Sage.

Doherty, W. J. (1988). Implications of chronic illness for family treatment. In C. S. Chilman, E. W. Nunnally, & F. M. Cox (Eds.), *Chronic illness and disability* (pp. 193–210). Beverly Hills: Sage.

Goldberg, A., Noah, Z., Fleming, M., Stanick, L., Childs, B., Frost, L., & Glynn, W. (1987). Quality of care for children who require prolonged ventilation. In K. Fisher & K. Gardner (Eds.), *Quality home health care: Redefining the tradition* (pp. 17–23). Chicago: Joint Commission on Accreditation of Healthcare Organizations.

Hatfield, A. B. (1987). Families as caregivers: A historical perspective. In A. B. Hatfield & H. P. Lefley (Eds.), *Families of the mentally ill: Coping and adaptation* (pp. 3–29). New York: Guilford.

Hatfield, A. B., & Lefley, H. P. (Eds.). (1987). *Families of the mentally ill: Coping and adaptation* (pp. 60–84). New York: Guilford.

Osterkamp, L., & Schafer, D. E. (Eds.). (1986, January/February). [Entire issue]. *Parent Care Resources to Assist Family Caregivers.* Lawrence: The University of Kansas Gerontology Center.

Power, P. W., Dell Orto, A. E., & Gibbons, M. B. (1988). *Family interventions throughout chronic illness and disability.* New York: Springer.

Rolland, J. S. (1988). A conceptual model of chronic and life-threatening illness and its impact on families. In C. S. Chilman, E. W. Nunnally, & F. M. Cox (Eds.), *Chronic illness and disability* (pp. 17–68). Beverly Hills: Sage.

Seltzer, M. M., & Mayer, J. B. (1988). Families as case managers. *Generations, 12,* 26–29.

U.S. Department of Health and Human Services. (1988). *Treating stress in caregiving families* (*Aging,* Rep. No. 358). Washington, DC: U.S. Government Printing Office.

6

Worksite Services and Benefits

Previous chapters of this book focused on responsibilities and problems faced by caregiving families and ways to support the family through health and social services systems. This chapter discusses another type of support—employer support for employees who are caregivers. Satisfaction and competence in the caregiving role can carry over into work productivity and satisfaction and vice versa.

Many professionals view flexible benefit packages, which employees can tailor to their family needs, and direct services for the children or older relatives of employees as contemporary phenomena. Employer interest in family support is driven by demographic trends such as an aging society, an increase in the number of single mothers, and the number of families where both parents work. By 2030, 65 million older Americans will require personal care (U.S. Department of Health and Human Services, 1986). Approximately 10 million will be somewhat disabled, requiring the help of others. Because Americans also are having fewer children, a smaller number of young people most likely will be entering the labor force. A growing portion of the labor force is women. Single mothers with children under the age of 18 are working. Many do not have a support system to care for their children during periods of illness or when they cannot find adequate child care. In many families, both parents are working, leaving no one at home to care for children, older parents, or mentally ill or developmentally disabled relatives.

As these demographic trends emerged, employers became concerned about the adequacy of their future labor force and began to recruit workers from nontraditional sources. Some corporations recruited older people out of retirement. Others trained and employed developmentally disabled people. Although these employer efforts are continuing, some employers realize that recruitment of older people and developmentally disabled people will not provide all the labor they will need. Adequate number of employees is not the only problem employers face. They worry about recruiting and keeping people with the particular skills their company needs. Older workers can fill some of these jobs and can be retrained for others, but will not solve all the corporations' personnel needs. With fewer people entering the labor market, competition will be stiff for those with particular skills. Thus, women, previously not considered a stable labor source, have become more important. Because women are usually the primary family caregivers, their caregiving needs have become more important because employers want to keep them in the labor force, even when their children are young, and prevent extensive absenteeism when these employees need time to care for family members.

Despite all the current pressures affecting employer concern about employees' caregiving problems, this issue is not a contemporary one. Employers always have responded to problems that affect the operation and productivity of their companies. This chapter briefly discusses historical employer responses, the risks and benefits to employers and employees of worksite response or nonresponse, and ways to develop worksite programs and integrate them into a community system of supports for caregiving families. Although some practitioners may believe that the history of employer response is unnecessary and the discussion of risks and benefits is interesting but irrelevant, this information is essential to practitioners who want to mobilize employer support within their communities. Practitioners must be able to sell employers on the benefits of supporting caregiving employees and their families and the costs of not providing such support.

HISTORY OF FAMILY/CAREGIVER SUPPORT
AT THE WORKSITE

According to Kamerman and Kahn (1987), employers first demonstrated concern about the welfare of employees and their families in the late nineteenth century. Employers became concerned about high turnover rates, their dependence on immigrants as a source of labor, and a growing union and government role in business. Whatever the reasons, employers provided a wide range of services and benefits, from housing and recreation to medical care, pension plans, and profit sharing. Some companies built "company towns" to keep employees together and foster a strong company spirit.

The depression ended employer interest in employee and family services and benefits because employers could no longer afford these "extras." Because the New Deal brought government-supported labor unions, companies did not want to offer benefits voluntarily before beginning a negotiation process, because they had to negotiate with the unions and pay for negotiated benefits. Although employee assistance programs (EAPs) developed gradually after World War II, beginning with employer concerns about alcoholism and drug abuse and gradually expanding to include medical problems, health promotion, and family-oriented policies, the next big spurt of employer concern began in the 1970s and continues today (Creedon, 1987). Most of the services and benefits offered in this contemporary period resulted from government mandates and incentives. Tax-free status of health insurance benefits and favorable treatment of pension funds that began in the 1920s and 1930s expanded to include favorable tax treatment for employee benefits such as stock ownership, educational help, and dependent care (Kamerman & Kahn, 1987). Thus, historically, employer willingness to provide services to employees and their families stemmed from two sources: (1) concern about maintaining the adequacy of their labor force (both in terms of numbers of employees and their skills); and (2) profit motivation, that is, finding ways to meet statutory and trade union requirements in ways that minimize cost and maximize profit for the company.

The Conference Board, a business information service organized to help senior executives and other leaders arrive at sound decisions, surveyed 75 companies that were leaders in recognizing the relationship between work and family life (Friedman, 1987). In the report, the board found that company concerns about family needs resulted from

- a need to recruit skilled workers
- increased productivity to compete with foreign countries
- absenteeism and tardiness
- an interest in an improved image
- acceptance of criticism that business does not care enough about employees
- a need to reward employees who deserve top positions but don't get them because competition is stiff (as a result of another demographic trend—too many members of the baby-boom generation in midlevel positions)
- pressure from women's groups for women managers
- demographics of the labor force, changing typical worker benefit and work schedule needs

These reasons for developing family-oriented policies and benefits showed continued concern about maintaining an adequate workforce. Employers seemed concerned about worker productivity and company image. Thus, the historical reasons for employer interest in the relationship between work and family are also the current reasons.

Contrary to speculation by some authors about the impact of government policies and programs, the report by the Conference Board did not mention employer concern about meeting government mandates or taking advantage of incentive funds. However, the survey was of employers who already had expressed an interest in the needs of employees' families.

CORPORATION RISKS, BENEFITS, AND COSTS

Employer willingness to develop family-oriented policies, benefits, and services is based on the employer's perceived risk of ignoring family needs, the benefits to the company of changes designed to support families, and the cost to the company of making changes. Much of the employer interest in family needs that the Conference Board found resulted from perceived risks. The risk that companies feared most was being unable to recruit and retain an adequate labor force. This fear emerged from experience and research, not just from demographic trends. For example, a 1984 study of a large Boston corporation found that both men and women with children under age 12 years missed 2 or more days of work per year more than those without children (Friedman, 1987). Absenteeism rates were lower when child care was at home rather than out of the home. Another study of a New Jersey corporation found that 77 percent of the female parents and 73 percent of the male parents had dealt with family problems at work (Friedman, 1987). Forty-eight percent of the women and 25 percent of the men admitted that time at work was sometimes unproductive because of their child-care problems. Absenteeism, tardiness, and early exit from work also resulted from difficulties workers experienced while trying to manage family and work roles. Forty-seven percent of the women with children under 5 years old and 12 percent of the men with children under 2 years old had considered quitting their jobs because of their care problems. Another study of a Connecticut company found that 4 in 10 employees reported that they spent an average of 10.2 hours per week caring for an older relative—16.1 hours for women and 5.3 hours for men (Friedman, 1987). Eighteen percent had not had a vacation away from responsibilities for more than 2 years. These employees said that their responsibilities interfered with other social and family needs and responsibilities. In a study of people caring for older relatives, employees reduced work hours or took a leave of absence to fulfill caregiving responsibilities (Subcommittee on Human Services of the Select Committee on Aging, 1987). This study showed that 11.6 percent of all caregiving daughters quit their jobs to provide such care.

Thus, the biggest risks faced by corporations that do not try to address their employees' family responsibilities include

- Loss of trained personnel and difficulty recruiting new workers. Because corporations now depend on women to meet labor force supply needs, they cannot afford for women (as the primary caregivers) to choose not to work only because they cannot meet caregiving responsibilities. This problem is particularly acute when families are caring for more than one person.
- Reduced productivity. Though difficult to measure, clearly absenteeism, reduced hours at work, and time spent at work making calls to resolve family problems reduce the productivity of employees. The effect of stress or reduced attention to work requirements is not as easy to measure, nor is it easy to measure the effect of one employee with unresolved family problems on other employees or on the productivity of his or her entire unit.

Friedman (1987) cited a newspaper article on a company that attributed a 23 percent decrease in employer turnover and 15,000 fewer work hours lost to an on-site child-care center. The article reported that another company found that its company day-care center reduced recruiting costs by approximately $50,000 per year. Regardless of the accuracy of such dramatic results, the employers perceived that improvements began when the day-care center opened for employee use.

Because corporate benefits from family support policies or services are difficult to measure, how does a practitioner persuade the employer to offer them? Is the risk of not helping troubled employees enough? Likely benefits, ease of implementation, and reasonable cost also may influence employers who are considering family-oriented changes. A likely benefit to the company is an improved image in the community, which not only helps in recruiting new workers, but may create a higher level of consumer interest in the company's goods or services. If a change can be made without altering the company's entire benefit structure or policies, can be done without extensive study or approval by a board of directors, and is low cost, it is much more likely to happen and happen quickly. Examples of changes are lunch-time sessions on caregiving for an elderly parent or on how to find good child care.

More extensive corporate changes are possible but require more planning. Friedman (1987) suggested that employees can achieve major changes only if senior executives endorse them. She also recommended patience, because the average time from idea to implementation was 2 years in the companies she studied. Selling the senior executives is not easy. The practitioner may shorten the process if he or she does some work in advance. If the practitioner providing family support services is already working in the company (or the company already purchases services for employees from the practitioner), the practitioner should be able to identify known problems, do a preliminary assessment of the severity of the problems for the company, and identify a range or continuum of possible company responses.

The practitioner may find videotapes useful. For example, one major telephone company developed a 30-minute videotape documentary, narrated by a well-known actress, for a public service TV network to increase public awareness of the emotional, physical, and financial problems that caregivers of the elderly face. The company sells its package to other organizations. By viewing the videotape, corporate executives can see that they do not have to start from scratch if they want to develop activities for caregivers as a short-term response while they examine long-term changes.

If the practitioner seeking corporate support for caregivers has no relationship with the company, then selling the executives may be more difficult. The practitioner may not have access to information about company problems or existing company policies. Thus, knowledge about general demographic trends in the community becomes more important. The practitioner should be able to cite labor force trends if such trends show a potential problem in recruiting and retaining workers. The practitioner also should point out instances in which the media discussed any problems the company experienced in selling products or services. For the employer with which the practitioner is unfamiliar, videotapes and "how to" manuals may be very important sales tools.

EMPLOYEE RISKS, BENEFITS, AND COSTS

When an employer does begin to offer family support services and benefits, the biggest problem is getting employees to use them.

Usually, managers of companies with EAPs only refer lower-level personnel who have problems on the job. Sometimes people who are not managers refer themselves if they are afraid they may lose their jobs. Thus, after the company develops services and benefits, the employer needs to provide outreach through a two-step process. First, the employer must consider what services and benefits to provide by conducting a survey of employee needs and service or benefit preferences. Second, the employer must identify community resources.

Professionals must construct a survey of employees carefully. Employees with long commutes, for example, might prefer child care or adult day-care close to home so they do not have to transport a young child or sick elderly parent long distances. No employee wants to admit to leaving a dependent relative in an undesirable care setting because the employee had to work. Yet, most people will admit dissatisfaction with certain aspects of a care environment if they can admit unhappiness with individual parts of the care program (Friedman, 1987). The survey should identify the employee's caregiving responsibilities, determine whether caregiving is overwhelming and affects job performance, identify informal help and services the employee already uses, identify the gaps in needed services, and determine how the company can help (Table 6-1).

The American Association of Retired Persons (AARP), has indicated that timing is important to a survey's success (Heath, 1987b). One survey should not immediately follow another survey. AARP has recommended that 1 month before distribution of a survey, the employer discuss the survey in an employee newsletter or distribute a memorandum that explains the survey. Two weeks after distribution, if 20 percent of the surveys have not been returned, AARP has recommended that the employer send out a reminder and extend the deadline 3 weeks. (At least 20 percent of the employees must respond.) The AARP developed these recommendations after testing a survey with the Aerospace Corporation, Drew University, Florida Power and Light Company, Ft. Logen Mental Health Center, Indian River Memorial Hospital, McNeil Consumer Products Company, Mutual of New York, and the Travelers Companies.

Once a company analyzes the survey results and practitioners identify community resources (see Chapter 2), both can compare available resources to the services employees want. Companies learn which service providers are reputable and which organizations are planning new programs (Friedman, 1987). According to the Conference Board report (Friedman, 1987), companies then tend to build on

Table 6-1. Sample Questions for Employee Survey

1. How long have you worked for the company?

    Less than 1 year ____   11–15 years ____
    1–5 years ____   Over 15 years ____
    6–10 years ____

2. Are you—

    Male ____   Female ____

3. What is your age?

    20–25 ____   36–40 ____   51–55 ____   66–70 ____
    26–30 ____   41–45 ____   56–60 ____   Over 70 ____
    31–35 ____   46–50 ____   61–65 ____

4. How many people live with you?

    0 ____   1 ____   2 ____   3 ____   4 ____   5 or more ____

5. What are the ages of the people who live with you? (Circle the number of people at each age level living with you.)

    Under 6   0   1   2   3   4   5 or more
    7–12   0   1   2   3   4   5 or more
    13–18   0   1   2   3   4   5 or more
    19–22   0   1   2   3   4   5 or more
    23–30   0   1   2   3   4   5 or more
    31–40   0   1   2   3   4   5 or more
    41–60   0   1   2   3   4   5 or more
    61–65   0   1   2   3   4   5 or more
    Over 65   0   1   2   3   4   5 or more

6. What is your relationship with the people who live with you? (Check relationship or write number if more than one.)

    Spouse ____   Brother or sister ____
    Child(ren) ____   Aunt or uncle ____
    Father or mother ____   Grandfather or grandmother ____
    Father-in-law or   Another relative ____
        mother-in-law ____   Friend ____

7. How many people in your household do you have caregiving responsibilities for?

    1 ____   2 ____   3 ____   4 or more ____

(continued)

Table 6-1. Continued

8. How many people, other than those who live with you, do you have some caregiving responsibility for?

   1 _____   2 _____   3 _____   4 or more _____

9. What is the nature of your responsibility for the people who live with you?

Type of Help	Hours Spent Daily	Hours Spent Weekly
Personal care	____	____
Meals	____	____
Housekeeping	____	____
Shopping	____	____
Transportation	____	____

10. What is the nature of your caregiving responsibility for people who do not live with you?

Type of Help	Hours Spent Daily	Hours Spent Weekly
Manage finances	____	____
Personal care	____	____
Meals	____	____
Housekeeping	____	____
Transportation	____	____
Home repair	____	____
Arranging for services	____	____
Companionship (visits)	____	____
Emotional support	____	____

11. If the people you are caring for have health or developmental problems, please identify them. (Check all that are appropriate; each column represents a different person for whom you are caring.)

Type of Problem	A	B	C	D
Mental health problem (specify _____)	____	____	____	____
Congenital heart disease	____	____	____	____
Other heart problems	____	____	____	____
Diabetes	____	____	____	____
Asthma	____	____	____	____
Other respiratory problems	____	____	____	____
Other handicapping conditions (specify _____)	____	____	____	____
Other developmental disability	____	____	____	____
Vision impairment	____	____	____	____
Hearing impairment	____	____	____	____
Stroke	____	____	____	____
High blood pressure	____	____	____	____
Circulation problems	____	____	____	____
Cancer	____	____	____	____
Drug/alcohol abuse	____	____	____	____
Memory loss	____	____	____	____
Uncontrollable elimination	____	____	____	____
Parkinson's disease	____	____	____	____
Arthritis	____	____	____	____
Other (specify _____)	____	____	____	____

(continued)

Table 6-1. Continued

12. Do other relatives or friends share your caregiving responsibilities or give you occasional relief?

    Yes _____   No _____

13. If friends or relatives help, what types of help do they provide?

Type of Help	Hours Spent Daily	Hours Spent Weekly
Manage finances	_____	_____
Personal care	_____	_____
Meals	_____	_____
Housekeeping	_____	_____
Shopping	_____	_____
Transportation	_____	_____
Home repair	_____	_____
Arranging for services	_____	_____
Visits	_____	_____
Emotional support	_____	_____
Temporary care so you can get away	_____	_____

14. If you purchase services, what types of services do you purchase?

Type of Help	Hours Daily	Hours Weekly
Financial management	_____	_____
Personal care	_____	_____
Meals	_____	_____
Housekeeping	_____	_____
Transportation	_____	_____
Home repair	_____	_____
Counseling	_____	_____
Home health care	_____	_____
Other (specify _____)	_____	_____

15. Have you experienced any problems with these services?

    Yes _____   No _____

16. If you have experienced problems, what do you dislike about the services you purchase?

    Way the provider responds to care receiver   _____
    Environment where service is provided   _____
    Hours service is available   _____
    Amount of service available/affordable   _____
    Some services unavailable in care setting   _____
    Other (specify _____)   _____

(continued)

Table 6-1. Continued

17. Has anyone helped you decide how to meet your caregiving responsibilities?

    Yes _____   No _____

18. If so, who helped you most?

    Doctor   _____
    Visiting nurse or other health care professional   _____
    Clergy   _____
    Social worker, psychologist, counselor   _____
    Family   _____
    Friends   _____
    Employee assistance counselor   _____
    Supervisor or co-worker   _____
    Other (specify _____)   _____

19. How have your caregiving responsibilities affected your health and feeling of well-being?

    Trouble sleeping   _____
    Sleep too much   _____
    Tired all the time   _____
    Gained or lost weight   _____
    Frequent illness   _____
    Constant worry   _____
    Feeling stressed   _____
    Feel good about care you provide   _____
    Not affected by caregiving   _____

20. Are you seeing a doctor for any problems related to your caregiving responsibilities?

    Yes _____   No _____

21. How have your caregiving responsibilities affected your ability to work and your ability to function on the job? (This survey is anonymous and cannot be traced back to you.)

    Absent frequently   _____
    Use leave for caregiving,
       not vacations/self   _____
    Reduced hours of work   _____
    Time spent at work
       arranging for care   _____
    Difficult to concentrate   _____
    Considered quitting work   _____
    No problems on job   _____
    More confidence in
       ability to handle
       responsibility   _____

22. Did you tell your supervisor about your difficulties?

    Yes _____   No _____

(continued)

Table 6-1. Continued

23. If you told your supervisor, how did your supervisor respond?

Unsympathetic, penalized you   ____
Sympathetic, but constrained by agency policies   ____
Worked out some flexible arrangements
   within own authority   ____
Worked out flexible arrangements with
   higher level management   ____

24. How could [name of agency] help? (Contents of this question will depend on employer's willingness to consider various options.)

Educational workshops on problems or developmental
   phases of people you are caring for   ____
Information about available services   ____
Support groups during lunch   ____
Better insurance coverage for dependents   ____
Worksite services for relatives
   (specify _____)   ____
Flex-time   ____
Job sharing   ____
Other (specify _____)   ____

existing services by creating new services where none exist or improving services that somehow are inadequate. Large corporations may have foundations that support programs or human resource departments that have analyzed possible corporate responses to family problems.

Practitioners trying to start a corporate program should begin with the research conducted by the company. The development of reputable services or well-known and preferred benefits increases the likelihood that employees will use what the company offers. Besides offering new services or benefits, AARP has strongly recommended that all companies whose employees have significant caregiving responsibilities (at least 20 percent of those responding) offer a caregiver fair and educational seminars. The caregiver fair requires about 10 weeks of planning and should include at least 18 community organizations. The organizations invited should include those providing home care (from meals to home health care); support and counseling services; housing; recreation; transportation; legal and financial information; and other general information (Heath, 1987a). A unique aspect of the educational seminars proposed by AARP is a session on time management, which includes a discussion on how to balance work and caregiving responsibilities (Heath, 1987c).

The risks to the caregiving employee of not seeking help when it is offered through worksite services or benefits are more complex than the risks normally faced by a caregiver (see Chapter 1). A caregiver who does not have services available may choose to reduce the number of hours at work, use leave for caregiving rather than vacations, or quit work entirely. On the other hand, a caregiver who chooses not to use services made available by an employer may find that the employer makes decisions for the caregiver. For example, just as employees found to have substance abuse problems may be fired if they refuse treatment, caregivers who will not use on-site day care, information and referral services, or special leave benefits or health benefits for dependents also may be at risk of losing their jobs.

This risk of "retaliation" by the employer makes many employees reluctant to discuss personal problems. The fear of retaliation for not managing work and family problems the way an employer suggests may far exceed the fear of reprimand or dismissal. Employees may be less fearful when the company offers cafeteria-style benefit plans rather than on-site services or perhaps even information and referral services. (Employees using information and referral services must tell someone about the problems they have in order to get the services they need.) Cafeteria-style plans offer at least one taxable benefit such as cash or vacation time and one benefit that is nontaxable such as different types of insurance, legal services, or coverage under a dependent-care assistance program. Special flexible policies also seem less threatening. Paid sick leave to care for an ill family member, additional personal days, and flex-time are low-cost ways to help family caregivers. However, these "less risky" approaches do not assure the employee access to needed services. Risks to the employee of not using any worksite services and benefits are alienation and isolation from managers and peers. The caregiver then becomes not only isolated at home, but also at work, with no one to turn to for help, with a career path blocked when advancement and the associated increase in income may be critical to help pay for extra medical bills, equipment, and other caregiving needs.

The benefit to the employee who uses worksite services or benefits is clear. On-site services for the dependent relative are easily accessible—the employee does not have problems transporting the relative to services that are in an area other than the worksite. On-site services for the employee (such as counseling and information and referral) also are easily accessible and the employee may not even have to take time off from work to use the services. Cafeteria-style benefit plans allow caregivers to tailor their benefits to meet personal needs and give the caregiver more resources to "purchase" needed services even if the resources are not cash.

Employees who take advantage of employer help and feel good about it will experience less stress. They will not jeopardize their jobs, and may increase their career opportunities because they can concentrate on their work. When companies begin new services or benefits, if they want to be able to assess the benefits derived from these changes, they might consider doing a repeat survey 1 year later. Employees as well as employers can benefit from worksite services (Table 6-2).

IMPACT OF PUBLIC POLICY ON EMPLOYEE BENEFITS

Employer willingness to help employees through family support policies, services, and benefits may result from concerns about recruiting and retaining workers and concerns about productivity. These "supports" are not structured in isolation, however. State and federal policies and programs can have a strong influence. Private pension plans usually supplement social security benefits. Private employers often follow the government's lead when economic or

Table 6-2. Benefits of Worksite Services

Type of Service	Employer Benefit	Employee Benefit
On-site service	Reduced absenteeism Less work time spent arranging care Recruitment and retention advantage	Easily accessible Less risk of losing job from absenteeism More career opportunity if not distracted
EAPs and information and referral	Recruitment and retention advantage Increased productivity Higher employee morale	Reduced stress Greater access to services
Flex-time	Low cost Higher employee morale Recruitment and retention advantage	Reduced stress Increased time with family; increased quality of life
Cafeteria-style benefits	Recruitment and retention advantage Higher employee morale	Ability to choose benefits to meet changing needs

political constraints preclude wage increases. When wages do not rise, employers often compensate employees by increasing benefits (Kamerman & Kahn, 1987). Tax advantages influence employers' choice of benefits as well as services they will make available and the way they offer these new items. For example, dependent-care assistance plans and child care as a tax-free benefit, authorized by federal legislation, encourage the development of on-site services. When companies want to build new sites, local regulations or ordinances that give preference to companies that offer child care to employees as well as to people in the neighborhood are strong incentives to provide that type of child care.

After the employer surveys employees to learn about their needs, identifies existing community resources, and learns what services or benefits employees prefer, the employer must take one more step. It must identify all the federal, state, and local laws, regulations, and ordinances that offer advantages to the employer if the employer provides certain services or benefits. The professional researching these governmental benefits also needs to assess which services or benefits employees prefer.

DIFFERENCES BETWEEN WORKSITE PRACTICE
AND PRIVATE PRACTICE

The biggest difference between social work practice at the worksite and in private practice is that at the worksite, employers focus on the individual as an employee. Employers are concerned about family issues only to the extent that the issues affect the employee's job performance. Because employers do not have a family focus, it is unlikely that an EAP would work with the entire family. It is much more likely that the EAP would work with the individual employee and help that employee find services and make arrangements for other family members. The EAP counselor would not have the advantage of home visits to observe family interactions and behavior.

Yet, despite their focus on the individual employee, large companies are leaders in the development of on-site child-care facilities and make contributions to stimulate the development of needed services even if the type of contributions varies somewhat with changes in public policy. Many employers recognize the stress and problems of managing work and child care. Some employers understand the problems associated with caring for a frail or ill older relative. It is primarily employers and organizations representing corporations, such as the Conference Board (Friedman, 1987), that demonstrate an understanding of the similarity and interrelationships between normal caregiving (that is, for children) and caring for someone who is chronically ill or impaired. All caregiving responsibilities require planning so the individual and the family can manage time more effectively. Effective time management allows for work, caregiving, recreation, special family time, respite, and so on.

Outside the worksite, many people view child care and care for chronically ill or impaired people as two completely separate issues. They consider the care of "normal" children a "developmental" issue. Parents need to place their children somewhere while they work, and that care environment should help the children achieve their potential developmentally. Outside the worksite, professionals do not think about the time management aspects of child care, because the only measurable impacts (such as absenteeism and productivity) are at the worksite. Friends and neighbors tend to dismiss feelings of stress associated with normal child care unless they suspect or witness abuse.

For professionals, these differences result in different expectations for practice. Practitioners outside the workplace who deal with chronically ill people focus on the clinical impact of chronic illness on other family members. Professionals also help primary caregivers find needed services and learn to manage time so that they can accomplish their caregiving responsibilities without jeopardizing their own well-being. The needs of other family members complicate the practitioner's job. Some practitioners who work with children either specialize in child development or focus on the needs of people or families caring for chronically ill relatives. Other practitioners specialize in working with families who have retarded children. Others concentrate on working with families who have an ill older relative. Thus, practice outside the job, although focusing on both clinical and time management issues, often tends to emphasize one person or the interactions between the caregiver and the care receiver, because of this professional specialization. Worksite practitioners, on the other hand, focus on time management, all the family members who affect the employee's ability to manage time, and helping workers find services that will allow them to devote more time to their jobs. However, worksite practitioners' interest in other family members extends only in terms of resolving conflicts between time needed to provide care to a family member and time needed at work. These professionals generally do not get involved in resolving relationship or family interaction problems that may be causing stress. If these problems result in alcohol or drug dependency, the EAP counselor often tries to steer the employee to a treatment center where professionals may help the employee come to terms with such problems.

Worksite support for caregiving employees probably should build on the strengths of practitioners inside and outside the organization to provide more comprehensive and effective support to employees. One means of worksite support is to use the worksite program as an information and referral service. The EAP counselor can discuss time management problems with employees when they are referred (or refer themselves) to the EAP because of problems with absenteeism and productivity. Discussions about time management will reveal caregiving problems and service needs. Although the EAP counselor could refer employees to services they need, it is more important initially to refer them to a case manager who will assess overall family needs and coordinate services for family members. As the case manager considers the developmental needs of the family, the EAP counselor can help the employee assess career development needs within the context of caregiving responsibilities. If the EAP counselor has a relationship with certain case managers and service providers, these providers may have special rates for the employees.

This distinction between EAP counselor responsibilities and case management responsibilities may become more important as more companies begin to use a managed health care program. Counselors inside the company will have to "ration" services available under plans that cap the number of visits each year to doctors, dentists, and mental health providers. (Companies are using these plans to control escalating health care costs so that they do not have to discontinue completely certain services and benefits.) This rationing may create ethical dilemmas for EAP professionals. The outside case manager, however, can pursue funding for all needed services. The EAP counselor would inform the case manager about what the managed health care plan covers. The case manager then would determine what the employee can afford beyond that plan and what other resources are available.

Another way to provide comprehensive employee support is to offer on-site counseling, case management, and direct services. Counseling is not uncommon, but it usually does not include other family members. Therefore, a company could expand counseling services to include family members; it also could offer case management services. However, these changes could be quite costly. Companies would need more counselors to provide the extended services. Thus, many companies might not be receptive to the idea of expanding services. In fact, corporate interest in providing some family supports stems from their being a low-cost way to help employees meet their needs and remain productive.

The role of the professional at the worksite probably would be that of a coordinator, getting guest speakers to provide information about certain diseases or conditions, rather than trying to provide all that information directly (Figure 6-1). Employee counselors do not have the time to specialize in helping families cope with caregiving responsibilities because they must deal with a range of problems affecting work performance. They probably would bring in other professionals to do skill training. Direct services offered might include support groups and career empowerment—planning and organizing work, improving peer relationships, setting career goals, and measuring career accomplishments.

PIONEERING COMPANIES

Companies that are leaders in work and family issues began their work in this area by investing heavily in research and the development of options for meeting identified needs. In 1983, Transamerica surveyed all employees about their child-care needs (Friedman, 1987). It then appointed a task force to analyze the survey findings and develop policy and program recommendations. With a

Figure 6-1. Role of Employee Counselors

54 percent response, the task force discovered four primary needs: (1) care for sick children, (2) monetary help with child-care costs, (3) information and counseling about child care, and (4) more available child-care services. Changes recommended by the task force, and implemented immediately, included the following:

• The company modified leave policies, allowing employees to use leave when other family members were ill. The amount of leave per employee increased more than 60 percent.

• The company created a resource and referral service by contracting with local resource and referral agencies.

• The company created an information-sharing program for parents by hiring a counselor under contract to the EAP.

• Transamerica participated in a consortium of companies to create a child-care center near the worksite.

• Transamerica created a child-care center for mildly ill children on a pilot basis. The company pays most costs. Employees must pay $10 the first day and $5 for each additional day.

The Travelers Companies surveyed its own employees and created a program for employees who are caregivers (Friedman, 1987). The Travelers Companies began, in 1979, by hiring a firm to evaluate national trends and recommend a way that the company could contribute to solving company and community problems. The evaluating firm recommended that the company concentrate on aging issues. Thus, the company created the Older Americans Program in 1980.

In 1985, staff of the Older Americans Program surveyed employees of the Hartford Connecticut Home Office who were age 30 years and older to learn about their caregiving responsibilities for relatives or friends age 55 years and older (Travelers Employee Caregiver Survey). With 52 percent of the sample responding (the sample was 20 percent of the employees), the survey revealed that 28 percent of the employees were caring for an older relative or friend. Most (73 percent) were caring for one person. However, 19 percent cared for two people. Eight percent of the employees responding served as caregivers for three or more people. More than half (54 percent) of the respondents helped to run the household of the care receiver. Most caregivers had been providing care for an average of 5.5 years. Most reported providing an average of 10.2 hours per week of care. Nearly one-half (49 percent) used outside sources for part of the care. Most employees had trouble finding needed services.

Programs developed for employees as a result of survey findings included

- a caregiver fair where experts from public and nonprofit agencies provided information to nearly 700 people
- educational services offered during lunch hours
- a lunchtime caregiver support group once a week
- videotapes on caregiving
- books on eldercare shelved in a special section of the corporate library
- articles on caregiving and aging run in the company newspaper, which is sent to every employee and retiree

Other employee benefits already available were

- flexible work hours
- unpaid leave of up to 4 weeks for pressing personal responsibilities
- an EAP
- a flexible spending account where employees could set aside pretax dollars in a special account used only for dependent-care expenses (children and older relatives)

The Travelers Companies responded to a newly identified need for information about caring for elderly relatives, but the ongoing benefits available to employees applied to those caring for children or elderly relatives. The Travelers Companies introduced an expanded flexible benefits program for its employees in early 1990. This expanded program includes a subsidy for child-care and eldercare expenses, with the greatest subsidy for the lowest-paid employees (covering up to 30 percent of the costs to an annual maximum of $1,200); family-care leave of up to 1 year, with continued coverage of medical, dental, and life insurance, and 3 paid days off per year to care for a sick family member; and a nationwide child-care and eldercare information and referral service for employees and retirees.

The Travelers Companies Foundation, in cooperation with the AARP, conducted a survey again in 1985 (Heath, 1987b). This survey was not of employees, but rather of 3.7 million U.S. households with caregivers providing unpaid help to someone age 50 years or older. Approximately 8 percent of the households contacted had a person currently serving as a caregiver or who had been a caregiver within the past 12 months. Telephone interviews with 754 of the caregivers revealed that the average caregiver provided care for 12 hours per week and had been doing so for 2 years. However, 25 percent spent more than 20 hours per week providing care. Forty-two percent of the caregivers worked full-time; 13 percent worked part-time. Most of those surveyed did not use formal services to help with their caregiving roles. When asked why they did not use services, most responded that they did not need the services (respite, 70 percent; support groups, 65 percent). When asked what they did want help with, many responded that they wanted to know about the aging process in general, medical/health developments, or legislative developments. Many also wanted help in dealing with the bureaucracy to get services for the care receiver.

The results of the survey raised some interesting issues. The types of services requested by caregivers are the ones most often provided by employers. Lunchtime information-sharing sessions or educational seminars are the most common short-term employer responses to needs of caregiving employees. The longer-term solutions offered by pioneering companies, such as dependent-care accounts that allow employees to set side tax-free funds so they can purchase services for the care receiver, respond to employee concerns about obtaining services for the care receiver. Of great concern in the survey results, however, was the caregivers' perceptions that they do not need services for themselves. Many professionals say that often caregivers do not acknowledge their own needs until they are in crisis (Osterkamp, 1989). A family-oriented practitioner, who understands the developmental needs of the caregiver and the family, can help caregiving employees seek help *before* a crisis occurs. Employees probably will not acknowledge their own needs to their employer. So again, the most effective way to offer this service probably is through referral to an expert who may be under contract to the organization.

One company that does refer families for case management services is IBM. IBM contracted for a feasibility study in 1986 to decide whether to offer employees, their spouses, and retirees an eldercare referral service similar to the child-care resource and referral program already available (Piktialis, 1988). The study revealed a need for personal help and information from a single source. The nationwide Elder Care Service, designed by IBM on the basis of the study, includes

- services of eldercare specialists, supported by an employer, who received training to help the employee throughout the process of searching for services

- consultation to help the caregiver clarify his or her needs and those of the older relative
- information about available local services
- an active review of local services by the expert, then referral to potential sources of help
- follow-up to ensure that employees' needs were met
- uniform service standards throughout the country for IBM employees

Thus, the service includes assessment, planning, referral, and monitoring—all part of a case management process. Sometimes, the service helps the family (through the caregiving employee) assume the ongoing case management role or refers the family to case management services. This referral includes a checklist to use in selecting case management agencies or private case managers (Piktialis, 1988).

The newest pioneer in work and family issues is the American Telephone & Telegraph Company (AT&T). A contract negotiated by the company and union representatives went beyond information sharing and traditional services for dependents or caregiving employees and began to offer benefits that support the caregiver as well ("AT&T Pact in Vanguard on Family-Care Benefits," 1989). The new contract created a $15 million Family Care Development Fund. The company will pay for the fund, but it will be jointly administered by the company and the unions. The fund provides seed money to help establish community programs for children and elderly dependents. According to company officials, employees can leverage the fund by combining it with money from foundations or other companies. Employees also can use the fund to pay for consultants who would study the feasibility of developing specific types of facilities. The contract also

- extended unpaid newborn-child leave for the mother or the father from 6 months to a year
- created a similar unpaid leave program for employees caring for seriously ill family members
- provided that the company will pay for up to 6 months of health care benefits and up to 1 year of life insurance benefits during unpaid leaves of absence
- allowed employees to set aside up to $5,000 for dependent care (tax-free) and offered family-care referral services and a special flex-time program that allows employees to take an extra paid holiday 2 hours at a time.

The fund that will help to create services, the dependent-care account that will help pay for services, and the referral service will greatly increase the employee's ability to meet the needs of the care receiver. The willingness of AT&T to pay the health and life insurance premiums during unpaid leaves of absence permits caregivers to provide care with reduced risks of jeopardizing their own health, coping abilities, or careers. These benefits recognize the caregivers' needs. It also is conceivable that employees could use the family-care referral service to locate and refer employees to professionals who will assess the broader needs of the family and the caregiver as an individual.

IMPORTANCE OF BROAD-BASED COMPANY EFFORTS

The importance of broad efforts such as the family policies proposed by AT&T cannot be overstated. Policies that give employees some flexibility, but do not help them resolve problems that conflict with work, can only be minimally effective. Policies or benefits that help employees care for one dependent, but ignore other dependents and ignore the impact of caregiving on the entire family, will not resolve conflicts between work and family responsibilities. Thus, even the companies that help employees address the needs of children and elderly relatives may not go far enough. Mentally ill or mentally retarded relatives may be young adults who fall into neither category, but who require extensive time or care. Special leave benefits or dependent-care accounts may not be adequate when employees have dependents who require lifelong care. Cafeteria-style plans that allow employees to choose more mental health, home health, or other coverage instead of leave benefits, life insurance, or other options may be worth exploring for those companies that are family oriented. Employees then can choose the types of coverage or benefits most needed at any point.

Corporations have the opportunity to move to the forefront of family issues. If private employers are willing to test different approaches, pay for staff to participate in conferences or forums to discuss what they have learned, and have company officials participate in local, state, and federal discussions about work and family issues, then employers will motivate other corporations and public officials to address these issues. Social work practitioners have an important role to play in corporate exploration of family support options. Social workers can bring a family-oriented, developmental perspective to the discussion of options.

REFERENCES

AT&T pact in vanguard on family-care benefits. (1989, May 29). *The Washington Post,* pp. 1, 9.

Creedon, M. A. (Ed.). (1987). *Issues for an aging America: Employees and eldercare (A briefing book).* Bridgeport, CT: University of Bridgeport, Administration on Aging.

Friedman, D. E. (1987). *Family-supportive policies: The corporate decision-making process* (A Research Report). Washington, DC: Conference Board, Inc.

Heath, A. (1987a). *Caregivers fair.* Washington, DC: American Association of Retired Persons.

Heath, A. (1987b). *Caregivers survey.* Washington, DC: American Association of Retired Persons.

Heath, A. (1987c). *Educational seminars trainer's manual.* Washington, DC: American Association of Retired Persons.

Kamerman, S. B., & Kahn, A. J. (1987). *The responsive workplace: Employers and a changing labor force.* New York: Columbia University Press.

Osterkamp, L. (Ed.). (1989). *Parent care.* Lawrence: The University of Kansas Gerontology Center.

Piktialis, D. S. (1988). The elder care referral service. *Generations, 12,* 71–72.

Subcommittee on Human Services of the Select Committee on Aging, House of Representatives, One Hundredth Congress. (1987). *Exploding the myths: Caregiving in America.* (Report No. 99–611). Washington, DC: U.S. Government Printing Office.

U.S. Department of Health and Human Services, Office of Human Development Services. (1986). (Fact Sheet). Washington, DC.

7

Community Acceptance and Response

$\mathbf{C}$aregiving families face many problems; models of practice—including a model of practice for worksite practitioners—can help families cope with the problems. However, practitioners depend heavily on the formal services available in their local communities. When help from family members and friends is insufficient to meet the needs of caregiving families, practitioners cannot offer assistance if formal services do not exist or if their clients do not have access to them. How do community leaders know when they have an adequate services delivery system? How do they create a system if it does not already exist?

Before a community can create an effective, well-used, and comprehensive system of support for caregiving families, citizens must believe that such a system is important; community leaders must identify and enlist appropriate and willing agencies and professionals to provide services; and community members must reach out to caregiving families and encourage them to use needed services. Social workers have a responsibility to advocate for, and help create, a process that will result in a comprehensive system of support for their clients. The first step in this process is to develop a broad public awareness of the needs of caregiving neighbors, relatives, friends, and respected community leaders.

PUBLIC AWARENESS AND EDUCATION

Communities can stimulate public awareness through mass media, special events, and information distributed by health, mental health, and social services providers. Examples of successful activities are growing. As mentioned in Chapter 6, in 1987, a major telephone company developed a three-part program to raise awareness throughout the United States about the needs of people caring for elderly relatives. This program includes

• A 30-minute documentary videotape about the feelings, needs, and frustrations of caregivers (Electronic Media Associates,

Inc., 1987). The telephone company made this documentary available to a public broadcasting network and cable and syndicated television. The company also offered the documentary to professionals, community groups, and employers.

• A manual with separate sections for professionals, community groups, religious organizations, and employers of caregivers. The first part offers professionals guidelines on how to evaluate services and equipment and suggests ways to raise awareness. The second part discusses coalition building, volunteer networks, and support groups. The third part explains the impact of caregiving at the worksite and gives examples of successful corporate activities.

• An audiotape, which gives practical advice to caregivers.

In 1988, the American Association of Retired Persons (AARP) conducted a mass mailing to professionals concerned about caregiving families to encourage multiple public and consumer awareness activities during National Caregivers Week (November 20–26, 1988). AARP hoped to enhance community knowledge and stimulate support of local caregivers. The package of materials mailed to professionals included a fact sheet about caregivers, suggestions for community activities, a poster and buttons calling attention to caregivers, a sample article for newsletters, and a sample agenda for a community forum. AARP suggested that the following community activities, though developed for caregivers of older people, would be useful to all caregivers (Mullen, 1988):

• sponsor a 1-day workshop that brings caregivers and service providers together to discuss concerns and resources
• display posters about caregiving
• invite caregivers to attend a local forum that highlights the problems caregivers face and community supports that are available
• organize a course; for example, AARP offers a training program on nursing for caregivers
• sponsor an open house for caregivers to visit agencies that offer supportive services; this activity could alleviate any misgivings about seeking help and could help a caregiver identify the agency with which he or she is most comfortable
• sponsor an information fair for caregivers where all providers display information and are available to discuss the services they provide
• develop a speaker series for caregivers on topics of concern to most caregivers (the Honolulu Gerontology Program described in Chapter 3 for example, hosts such a series, as do other employers)

- place information on caregiving in congregational bulletins and encourage clergy to recognize caregivers
- encourage local newspaper staff to write stories about caregivers
- involve local political leaders—AARP suggests that community leaders invite officials to meet with caregivers in a public meeting; moreover, professionals also might develop relationships with key aides, submitting information about new approaches to them, and inviting political leaders to important events through their aides
- plan an awards ceremony because events honoring caregivers and caregiving families not only increase public awareness by spotlighting their contributions, but they also build self-esteem among the honorees, rewarding and encouraging the caregivers

These activities can generate an increased public and professional awareness about eldercare problems. However, haphazard scheduling of activities will not necessarily result in an informed public. Even if citizens are more aware of caregivers' problems and the services available in their community, this awareness may not translate into continued support for existing services or resources to develop other needed services. The key is to develop strategies with short- and long-term goals and then to structure activities that will help meet these goals. Goals at the national level will be different from goals at the local level, however. The ultimate goal is to build an effective, well-used, comprehensive system of support for caregiving families (Table 7-1). Activities to achieve this long-term goal include research, demonstration, and evaluation projects to determine what is "most effective" and what results in a system that is "well used"; an outreach strategy and a training strategy for professionals; and a political strategy to enlist the support of community leaders.

Strategies based on the developmental approach suggested in this book must focus on the family rather than only on the caregiver or the care receiver, and should spotlight caregiving as one part of the family members' lives. Although a long-term objective is to improve professional response to the needs of caregiving families, a short-term objective, for example, might be to reach professionals—to interest them in the developmental approach. Ways of reaching professionals include an awareness strategy that uses mass mailings such as the AARP mailing, special shows on public television or other television stations, and a training strategy by developing and

Table 7-1. Creating an Effective, Well-Used, Comprehensive System of Support

Intermediate Goal	Short-Term Goal	Awareness Strategy	Research/ Evaluation Strategy	Training Strategy	Outreach Strategy	Political Strategy
Increase awareness and acceptance of caregiving families and their desire to help	Increase public awareness Increase acceptance of caregiving families	Television show Radio shows Caregiver fair/part of health fair Information distributed through doctors, hospitals, and other providers Volunteers in neighborhoods to discuss information	Test methods of presenting caregiving issues to elicit positive response Develop approaches for identifying strategies appropriate to individual communities	Train volunteers to disseminate information Train agency personnel in identified strategies	Hotline to follow up television and radio shows Information on resources and support groups	Spotlight poor type of community response to serious caregiving problem and request response from candidates or political leaders
Improve professional response	Increase professional awareness of needs of caregiving families Improve professional practice with caregiving families	Mass mailings Public television Special, well-advertised radio shows Television shows about a professional working with a family Market curricula through the Council on Social Work Education (CSWE) Awards	Develop and test ways to reach a professional audience Develop and evaluate best approaches Develop curricula for social work, nursing, and so forth Develop continuing education series	Provide continuing education classes on needs of these families Provide continuing education on best practices Offer generic caregiving curricula and curricula on illnesses and problems Offer student internships	Special chapter bulletins Graduate student help Recruit college interns for practice Educational programs by an agency	Arrange meetings between professionals and key political leaders Work with aides of candidates—introduce issues into campaign

marketing continuing education classes. Another long-term objective is to increase public awareness, acceptance of caregiving families, and desire to improve community response. One of the short-term objectives might be to stimulate public awareness of the millions of caregiving families and their multiple needs through an awareness strategy to "sell" the idea to a well-known news reporter. A special television show can convey much information and stimulate awareness. Such a show should spotlight families who care for elderly, developmentally disabled, and mentally ill people; people with acquired immune deficiency syndrome (AIDS); and those people who care for alcoholics or drug abusers, in addition to families who care for more than one person. For this short-term goal to be most effective, professionals should use an outreach strategy—either a hotline should be made available following a television show or viewers should be given an address to write to for more information. Information on where to turn for community resources or how to volunteer should be available.

An important difference between the telephone company and AARP activities described at the beginning of this chapter and activities created under a developmental approach is that the telephone company and AARP activities are only for elderly people. However, under a developmental strategy, a caregiver fair (part of an awareness strategy) would bring together service providers for all populations—preferably with a central information point for those people who care for more than one person or care for someone with more than one diagnosis or problem. To be most effective, the caregiver fair should not reach only one group of people, such as employees in one company. Instead, the fair should be a well-planned, well-advertised community event. Employers interested in making a contribution could offer to house the fair and pay for the reproduction of materials. This type of fair also could serve as the first step in achieving a long-term goal of developing a single community entry point for all caregiving families. The service networks for the elderly and developmentally disabled people and children often have single entry points for each system through an information and referral agency. The worker in a single community entry point would determine whether a family is caring for one person, more than one person, or someone with multiple problems and would decide whether referral to a case manager is a more immediate need than referral to a specific service or service delivery system. Such a single entry point also would enhance the success of public awareness and education efforts, because those people seeking help as a result of media reports or other public awareness activities only would have to go to a single source to receive basic information. Efforts to stimulate public awareness and to get caregiving families to seek help probably will fail if these families must make multiple calls to find their way through a bureaucracy.

Although this chapter conceptualizes an "awareness" strategy for a public awareness and education objective, only a professional "communicator," such as a public affairs consultant, can develop the best strategies. Public affairs consultants know how to mobilize media power (Fitzpatrick, 1989). Similarly, researchers and evaluators should help develop the research and evaluation strategy. Educators should participate in the development of a training strategy. Besides the special awareness activities that require expert help, professionals who work in agencies serving as key contact points in the community can increase public awareness and the willingness of caregiving families to use available services. If doctors' offices, hospitals, and mental health and social services agencies distribute information to clients, they lend credibility to the caregiving family's need for help and portray confidence in the type of services that are available.

PROFESSIONAL AWARENESS AND TRAINING

Ways to increase the awareness of medical personnel about the needs of caregiving families and ways to improve the types of curricula that schools of social work offer to medical personnel to help them feel comfortable in referring caregiving families to social workers were discussed in Chapter 5. However, that chapter did not address ways in which to recruit social workers into a developmental, family-oriented curriculum and practice by increasing their awareness of and interest in the needs of caregiving families. Professional awareness and marketing or training materials are both part of a long-term objective to improve professional response.

Special television news shows on topics of interest to social workers and perhaps well-advertised radio shows may increase professional awareness and public awareness. Special outreach activities can supplement these efforts to increase professional awareness. For example, special bulletins from and workshops on the needs of caregiving families offered by chapters of the National Association of Social Workers (NASW) and other human services organizations may elicit interest. As schools of social work develop curricula, the

Council on Social Work Education (CSWE), NASW, and other social welfare organizations need to market adoption of the curricula and develop materials for recruiting students into these programs. However, even curricula for schools of social work are not enough. Social work leadership with national associations representing nursing, schools of medicine, and other health and mental health professions could result in greater awareness and sensitivity among these professions and the development of appropriate roles for each profession. Current family-oriented practitioners would benefit from continuing education classes that should develop alongside special curricula for graduate schools.

COMMUNITY ORGANIZATION

Although professionals must increase public and professional awareness of the needs of caregiving families and improve professional techniques for helping those families, neither of these activities is sufficient to create a community support system. The curricula development and leadership with other professions are forms of community organization and advocacy by the social work profession. However, community organization and advocacy by social workers in the communities where they live are equally important. Such organization is critical to the development of a comprehensive system of support for caregiving families and is an important part of the professional role. The professional cannot help caregiving families if the formal services families need are not available in the community. Thus, is it the professional's responsibility to identify the families' needs and to advocate for the development of services and resources.

The first step in gaining support for needed services is to demonstrate that caregiving families who deal with different medical problems share the same needs for supportive services. Although this step alone will not result in new services, it shows the extent of need and the wide range of families that would benefit from the services. Thus, political leaders, and the general public, will not feel that social workers are requesting costly services for only a few families. A General Accounting Office (GAO) study of families who cared for children with different illnesses showed that the families identified similar support needs (General Accounting Office, 1989a). In that study, parents of chronically ill children were surveyed. The children were afflicted with severe forms of 10 medical conditions:

(1) juvenile diabetes, (2) asthma, (3) spina bifida, (4) cleft palate and other craniofacial problems, (5) congenital heart disease, (6) leukemia, (7) kidney failure, (8) sickle-cell anemia, (9) cystic fibrosis, and (10) muscular dystrophy. The GAO study found that the needs for support services were uniform and were not affected much by the condition. At least one-half of all respondents to the GAO survey indicated that they needed four services: baby-sitting, counseling, day care, and transportation. Baby-sitting and day care could serve as respite services that allow a caregiver to work or to pursue his or her own activities.

Thus, to mobilize community support, the professional must identify the supportive services needs of all caregiving families (for elderly people, chronically and terminally ill children and adults, mentally ill and developmentally disabled people, alcoholics, drug abusers, and people with AIDS). The GAO identified caregiving families through contacts with hospital discharge units, because GAO was focused on services available through the Maternal and Child Health Services Block Grant. However, a complete inventory of needs and available services would have to go beyond the GAO survey—to a sampling of doctors, home health agencies, and health, mental health, and social service agencies. Once the professional identifies families, he or she will need to survey a sampling of families with different types of problems (Table 7-2). The survey should seek information on the supportive services needs of all family members. For example, parents may need baby-sitting or day-care services for a healthy child so they can take a chronically ill child to the doctor or visit that child in the hospital. The person who is ill, the primary caregiver, and other family members all may need counseling. A survey that shows widespread need in a community also means there is a big constituency for community leaders who want to develop services and resources based on the identified needs. The survey itself also serves to raise awareness. Social workers can introduce these supportive services needs in political campaigns to encourage politicians to make commitments to focus resources on caregiving families. Social workers can arrange meetings between experts and key community leaders to discuss various solutions.

While experts are surveying caregiving families, they also need to be surveying service providers—both formal and informal (for example, volunteer organizations)—to determine what types of services they offer and whom they serve. Service providers include health, mental health, and social services agencies; private, non-

Table 7-2. Sample Questions for Caregiving Families

1. Because your [family member's relationship] was diagnosed with [illness/chronic condition/handicapping condition], has it been difficult or easy for you to obtain the medical and nonmedical services, listed below, for your [family member's relationship] and family? [Professional: Check appropriate column.]

Services	Services Not Needed (1)	Very Difficult to Obtain (2)	Difficult to Obtain (3)	Neither Difficult nor Easy (4)	Easy to Obtain (5)	Very Easy to Obtain (6)
Medical services						
Physician home visits						
Skilled nursing visits						
Home health aide visits						
Physician office visits						
Medical equipment						
Medical supplies for equipment						
Medications						
Food for special diet						
Training in therapies to be provided by family member (from skilled medical personnel)						
Other _____						
Nonmedical services						
Respite care						
Homemaker services						
General transportation						
Transportation for specific services and needs						
Shopping						
Chore and home repair						
Day care (for child or adult)						

(continued)

Table 7-2. Continued

Services	Services Not Needed (1)	Very Difficult to Obtain (2)	Difficult to Obtain (3)	Neither Difficult nor Easy (4)	Easy to Obtain (5)	Very Easy to Obtain (6)
Counseling						
Case management						
Training in behavior management						
Baby-sitting						
Rehabilitative and other therapies						

2. If your [family member's relationship] was discharged from the hospital recently, has it been difficult or easy since [his or her] discharge for you to obtain the medical and nonmedical services listed below for your [family member's relationship] and family?

Services	Services Not Needed (1)	Very Difficult to Obtain (2)	Difficult to Obtain (3)	Neither Difficult nor Easy (4)	Easy to Obtain (5)	Very Easy to Obtain (6)
Medical services						
Physician home visits						
Skilled nursing visits						
Home health aide visits						
Physician office visits						
Medical equipment						
Medical supplies for equipment						
Medications						
Food for special diet						
Training in therapies to be provided by family member (from skilled medical personnel)						
Other _____						

(continued)

Table 7-2. Continued

Services	Services Not Needed (1)	Very Difficult to Obtain (2)	Difficult to Obtain (3)	Neither Difficult nor Easy (4)	Easy to Obtain (5)	Very Easy to Obtain (6)
Nonmedical services						
Respite care						
Homemaker services						
General transportation						
Transportation						
Shopping						
Chore and home repair						
Day care (for child or adult)						
Counseling						
Case management						
Training in behavior management						
Baby-sitting						
Rehabilitative and other therapies						

3. If you had trouble obtaining needed services, what was the reason?

Reason	Not Applicable (1)	Not a Problem (2)	Problem (3)	Somewhat of a Problem (4)	Very Serious Problem (5)
Insufficient funds or insurance coverage					
Lack of information about services					
Too difficult to deal with "red tape" or agency requirements					
No one to help find appropriate and good-quality service providers					

(continued)

Table 7-2. Continued

4. If you had trouble paying for needed services, which of your resources were insufficient?

Resources	Not Applicable	Resources Were Sufficient	Resources Somewhat Insufficient	Resources Insufficient	Resources Very Insufficient
Income					
Insurance coverage purchased individually					
Insurance purchased through employer					
[Family member] not covered by insurance					
Medicare					
Medicaid					
Other					

profit agencies, such as the Red Cross, Boy Scouts, and Girl Scouts; and religious organizations. Many professionals do not consider informal or volunteer services stable enough to include in such a survey. However, one long-term approach was successful in organizing informal support with volunteers and integrating that support with formal services. In 1983, the Robert Wood Johnson Foundation (1989) launched a 3-year program to strengthen the role of informal caregivers (family, friends, and neighbors) through interfaith coalitions. The 25 coalitions funded were to recruit, train, and match volunteers with disabled or elderly people in the community. The coalitions recruited volunteers from religious organizations within the selected communities.

During the 3 years, 900 congregations recruited and trained more than 11,000 volunteers who helped 26,000 people. Fewer than 36 percent of the people they helped received services from a formal agency. Two significant services that volunteers provided were (1) respite for family members who provided full-time care to disabled or elderly people and (2) transportation, a service needed by 68 percent of the care receivers. At most interfaith volunteer caregiver sites, volunteers also provided shopping, advocacy and referral, friendly visiting, and telephone reassurance. At more than half the sites, they also provided home care and help with meal preparation. One of the most significant aspects of the project, besides providing services that might not be available otherwise, was the relationship that developed between coalitions and local service agencies. When the care receivers' problems were more than a volunteer could handle, the coalition referred the person to an appropriate formal agency. When formal agencies felt that clients' needs could be met by a volunteer, they referred people to the coalition. Formal agencies referred nearly one-third of the people served through the project.

Staff and coalition organizers learned about recruiting and training volunteers, and integrating their services into the community. They attributed part of their success to the involvement of key community leaders. Formal agency staff felt that the key to the coalitions' success was their ability to be flexible. Formal agencies do not have such flexibility. Volunteer caregivers can provide one-time services or services that are important, but for which no financial coverage is available. Eligibility criteria do not constrain the coalitions. Thus, the coalitions provide services that families or friends cannot provide or for which they cannot pay. The coalitions also fill gaps in available formal services.

Out of this experience, a grassroots organization developed the National Federation of Interfaith Volunteer Caregivers (Robert Wood Johnson Foundation, 1989, p. 18). By the end of 1988, this organization had more than 250 organizational and individual members. The federation eventually plans to develop five regional offices to provide outreach and support. However, the federation can offer some help to communities now. Membership in the federation provides access to the network's training materials, newsletters, and other information. The federation will help a community group organize or strengthen an Interfaith Volunteer Caregiver Project. Professionals clearly need to include this type of informal and volunteer organization in a community survey.

Besides surveying caregiving families and service providers as part of the community effort to integrate all formal and informal services, experts also should survey local employers to determine if employers want to develop a comprehensive system at the local level (Table 7-3). As more employers begin to construct policies, benefits, and services to help families cope with work and family conflict (especially time management), they become part of the community's resources. Thus, community leaders need to integrate these resources with other formal and informal services.

Following the surveys, the professional should be able to construct a community profile that answers questions such as

- Does the community have a single services entry or contact point for all caregiving families, separate entry points for each

Table 7-3. Sample Questions for Employer Survey

1. What kinds of services or benefits do you offer that may help employees when they are providing care for an ill or dependent family member?
2. Were any of your policies specially designed to help employees whose family responsibilities may affect their work performance?
3. If you wanted to make or to expand your contribution to your community or your employees in a way that would help caregiving families, how would you prefer to do so? (Circle the lettered options that you would like to make available.)
    Ease Problems with Time for Employees
        a. Flex-time
        b. Part-time work
        c. Job sharing
        d. Work at home
        e. Sick child care or eldercare leave
        f. Extended parental leave and adoptive leave
        g. Personal family leave
        h. Time off to serve as community volunteers
    Donate to Local Programs
        a. Money
        b. Corporate goods/services
        c. Staff time
    Create services at your worksite
        a. Child care
        b. Adult day care
        c. Contract with service organizations to serve employees
        d. Provide employees with information and referral to needed services
    Offer financial help
        a. Improved or cafeteria-style benefit packages
        b. Flexible spending accounts with salary reduction for dependent care

service system (for example, for the elderly, the developmentally disabled), or no visible entry points?

• Are all services accessible to everyone; are some services for each care setting (in-home, in the hospital, residential) accessible to everyone; or is access extremely limited for some types of services?

• Are all or most providers part of a comprehensive community system or do they operate independently?

• If providers operate independently, do they normally refer clients to other service providers, when appropriate?

The surveys also should help to identify key community leaders. If service providers organize themselves into coalitions or boards, then the presidents or chairpersons of these organizations are community leaders. The board members of any organization representing corporations are community leaders. All people who can influence decisions in a major sector of the community are key community leaders. Once professionals identify these community leaders, they can organize these leaders and help them use the following techniques that gained support for caregivers of people with Alzheimer's disease (Pfeiffer et al., 1989):

- building coalitions that include all the key community leaders (politicians, key service providers, corporate leaders, religious leaders, and volunteer leaders)—these coalitions should participate in the initial planning phase for the development of a community system
- learning about and understanding the goals of each collaborative organization and how each organization can best contribute to the coalition's activities while working to achieve its own goals
- developing strategies that allow every organization or program to benefit

If professionals can identify community leaders before constructing the surveys, then the leaders can help to frame the questions and select the people to survey. If social workers cannot identify leaders until the surveys are completed, then the surveys will provide information for planning an appropriate community response. Community organization activities do not end with the identification of the service needs of caregiving families or a determination of the willingness of service providers, volunteers, and employers to provide needed services. Community leaders must become a collective decision-making body that systematically reviews survey information through the help of staff support and makes policy decisions about the development or coordination of services. This group can designate existing staff in their agencies to help this collective decision-making body, or the group can pool resources or solicit help from governmental authorities or the state legislature to hire staff dedicated to supporting informed decision making.

A model of effective community decision making that has evolved for more than 43 years is the Juvenile Welfare Board of Pinellas County, Florida. In 1946, citizen leaders of Pinellas County succeeded in getting the state legislature to pass legislation allowing the county to create a countywide special taxing district for children's services funded through a property tax. Implementation was subject to a referendum, which passed by a four-to-one margin. The current Juvenile Welfare Board comprises community leaders, including three ex-officio representatives—the juvenile court judge, the vice chairman of the county commissioners, and the superintendent of schools—and five citizens appointed by the governor (personal communication with J. Mills, Executive Director, Juvenile Welfare Board of Pinellas County, Florida, October 25, 1989). Currently, the chairperson of the board is a social worker in the public schools. Other appointed board members include a pediatric physician, the vice president of a financial services company, a community volunteer, and the director of the county jail services program (also a social worker).

The board has an annual budget of $19.5 million. It provides no direct services, but plans and contracts with 44 agencies and 86 county programs throughout the county (mostly not-for-profit agencies). The board's historical emphasis has been on prevention and early intervention. Its first priority is to deal with adolescent pregnancy, adolescent substance abuse, physical abuse and neglect of children, family dysfunction, and truancy and dropouts. One of the services included under this priority is a specialized children's support program for families with a terminally ill member. Most of the board's second-level priorities, for which the board will maintain and slowly increase resource commitments, are programs dealing with chronically ill children, developmentally disabled children, emotionally disordered children, and physically handicapped children. This priority also includes funds for unsupervised children, that is, day care. In 1987 and 1988, day care received the most funding of the second-level priorities (Juvenile Welfare Board of Pinellas County, 1988). Even when one subtracts the $2.8 million for day care from funds spent for these second-level programs, $2.7 million was spent on services for children with chronic or potentially chronic problems and their families. When one considers that of the $3.5 million spent for the first-priority preventive and rehabilitative services some of the services designed to prevent family dysfunction will be used by families who have a child with chronic problems, it is obvious that a comprehensive approach does not need to shortchange these families.

Besides funding services directly, the board's staff also serves the community. The staff includes an executive director who is a social worker, four programmatic units, an administrative unit, and staff support for seven advisory committees. Community planning and development staff maintain a special database and serve on approximately 30 committees throughout the community and integrate information from citizens and the multiple organizations serving on the committees to help with planning. Funding and evaluation staff monitor programs funded by the board. Members of the staff development and training unit provide training for professionals and caregivers throughout the county who are working with children and families. They coordinate training with the school system, professional associations, and local colleges and universities. Community relations staff help the public understand the services of the Juvenile Welfare Board and, more generally, the many needs of families and children. The purpose of the services advisory committees is to get professional and public input for critical services coordination and policy development. Current committees include abuse neglect and dependency, day care and early childhood, economic services, juvenile justice, legislative, mental health/substance abuse, and health.

The integrated community approach allowed the Juvenile Welfare Board to identify unmet needs in the county (for planning purposes) as well as accomplishments with those clients who did receive services. For example, unmet needs (people waiting for services funded by the Juvenile Welfare Board) in Pinellas County included the following (Juvenile Welfare Board of Pinellas County, 1981, p. 36):

Need Area	Children on Waiting List as of 12/31/88	Children on Waiting List as of 12/31/87
Chronically ill children	0	0
Developmentally disabled children	14	26
Emotionally disordered children	110	54

Accomplishments included the following:

• With early intervention, 100 percent of the emotionally disturbed children maintained their placement for at least 1 year.

• Eighty-five percent of the children who completed a therapeutic day-care program were mainstreamed into regular kindergartens, preschools, or family day-care homes.

• One hundred percent of the handicapped children who completed a special community center program were mainstreamed into the general program population (Juvenile Welfare Board of Pinellas County, 1989).

The steps after creating a collective decision-making body are illustrated well in the Juvenile Welfare Board model. The decision-making body must decide on its budget (discrete or collective) and how to allocate the resources over which it has control. The budget could include funds allocated by government, private, or charitable sources, and fees that consumers are willing and able to pay. If community leaders anticipate consumer fees as part of the budget, then they will need to arrange for market research to determine what services caregiving families are willing to buy and how much they will pay for the services (Pfeiffer et al., 1989).[1]

Finding all available funding sources is a major challenge. Identifying federal, state, local, foundation, and private-sector funding is difficult. No one program or category of programs or services reveals all the funds that caregiving families can use. Social workers are encouraged to develop a registry of all community services (see Chapter 2). In developing a comprehensive community system, however, the social worker needs to examine all possibilities. Existing services and possible funding sources can be used in a variety of ways to meet the needs of different types of caregiving families.

Programs for caregiving families of elderly and developmentally disabled people are the most developed. For people with developmental disabilities, 22 states operate extensive family support programs (Agosta & Bradley, 1985). Nine of these states primarily offer cash assistance. In the 33 states that offer supportive services programs, more than 19 types of services are available. Eleven of the states provide unique services that are unavailable through another program. For families who care for an elderly relative, 24 states offer a variety of services. Another 23 states offer a combination of economic incentives or cash assistance and services (Biegel et al., 1986). Most programs target one or two populations (Tables 7-4–7-6). However, a recent GAO survey of 24 respite programs for children in five states revealed nine programs that do provide broader coverage. These broader programs serve most or all the following groups: mentally retarded, visually impaired/blind, physically handicapped, chronically ill, speech or hearing impaired, abused/neglected, and foster children (General Accounting Office, 1989b). Agencies that administer these programs include social/human services, mental health/retardation, health, welfare, developmental disabilities, and education.

---

[1]For further information about this unique program, contact James E. Mills, ACSW, Executive Director, Juvenile Welfare Board of Pinellas County, 4140 Forty-Ninth Street, North, St. Petersburg, FL 33709.

Table 7-4. Federal Programs Covering or Offering Services to Caregiving Families

Program	Eligible Population	Type of Assistance	Contact
Social Security	Disabled insured workers under age 65 Retired insured workers Spouses of eligible retired or disabled workers who are age 62 years or older or care for the worker's child who is under age 18 years Age 62 years or older divorced spouses of eligible person who was married to the person for 20 years (1978 and before) or 10 years (after 1978) Dependent, unmarried children of eligible person or deceased insured person if child is under age 18 years; 18 years or older but has a disability that began before age 22 years; or age 18–21 years and attending school full-time Surviving spouses of deceased workers if widow/widower is age 50–59 years and becomes disabled within period specified by law Surviving spouses of deceased insured workers, regardless of age, if they are caring for an entitled child who is under age 18 years or is disabled Dependent parents of deceased insured workers age 62 years and older	Insurance payment figured on basis of average wages earned	Local social security office
Supplemental Security Income (SSI)	Aged, blind, or disabled individuals who meet the standard for low income; states may provide supplemental payments for special types of living arrangements (for example, personal care homes)	Monthly guaranteed income based on defined level of need	Local social security office

(continued)

Table 7-4. Continued

Program	Eligible Population	Type of Assistance	Contact
Medicare	Social security beneficiaries age 65 years and older and those permanently disabled Dependents of permanently disabled eligible persons People suffering from end-stage renal disease	Hospital insurance (Part A) covers inpatient hospital services; extended care in skilled nursing facility; and services in the home through a participating home health agency Supplementary medical insurance (Part B) provides optional coverage for those who enroll, covering physician services, outpatient hospital services, diagnostic tests, outpatient physical therapy, speech pathology, medical equipment, supplies, home health	Health Care Financing Administration or local social security office (see appendix A)
Medicaid (joint federal/state)	People with low incomes Aged, blind, or disabled "Medically needy" at state option (those with incomes too high to quality for welfare but too low to cover medical expenses)	Required services: physician, hospital, skilled nursing home care, health screenings and follow-up treatment for children, laboratory and x-ray services, home health care services, family planning services, rural health clinic services Optional services: dental care; eyeglasses; clinic services; prescribed drugs; care in an intermediate-care facility; and services by optometrists, podiatrists, and chiropractors	State Medicaid agency (see appendix B)
Social Services Block Grant (Title XX)	Determined by state	Many services designed to achieve goals specified by legislation: self-support; self-sufficiency; protection of children and vulnerable adults from abuse, neglect, or exploitation; prevention or reduction of inappropriate institutional care by referral to community-based care, home-based care, or other forms of less-intensive care; and securing referral to institutional care, when appropriate	Designated single state agency—state department of human services or resources (see appendix C)
Older Americans Act	All people age 60 years or older without regard to income	Planning and coordination of community services Direct services include in-home services, congregate meals, residential repair and renovation, legal services, transportation, information and referral, escort, and outreach services; services provided in individual communities are determined locally	State or area agency on aging (see appendix D)

(continued)

Table 7-4. Continued

Program	Eligible Population	Type of Assistance	Contact
Services available through Department of Veterans Affairs	Veterans with injuries incurred in the line of duty Veterans discharged or retired for a disability incurred in the line of duty or those receiving compensation and requiring treatment for a non-service-connected condition Veterans unable to pay or older than age 65 years (not discharged or retired as a result of service-related condition) Wives and children of veterans with permanent total service-connected disabilities (veterans living or deceased as a result of the disability)	VA provides services directly or through contract in hospitals, nursing homes, psychiatric and domiciliary facilities. Services include inpatient care, skilled and intermediate nursing care, psychiatric services, domiciliary care, social services, and rehabilitation[a] VA also provides monthly benefits to housebound veterans to purchase "aid and attendance" service Veterans whose disabilities are not service connected have a lower priority for VA nursing home care than those with service-connected disabilities, and those with incomes in excess of prescribed amounts only may receive VA care to the extent that space and resources permit	Local VA Medical Center (see appendix E)
Vocational Rehabilitation Program	Physically and mentally disabled people who have a reasonable expectation of obtaining employment as a result of vocational rehabilitation, usually non-elderly adults	Services include evaluation, counseling, placement, training, physical and mental restoration services, and transportation. Vocational rehabilitation also may pay for hospitalization; convalescent or nursing home care; prosthetic; orthotic or other assistance devices; education; attendance services; interpreter services for the deaf; and outfitted vehicles	State rehabilitation office
Maternal and Child Health Services Block Grant (Title V)	Mothers and children with low income or limited availability of health services	Authorizes home- and community-based services for children with special health care needs; block grant funds also were used to establish a national information network that includes an 800 number	Title V agencies (see appendix F)

(continued)

Table 7-4. Continued

Program	Eligible Population	Type of Assistance	Contact
Developmental Disabilities Program	People with severe, chronic disabilities that are attributable to a mental or physical impairment or combination of these impairments that is manifest before age 22; that are likely to continue indefinitely; that result in substantial functional limitations in self-care, language, learning, mobility, self-sufficiency; and that reflect the need for a combination and sequence of special, interdisciplinary, or generic services, which are lifelong or of extended duration	Coordination of services through state planning and by ensuring that all agencies receiving funds under the Basic State Grant Program have an individualized habilitation plan for each developmentally disabled person receiving services and provide for an annual review of each plan To participate in the Basic State Grant Program, a state must have a protection and advocacy system that can take action to protect the rights of developmentally disabled people in the state; these systems must be capable of litigating; however, most problems are resolved through direct referrals, negotiation, administrative actions and other nonlegal remedies	State administering agencies and state protection and advocacy agencies (see appendixes G and H)
Education of the Handicapped Act	All handicapped children age 3 through 21 years	The act mandates the free provision of needed public education. It does not mandate other services, but does authorize the provision of related services. Related services may include early identification screening, assessment, and parental counseling. The 1986 amendments authorized funds to assist states in developing a statewide comprehensive, coordinated, multidisciplinary, interagency program of early intervention services for handicapped infants and toddlers and their families.	State Office of Special Education (see appendix I)
Head Start Program	Low income At least 10 percent of enrollment must be handicapped children	Besides child development, Head Start provides comprehensive education, health services, social services, and parent involvement; medical evaluations identify any handicapping or health conditions, then Head Start offers follow-up activities	Head Start Bureau[b]

(continued)

Table 7-4. Continued

Program	Eligible Population	Type of Assistance	Contact
Temporary Child Care for Handicapped Children and Crisis Nurseries	Competitive grant award process to states means that eligibility of handicapped or chronically ill children is proposed by each grantee and provided on a sliding fee scale with hourly or daily rates	Grants to states to establish demonstration programs that provide two types of services: (1) in-home or out-of-home temporary nonmedical child care for handicapped children and children with chronic or terminal illnesses (Section 203 of Title II of the Children's Justice and Assistance Act, now Section 5117a); and (2) crisis nurseries for abused and neglected children, children at risk of abuse and neglect, or children in families receiving protective services (Section 204 of Title II of the Children's Justice and Assistance Act, now Section 5117b)	See appendix J for list of 1988 and 1989 grantees
Department of Defense Family Support Program	Retired active duty personnel and their families; overseas civilian employees of the military	Multiple family support services	See appendix K

^aMany VA medical centers now offer services for caregivers, including educational services while the patient is hospitalized.

^bHead Start grantees change often. For current information, contact the Head Start Bureau, 330 C Street, SW, Room 2050, Washington, DC 20201, (202) 245-0572.

Table 7-5. *Recent State Programs and Services for
            Caregiving Families*

Service and Contact	State	Eligible Population	Funding
Respite (Williams & Lidoff, 1985)	Alaska	60 years and older	State funds
	California	Elderly	2176 Medicaid waiver
	Colorado	All eligible for 2176 Medicaid waivers	2176 Medicaid waiver
	Connecticut	Recipients ages 0–9 years are most frequent users	State funds
	Delaware	75 years and older	Older Americans Act, Title IIIB
	District of Columbia	Unclear	Medicaid
	Florida	Elderly	General state funds and local match
	Georgia	Unclear	2176 Medicaid waiver
	Hawaii	Elderly	State funds and Medicaid waiver
	Idaho	Unclear	State funds; Older Americans Act, Title IIIB; Social Services Block Grants; Local funds; Medicaid waiver
	Illinois	Unclear	State funds
Department on Aging	Kansas	Unclear	2176 Medicaid waiver
	Maine	75 years and older	State funds
	Michigan	Unclear	1-Year model project; Older Americans Act, Title IIIB
	Minnesota	Unclear	2176 Medicaid waiver
	Utah	Unclear	State funds; Older Americans Act, Title IIIB
	Vermont	Unclear	State funds
	Washington	Unclear	State funds
Division of Aging	Missouri	Unclear	2176 Medicaid waiver
	Montana	Unclear	2176 Medicaid waiver
	New Hampshire	Unclear	State funds

(continued)

Table 7-5. Continued

Service and Contact	States	Eligible Population	Funding
Department of Human Services	New Jersey	Elderly	2176 Medicaid waiver
	New Mexico	Elderly	State funds (demonstration, not ongoing program)
	New York	Elderly	State funds
	North Carolina	Caregivers of special-needs people	State funds; Older Americans Act, Title IIIB
	North Dakota	60 years and older and rural elderly	2176 Medicaid waiver; Social Services Block Grant; state funds
	South Carolina	Poor rural elderly	Social Services Block Grant
	South Dakota	Unclear	Older Americans Act, Title IIIB; Social Services Block Grant
	Texas	Unclear	Medicaid; Social services Block Grant; Older Americans Act, Title IIIB
Department of Social and Health Services	West Virginia	Most beneficiaries are male spouses from urban areas	2176 Medicaid waiver
Office on Aging	Wisconsin	Five categories, including elderly and developmentally disabled	State funds; Older Americans Act, Title IIIB

Social workers who want to develop a comprehensive community system can try different approaches to integrating funding sources and services, depending on the existing community system. If the community has moved toward integrating services for many populations, social workers will want to expand this approach. If the community has individual service systems and providers for each client group, a single entry point for caregiving families to access all service systems and providers might be preferable to trying to integrate providers with a single focus on one client group. Whatever approach the community chooses, once community leaders establish the budget, the decision-making body must determine which service needs they will meet, define the services that the community will

Table 7-6. Examples of State Services Offered to Developmentally Disabled Retarded People

Service	State	Population
Cash assistance (Agosta & Bradley, 1985, pp. 100–102)	Connecticut	Developmentally disabled
	Idaho	Developmentally disabled under age 21 years
	Indiana	Developmentally disabled
	Louisiana	Mentally retarded
	Minnesota	Mentally retarded
	Nevada	Profoundly retarded
	North Dakota	Developmentally disabled under age 21 years
	South Carolina	Mentally retarded
Support services (Agosta & Bradley, 1985, pp. 100–102)	California	Developmentally disabled
	New Jersey	Mentally retarded
	Ohio	Developmentally disabled
	Oregon	Developmentally disabled under age 6 years
	Pennsylvania	Mentally retarded
	Vermont	Mentally retarded
	Washington	Developmentally disabled
Cash and support services (Agosta & Bradley, 1985, pp. 100–102)	Florida	Developmentally disabled
	Maryland	Developmentally disabled under age 22 years
	Michigan	Cash—severe mental or multiple impairment, autism, under age 18 years; Support services—developmentally disabled
	Montana	No set priority, but preference for young with severe disabilities
	Nebraska	Developmentally disabled
	Rhode Island	Mentally retarded, mental illness, chronic impairments
	Wisconsin	Children with severe disabilities

offer, identify all providers and their target populations, and then negotiate agreements with providers on the numbers of people from each target group they will serve and decide what strategy the community will use to fill gaps in services and programs. One gap-filling option the community may want to consider is paying family caregivers. In making this decision, states and communities must assess the limited evidence on the effects of paying family caregivers and the community's need for more caregivers. Most women, previously the presumed caregivers, are working because their families need the money. This compensation provides them with the opportunity to stay home and care for a loved one if they choose to do so. (Family members are more likely to provide continuous care for someone who is severely impaired than is a formal agency.) On the other hand, communities do not want to encourage family members to provide such care if they are not trained or are unable to provide appropriate care. Only two states offer programs that pay family caregivers. However, these states also have developed mechanisms for limiting the growth of the programs so that people already providing care voluntarily would not seek compensation, which would dramatically increase state costs (Linsk et al., 1986).

Once community leaders decide on a budget, an approach for integrating services, and priorities, they need to determine what their staffing needs are and how they want to operate on an ongoing basis. Although the initial decision making and cooperation are critical to the establishment of a comprehensive community system of support for caregiving families, the system will not continue to respond to community needs unless someone monitors changes in needs and the types of services families want. Someone must continue coordination activities with service providers and seek new resources for emerging needs. Although a community might not want to have a staff as large or as sophisticated as the Juvenile Welfare Board of Pinellas County, some type of continuing staffing is essential.

Especially important to the planning and continuity of such a system is quality assurance. Family access to supportive services may not be beneficial without mechanisms to assure the quality of the services. If the services supplied to the care receiver do not meet his or her needs, he or she may not be eligible for other services. The person referring the care receiver to a provider may assume that the care receiver is well cared for. Or, the care receiver could be the victim of abuse or neglect—worse than if he or she received no services at all. Quality assurance mechanisms need to be built into the developing system and monitored for effectiveness. A variety of quality assurance mechanisms are used in some federal and state programs for workers who provide home care (Macro Systems, Inc., 1988).

Standards

Some programs or states require minimum training for certain types of workers. Personnel, who are part of the medical system, and home health aides often must meet such standards. Additionally, social workers, psychologists, and nurses must meet standards to be accredited by their own professional accrediting bodies and often must comply with standards set forth in state licensing laws. Personnel who work in supportive services systems generally do not have to meet specified standards. For example, chore workers and respite care workers do not have to meet any standards for training. Often, even homemakers and personal care workers do not have to meet any standards.

States with certification programs usually tie the certification to worker training standards. Workers generally must complete a state-approved training program and submit documentation to become certified. Most states only certify workers involved in providing home health care. Again, supportive services workers and non-medical homemakers do not have to be certified, with exceptions. For example, New Jersey requires certification for home care workers under the Older Americans Act, Title III, and the Social Services Block Grant. Licensure of provider agencies by a state means that the agencies must not only meet specified standards, but also that the state will review their compliance with standards periodically (usually annually). Licensure of individual professional providers does not include the same types of reassessment. Generally, professionals must complete a specified number of hours of continuing education to maintain their licenses.

Supportive services programs more often use state or program approval, rather than the more formal mechanisms for ensuring quality. To obtain approval, providers register with the state program and agree to comply with requirements. For example, California maintains a registry of approved individual providers and conducts background checks. Programs funded by Social Services Block Grant only purchase services from approved agencies.

Other approaches to assuring quality in home care include accreditation of providers by an independent body (for example,

Joint Commission on Accreditation of Health Care Organizations, National League for Nursing, and National Home Caring Council); a client bill of rights that limits the provider's authority to act without client knowledge and approval; and a code of ethics for workers that defines what the public expects of them.

Monitoring

Once states or communities develop quality assurance mechanisms, they have to monitor and enforce the requirements for the mechanisms to be effective. Monitoring approaches include annual reviews to ensure compliance with program standards; supervision of workers (either on site or by telephone); unannounced home visits when the worker is there; regular reassessments of client needs and development of a written care plan based on those assessments; and the use of case managers to coordinate and monitor services for the client. Other monitoring approaches used sometimes include a provider quality assurance advisory body, which includes current or former clients in the planning and evaluation of services, and a hotline to address complaints.

Enforcement

Unfortunately, the options for enforcing quality tend to harm the clients and the provider. States may cancel contracts with providers, withhold funds, recover funds, reassign clients elsewhere, and stop referrals to a provider. These mechanisms, although protecting care receivers from inadequate care, also reduce the number of providers available when there is already an inadequate number of providers. When providers abuse or neglect care receivers, criminal penalties apply.

When planning a comprehensive system, the community needs to develop quality control for the entire range of in-home, out-of-home, and residential care provided by professionals, paraprofessionals, and volunteers. Quality assurance is a major issue for states and communities that choose to compensate family caregivers. Care receivers are much less likely to complain about or take action against members of their own family who are not providing enough care or not providing care in a way preferred by the care receiver. The best way to initiate planning for quality assurance is to emphasize empowerment of the care receiver and the caregiving family. This means the family not only needs to know how often a service provider should come to their home and for how long, but also what to expect from each provider in terms of service, treatment regimens, and so forth. Thus, to empower caregiving families, the professional needs to train them to understand and handle the illness or condition, communicate appropriately, and solve problems. The professional also needs to train the family to be prepared (what to expect); discuss unsatisfactory service with a worker; request other types of services; and consult with a professional about the provider at appropriate times. If the family fears provider reprisal against the care receiver, then the family must know they not only may, but should, involve the professional in resolving service problems.

The community's responsibility is to build requirements for training into any certification or licensure program. The community might offer a hotline number so consumers could report serious problems. If enough resources are available, the community might develop a program similar to the Ombudsman Program mandated by the Older Americans Act Amendments. The Ombudsman Program staff investigate complaints made by or for older patients in nursing homes, foster homes, and group homes. Some states also use the program to investigate problems older people experience with home care. For such a program to work for all types of caregiving families and clients of all ages with a variety of problems, the program unit might need professionals who either specialize in understanding certain types of care or the problems of certain types of care receivers. The unit also needs enough funding to be fully staffed.

The biggest challenge to the community both in planning services and ensuring the quality of those services is to prevent a fragmented, uncoordinated system. Individual responsibility for services in hospitals, nursing homes, each residential setting, and each type of service provided in home means that each new provider must learn about the needs and preferences of the caregiving family, unless a case manager or some type of community process already ensures and monitors coordination. It also means that the family has to learn about the quality assurance mechanisms which differ for each of these service settings or providers.

The opportunities and challenges for social workers and other professionals are tremendous. Curricula in schools of social work need to train social workers about a disease or problem and how to train the caregiving family to serve as case manager, to solve problems, and to communicate. Training the family in quality assurance is an added dimension. As opposed to being labeled as a profession that promotes dependency on public programs, social work has the opportunity to become the profession of optimists. Social work can be the profession that helps people in need take charge of their lives, whether it is to overcome problems they are facing now or whether it is to anticipate possible problems and plan for them (lifecare planning). Social workers can help clients become and remain confident about their ability to control their lives and achieve the goals developed after a realistic assessment of their personal resources and family responsibilities.

To achieve this "optimism," social workers may not only need to be comfortable with issues related to death and dying, but also may have to recognize their ongoing need for support (Leukefeld, 1988). It is unrealistic for professionals to assume that they can cope with constant illness, distress, or death because their professional training taught them to help people in crisis. Professionals must remember that they, too, are human, have feelings, and need help coping with grief. Although support groups for social workers are used at times for workers dealing with cancer patients or AIDS patients, these groups are not routinely established for professionals dealing with chronic illness, handicapping conditions, and death. For social workers to be able to help others effectively, they must be able to help themselves so their own emotions do not interfere with their interactions with patients.

To achieve a leadership role in developing a comprehensive system of care for caregiving families, social workers will have to develop new curricula and continuing education. They also will have to examine the accreditation procedures for schools of social work, the Academy of Certified Social Workers, and state licensure laws. New curricula and credentials are being developed for people who work with children, gerontologists, and others. It is time to question whether separate qualifications are necessary for each population group and to ask whether special qualifications are needed when one works with families with a member suffering from chronic illness, terminal illness, or a severely handicapping condition. The existing quality assurance mechanisms for social workers may be so general that some mechanism, or addition to existing mechanisms, may be necessary to give the public confidence that social work training and supervision does prepare social workers to work with caregiving families.

REFERENCES

Agosta, J. M., & Bradley, V. J. (Eds.). (1985). *Family care for persons with developmental disabilities: A growing commitment.* Boston: Human Services Research Institute.

Biegel, D. E., Morycz, R., Schulz, R., Shore, B., Christopher, P., & Flynn, B. (1986). *Family elder care incentive policies* (Final Report to the Pennsylvania Department of Aging). Pittsburgh, PA: University of Pittsburgh University Center for Social and Urban Research.

Electronic Media Associates, Inc. (Producer). (1987). *Caregiving: The challenge of elder care multimedia program* [Film]. New York: Producer for Southwestern Bell Telephone.

Fitzpatrick, M. D. (1989). Managing media relations. *Public Welfare,* 33–35.

General Accounting Office. (1989a). *Health care home care experiences of families with chronically ill children* (Report to the Chairman, Committee on Finance, U.S. Senate). Washington, DC: U.S. Government Printing Office.

General Accounting Office. (1989b). *Respite care: Insights on federal, state, and private sector involvement.* Statement of Franklin Frazier, Director of Income Security Issues (Disability and Welfare), Human Resources Division, before the Subcommittee on Select Education, Committee on Education and Labor, House of Representatives, Washington, DC.

Juvenile Welfare Board of Pinellas County. (1981). *Social indicator report* (Report Vol. 10, No. 2). St. Petersburg, FL: Author.

Juvenile Welfare Board of Pinellas County. (1988). *Annual report 1988.* St. Petersburg, FL: Author.

Juvenile Welfare Board of Pinellas County. (1989). *Building healthy families in Pinellas—A county that supports success.* St. Petersburg, FL: Author.

Leukefeld, C. (1988). AIDS counseling and testing. *Health and Social Work, 13,* 167–169.

Linsk, N. L., Osterbusch, S. E., Keigher, S., & Rasinowitz, L. S. (1986). *Executive summary paid family caregiving: A policy option for family service agencies* (Report to the Illinois Association of Family Service Agencies). Chicago: University of Illinois.

Macro Systems, Inc. (1988). *Review of state quality assurance programs for home care* (Report to the U.S. Department of Health and Human Services, Office of the Assistant Secretary for Planning and Evaluation). Washington, DC.

Mullen, E. K. (1988). Unpublished "Dear Colleague" letter and materials. [Available from Women's Initiative, American Association of Retired Persons].

Pfeiffer, E., Cairl, R., Middleton, L., Alexander, L., Kleine, E., & Elbare, J. (1989). *Alzheimer's disease: Caregiver practices, programs and community-based strategies.* Tampa: University of South Florida, Suncoast Gerontology Center.

Robert Wood Johnson Foundation. (1989). *Interfaith volunteer caregivers: A special report* (Report No. 1). Princeton, NJ: Author.

Williams, W. S., & Lidoff, L. (1985). *State support for respite care: Report of an exploratory survey.* Washington, DC: The National Council on Aging.

8
Where Do We Go from Here?

Some social workers, when they reach this chapter, will say either that the approach is not new (because social workers always have been concerned about a family's ability to "cope" with problems) or that the only way the approach will work is if governmental agencies develop and pay for services. These answers are too simple. Agencies may know how to stimulate greater awareness among professionals about the needs of caregiving families. Professionals know how to help families in crisis improve their coping abilities. However, this knowledge does not constitute a close examination of models of practice based on changing family demographics and life-styles and on newly emerging types of practice in a variety of settings. Without such an examination of current practice and its success, social workers cannot realistically advocate for third-party reimbursement of services based on the way services help clients develop and achieve goals or advocate for governmental funding of services for low-income clients. In an editorial for *Health and Social Work,* Thomas Owen Carlton (1989) wrote,

> It is far from certain that educators and practitioners really love change all that much. If they did, it seems that the nature of social work education for health care practice would be very different than it currently is. However, the need to develop leadership strategies that lead to change is of paramount importance, for the health-care system in the United States is itself in the midst of massive change, and has been for some time. One has only to scratch the surface to find shifting patterns of service delivery, fundamental diversification and modification of time-honored functions and roles, the shift from traditional modes of team practice and collaboration to case management, and above all, the radical reorganization of funding for health care. (p. 151)

The issue of leadership extends beyond health care. Just as all families with a chronically ill or handicapped member face many of the same stresses, their medical or health and supportive services needs intertwine. People who receive ample supportive services may not demand as much from the health care system. For example, homemaker or home visitor services may meet the needs of the care receiver and the caregiving family. If those services are unavailable, the family may demand home health care. The interrelationship is clear when some medical clinics choose to develop and extend supportive services to the community at large (Center for Research, 1988).

IMPLICATIONS FOR PROFESSIONAL PRACTICE AND RESEARCH

Social workers and other professionals cannot afford to specialize so much that they cannot help caregiving families obtain an appropriate mix of health, mental health, and social services, or cannot teach caregivers of people with different problems to help and learn from each other. The immediate goal for the helping professions is to broaden the professionals' perspective and knowledge base. The short-term goal for the helping professions must be to develop and test approaches that maximize individual and family functioning and independence. What services and which professional skills directly affect individual and family coping? What patterns of practice/approaches are effective with different types of caregiving families? This book identifies some exemplary approaches.

Few practitioners feel comfortable with research that requires random placement of clients into groups that receive services and groups that do not. Many practitioners are uncomfortable with the notion of accountability—either to the agencies they work in or to governmental bodies that pay for services they provide. Some practitioners assume that because they know their services help, and because they are accredited, everyone should accept the "effectiveness" of the services they provide. However, "quality assurance" (for example, accreditation) and "effectiveness" are not synonymous. *Quality assurance* means that practitioners provide the services with at least a minimum level of skill. *Effectiveness* means that the services help clients achieve agreed upon goals. Not only should professionals broaden their practices to serve different types of families with similar needs, and work to integrate health, mental health, and social services, but it also is imperative that social work, as a profession, develop a professional plan that includes the testing and evaluation of new approaches. The goal of this testing is to improve service provision, management, policy development, and advocacy.

Light and Lebowitz (1989) indicated that the long-range objectives for research on Alzheimer's disease are "to develop more effective ways of characterizing the disorder and its subtypes, to identify its etiology, and to develop effective treatment and prevention strategies" (p. vii). These objectives represent a good agenda for an integrated approach for health, mental health, and social service researchers. The long-range goals, not only for prevention, but also for a fulfilling life, must be even broader and should begin before a family faces a crisis.

Just as it is advisable to plan for potential incapacity to ensure a fulfilling life, it is wise to assess personal and family capacity for caregiving and plan for possible caregiving responsibilities. In 1986, Bass (1986) proposed a decision-making model for those who wanted to plan for possible incapacity. This model focused on the individual as a potential care receiver, and not on the family. If one adds planning for caregiving responsibilities and developmental planning to this decision-making process, then the process becomes somewhat more complex (Figures 8-1 and 8-2). Although many professionals question people's willingness to plan for possible incapacity (many people do not even have wills), as families witness the effects of incapacity on family members, they should become more receptive to the notion of planning. Millions of American families face caregiving responsibilities. As they become uncomfortable with their problems, professionals can stimulate the desire to plan for future

Figure 8-1. Lifecare Planning: Decision Making with Professional Intervention

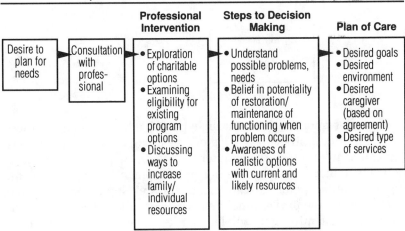

Figure 8-2. Lifecare and Developmental Planning: Decision-Making Pathway for Individual and Family

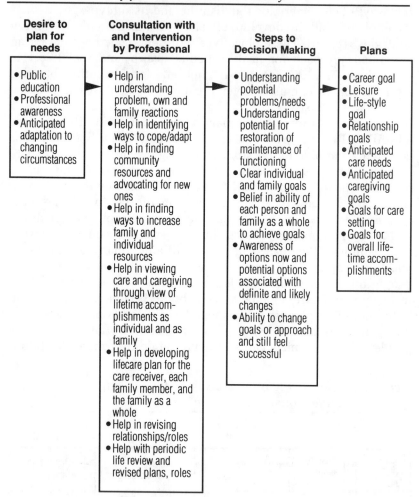

Desire to plan for needs	Consultation with and Intervention by Professional	Steps to Decision Making	Plans
• Public education • Professional awareness • Anticipated adaptation to changing circumstances	• Help in understanding problem, own and family reactions • Help in identifying ways to cope/adapt • Help in finding community resources and advocating for new ones • Help in finding ways to increase family and individual resources • Help in viewing care and caregiving through view of lifetime accomplishments as individual and as family • Help in developing lifecare plan for the care receiver, each family member, and the family as a whole • Help in revising relationships/roles • Help with periodic life review and revised plans, roles	• Understanding potential problems/needs • Understanding potential for restoration of maintenance of functioning • Clear individual and family goals • Belief in ability of each person and family as a whole to achieve goals • Awareness of options now and potential options associated with definite and likely changes • Ability to change goals or approach and still feel successful	• Career goal • Leisure • Life-style goal • Relationship goals • Anticipated care needs • Anticipated caregiving goals • Goals for care setting • Goals for overall lifetime accomplishments

needs and responsibilities through public education and professional awareness strategies. Once people are ready to plan, the next
step is consultation with, or intervention by, a professional. In a
model that incorporates planning by the potential care recipient,
planning by the potential caregivers, and developmental planning
for the family, the professional must first consult with each individual, then the family as a whole. The key role of the professional

continues to be facilitating decision making and helping the family implement the decisions, whether decision making results in a plan or helps families resolve specific problems.

This role is the key professional role in a developmental approach even though professionals have multiple responsibilities. For example, as part of a survey of 453 community-based acquired immune deficiency syndrome (AIDS) service organizations, providers identified five of their functions that they considered most important (Alperin & Richie, 1989). These functions were (1) case management, (2) securing or developing resources, (3) providing support during a crisis, (4) training, and (5) advocacy, all functions that support the key professional role. The functions either support decision making (through the development of a case management plan and support during crises) or they support plan implementation by securing needed resources, advocating for new resources, and training family members.

The research implications of this type of planning and decision making are clear. Researchers must continue to assess the impact of chronic illness and disability and caregiving responsibilities on the care receiver, primary caregiver, individual family members, and the family as a whole. For example, the impact on the caregiver of the Alzheimer patient's inability to recognize or acknowledge the primary caregiver still is not understood (Light & Lebowitz, 1989). Once the impact is known, the research issues are whether developmental planning will reduce the negative emotional consequences of problems faced by caretakers of Alzheimer's patients and their families and whether the planning improves the caregiver's or family's coping and response. Although no amount of anticipatory coping can change the course of Alzheimer's disease (Light & Lebowitz, 1989), for example, or change the emotions of family members who love the victim, it is possible that planning could reduce maladapted responses or shorten the time that a family member spends on these types of responses. Planning may shorten the time it takes family members to start coping because they already know what they need to do. Other research issues concern the degree to which the lack of specific services or cash assistance to carry out developmental plans negates the benefits of planning and which planned services or types of economic assistance are critical to success. Do the impact of problems and caregiving responsibilities, the success of developmental planning, and the importance of specific services and benefits vary by the gender and age of the primary caregiver or the developmental stage of the family?

One step beyond planning for chronic illness or disability is general planning for the family, which integrates planning for "normal" family functions with the type of planning described in this book. Thus, care for "normal," healthy children is a family responsibility that requires planning. Because child care is a 24-hour-a-day responsibility, virtually all families need help sometimes. Only leading employers who provide family benefits demonstrate an understanding that normative care and care for chronic illness impact the same family system, and they have structured benefits accordingly. Families that are otherwise normal, but are at risk of abusing children or elders, would receive help in planning, deciding on goals, and obtaining needed services just as families with a chronically ill or disabled member would receive these same services.

Another step is planning for the family with a substance abuser. Few people perceive substance abuse as a chronic illness. However, most professionals understand the impact of substance abuse on the abusers' families. Work with such families used to emphasize teaching the family not to contribute to the substance abuser's dependency. Professionals have long recognized the poor communication problems and interpersonal relations in these families and recently have begun to focus on working with the entire family. However, many families still receive help from self-help groups such as Al-Anon and Alateen, and not from intensive work with professionals (Collins, 1990). Al-Anon is an independent organization for spouses, close relatives, and friends of alcoholics. Alateen is for the adolescent children of alcoholics. Both groups are allied with Alcoholics Anonymous. The purpose of these groups is to help family members and friends understand alcoholism and their own reactions, and learn how to cope with their alcoholic family member. Early studies suggested that a high percentage of children with alcoholic problems have psychosocial problems (Johnson & Rolf, 1990). The developmental model could help these families improve their communication and problem-solving abilities and might help prevent further family dysfunction.

ORGANIZING FOR PRACTICE

The developmental, family-oriented model offers social workers a variety of career opportunities. No single service setting is mandatory for a developmentally based practice, although some settings may be more conducive to offering a full range of services than others. Moreover, two models for social work practice in lifecare planning exist (Bass, 1986).

Model 1

The first model is a social work agency that specializes in helping families plan to meet caregiving responsibilities, lifecare needs, and developmental needs. Because specialization is new for family services agencies, much preliminary work should be done before the agency opens its doors. First, the director needs to determine what help the organization will need from other types of professionals and identify those professionals in the community. As with lifecare planning, financial planners can help families invest their resources and require that resources be used for care or to support family caregivers. Financial planners also could help to develop and structure trust funds to pay for both the planning and the services needed to carry out plans. The person administering any trust arrangement becomes a key player in all planning. The administrator may be a family member, a bank trust officer (some are social workers), or a designated relative or friend.

Another professional essential for lifecare planning and useful in all types of planning is an attorney. If personal lifecare plans and family caregiving plans specify service settings, services, responsibility for different aspects of caregiving (so no single family member must assume all responsibility if more than one member is available), and responsibility for decision making (including revision of plans as family members' abilities to provide care change and as care needs change), an attorney can turn the plans into legal documents.

Establishing relationships with other community professionals who work with individuals or families also is important to a lifecare planning agency. For example, both the employee assistance counselors in corporations with family policies and the hospital social workers, who follow their clients through testing for and diagnosis of medical problems, are essential links in a community system of services that support developmental planning, lifecare planning, and planning for caregiving responsibilities.

Once an agency establishes relationships with professionals and key community leaders, the agency role varies by community. If the community has conducted needs assessments and resource assessments and has tried to fill service gaps, the agency then can work within the established system. The agency will market services to other professionals, list their services with an information and referral service, and take part in any existing strategy to promote public awareness. If the community does not have an established system, the agency can either assume a leadership role to help develop a comprehensive community system or can assume responsibility for a user needs analysis to assess the needs of caregiving clients and their families and the resources available to meet those needs (Winston, 1984). The social work agency will try to match services to client needs and coordinate all services through planning processes and continuing consultation or case management (if the family wants that kind of help). If the social work agency decides to offer the developmental services described in this book, the agency may need more than a user needs analysis with existing clients—it may need a marketing plan. A private practitioner could offer services as part of a comprehensive system and could help to develop such a system. However, the private practitioner then would be solely responsible for developing and marketing these services.

Model 2

A second model for social work practice in lifecare planning would be an agency that places specialists in the developmental approach with other agencies. The agency would be responsible for recruiting, training, and placing social workers. The agency also would be responsible for marketing. The agency could earn a fee from the organization that hires the social worker, or the social worker could be a permanent employee of the social work agency. The agency then would continue to receive a portion of the fee. Under this approach, the social worker would probably earn less, but also would have less risk because the agency would find a new placement if one did not work out. A private practitioner could take advantage of the second model if the social work agency (same or different) also made referrals for organizations that did not want to hire the social worker, but did want to refer clients to an individual for specialized services. In this type of arrangement, the social worker would have to pay a regular fee to be listed by the agency.

Key to the success of any private agency is marketing. Start-up costs for a developmental program should include the cost of a marketing specialist because the agency must define services so the general public understands what they are, the agency should identify providers likely to compete with any portion of the services being offered, and the population targeted for services must understand that the services are for them. The agency also must be aware of several other marketing considerations (Table 8-1).

IMPLICATIONS FOR NATIONAL, STATE, AND LOCAL GOVERNMENTS AND FOR CORPORATIONS

A major issue for social welfare agencies is how a developmental approach could be used in publicly funded programs for the poor, near poor, endangered individuals, and people who face higher risks (such as elderly people). In some localities, social services and child and adult protective services, for example, have moved from a single focus on removing the victim from harm to a focus on helping families cope with problems so that abuse will not occur. This focus is still a long way from a developmental approach. In the health arena, programs such as Medicaid and Medicare that pay for health care would have to move toward a more preventive focus at a time when resources for catastrophic illness are limited. The health, mental health, social services, and economic support systems are all discrete systems. Although some federally funded systems provide separate block grant funds to states, most systems have separate organizations and networks at the local level. Although services integration projects have used colocation of services, case management, and other approaches to successfully integrate targeted services for specific clients (for example, elderly people, Aid to Families

Table 8-1. Marketing Considerations for Private Agencies

Issue of Concern to Caregiver	Type of Concern
Ease of Access	Can the services be brought to the caregiver or must the caregiver travel to the service? If the caregiver must travel, will he or she receive help arranging care for the family member and finding transportation?
Cost	Can the caregiver or the family afford the services? If not, are the services covered by any insurance plan or publicly funded program? Are community resources available to fund the services (such as a charity)?
Flexibility	Can the agency accommodate scheduling problems, for example, of working caregivers? Can special arrangements be made to help a caregiver in crisis?

with Dependent Children, single heads of households, and disabled individuals), a successful model that integrates all supports for people and for families on a continuing basis has yet to be developed.

Although funding is an issue, it should not be such an overriding issue that it prevents a developmental approach. In the early 1980s, several states recognized the importance of adequate funding for the prevention of child abuse. These states established Children's Trust and Prevention Funds. By 1984, 20 states had made available such trust funds for child abuse prevention activities. In 1984, Congress enacted the Challenge Grant Program, which provides federal matching funds to "challenge" states to establish trust funds and other mechanisms for funding child abuse prevention activities. The Department of Health and Human Services anticipates that nearly every state will offer this type of trust fund by the end of fiscal year 1990 (Stewart, 1989). States or communities could develop trust funds for specialized services or establish individual small trust funds so that individuals or families could create and carry out developmental, lifecare, and caregiving plans.

What is essential now and must precede efforts to reform public programs is a national will to accomplish the "impossible." The ultimate goal for professionals, communities, and the United States must be policies that help professionals and communities integrate health, mental health, social services, job opportunities, and cash assistance to support families, so that individuals and the entire family may achieve their maximum potential based on the goals they set for themselves.

MOVING TOWARD A NATIONAL POLICY

A national policy requires a "national will" and the integrated efforts of providers and funding agencies. To achieve a national will, professionals and policymakers must understand citizens' attitudes about responsibilities and problems facing their families. The Roosevelt Center for American Policy Studies (1989) completed one of the best efforts to assess the attitudes of American citizens on work and family issues. During May 1989, the center convened 813 citizens at 12 regional sites throughout the United States to discuss alternative policies for balancing work and family responsibilities. The center recruited citizens for these assemblies through newspaper ads; radio announcements; and contacts with civic, business, labor, education, and public service organizations. Respondents filled out applications and the final selection resulted in an assembly as representative of the local demographic and political community as possible. Participants were 44 percent Democrats, 27 percent Republicans, 26 percent Independents, and 3 percent other. They classified themselves as 54 percent moderates, 16 percent conservatives, and 29 percent liberals. Sixty percent were females and 40 percent were males. Before the forum, participants read 80 pages of briefing materials, ranked their work and family concerns, chose policy options, and reconciled preferred policy options with federal budget realities.

The findings indicated that participants felt, with some urgency, that help should be available for families caught between work and family responsibilities. They felt that business has a major responsibility to help employees. Eighty-two percent of the respondents said that employers should change their personnel policies to help employees. Most felt that some level of government should be responsible for helping both poor and middle-class families. Eighty percent wanted government help; 65 percent felt that help should be provided to middle-class families. Two-thirds felt that federal, state, and local governments should pool their resources and work together.

Policy options on family and medical leave issues that were presented to participants varied from no federal role to tax incentives for businesses that create generous leave policies, to mandating 6 months of partially paid leave for all American workers. Seventy-four percent of the participants called for a federal labor standard. Sixty percent supported the most stringent regulatory option—6 months of family leave at half pay. Participants would pay for this option by asking each employer and employee to pay $80 per year per person into a fund. Most participants felt that maternity or paternity leave should be available as well as leave for personal illness and the serious illness of a spouse, child, or parent.

Options on child-care issues that were presented to participants included tax incentives for businesses to subsidize or develop on-site child care, tax credits for families, more funding for developmental programs such as Head Start, and subsidized care for low- and moderate-income families with regulated safety and quality standards. Participants overwhelmingly selected minimum federal (63 percent) or state (23 percent) standards. Sixty-four percent also supported tax incentives for businesses. Fifty-six percent supported a $2.5-billion package of federal subsidies for public early education programs, including Head Start.

Options on eldercare and long-term care issues included a new federal insurance program, Medicare coverage of long-term care, expanded Medicaid coverage of long-term care for the poor; Individual Medical Accounts (similar to Individual Retirement Accounts), and tax incentives to encourage the creation of private long-term care insurance coverage. No single option received overwhelming support. However, two similar options, a new federal insurance program and expanded Medicare coverage, received a combined total of 59 percent of the participants' support. The center estimated that the increased federal cost would be $20 billion (Roosevelt Center, 1989).

Although it is impossible to assume that these citizens represent the entire United States (they selected themselves to participate in such a process), the degree of interest in and concern about family issues shows a clear willingness to tackle the problems facing caregiving families. Citizens expect government to play a lesser role financially in work and family responsibilities, except for programs such as Head Start ($0.5 billion for tax incentives to encourage businesses to establish family and medical leave and $0.5 billion for tax incentives to encourage businesses to subsidize or establish child care). Citizens did foresee a significant government role in ensuring safety and quality of care. They were willing to invest heavily in health and long-term care for older people ($20 billion in new spending). Assembly participants also recognized the importance of helping all families, not just those who are now poor. The potential for a national will clearly exists.

POLICY OPTIONS

Once social work professionals coalesce to develop a national will and mobilize the national community, leaders must make many policy decisions before they achieve national support for caregiving families. For a comprehensive community system to be available to all families, options (other than national health and long-term care coverage for everyone) may require different strategies for different groups of people. Three options need to be addressed.

Option 1

Is it better, financially, for the United States to create different financing mechanisms for poor citizens who are not employed, poor citizens who are employed, and middle-class citizens, or to create a single mechanism? If different mechanisms are the choice, how can different financing mechanisms be used to support coverage of the same services and care for different populations?

Some of the problems to resolve when discussing the financing options relate to evolving changes in the health care system. Private insurance coverage of working people and their dependents is decreasing. With health care costs and the cost of insurance rising rapidly, employers are increasing deductibles or requiring deductibles for more family members. These regulations control unnecessary health care use, but put a burden on those who must have more care. Cafeteria-style plans, although useful to those who do not need all types of coverage, reduce the ability of insurance companies to spread the risk or reduce the cost for people who need many types of care. Those who cannot afford adequate coverage may not have insurance or may leave their dependents uninsured. These are problems for most workers who are employed by firms with more than 500 employees; yet, 75 percent of all U.S. firms have fewer than 10 employees. Fifty-four percent of these firms do not offer health insurance coverage (Griss, 1988–89). No amount of personal leave, suggested by the citizen assemblies, will compensate for lack of health care coverage. Although new regulations for employers are an option, many states already have regulations for private insurance companies. Additional regulations could drive small employers out of business. Some states, for example, require reimbursement of mental health treatment and treatment for alcohol and drug abuse.

William A. Schreyer (1989), Chairman and Chief Executive Officer of Merrill Lynch and Company, Inc., has proposed the following financing mechanisms for long-term care: government coverage for the poor and an asset accumulation savings account and a group insurance policy for all workers. Each worker and employer would contribute pretax dollars (that would be tax deferred) to be divided between the savings account and group insurance. These accounts would be portable—that is, they would not change with each employer. It is unclear whether this proposal would drive small employers out of business or whether the amount of employer contribution to the larger fund could vary by the employer's size. With portable coverage, it should be possible for all workers to have coverage for similar services. It seems possible that government contributions to the same funds could be used to cover services for the poor. A key social work role, besides ensuring equity in coverage of services, is to ensure coverage of services that are not medical— that is, coverage of necessary supportive services.

Option 2

Should the United States continue to finance, and communities continue to operate, separate service delivery systems for each population or each type of chronic problem? The Department of Education and the Department of Health and Human Services identified 16 federal programs that states can use to support early intervention for children and youths with handicapping conditions. These programs also support other services for these children and youths, but do not include all the programs for other populations with chronic illnesses or handicapping conditions. The programs have varying eligibility requirements and degrees of state flexibility to select service priorities, populations to serve, and funding approaches. When states try to coordinate the programs, they usually only coordinate three or four funding sources—usually health and education (Gallagher, Harbin, Thomas, Wenger, & Clifford, 1988).

A key question is, Is it feasible to "scrap" existing and evolving service delivery systems and create a single system? Because national funding policies usually dictate the types of systems established in each community, this question requires realistic analysis. If it is not feasible to create a single funding stream or, even with a single funding stream, is impossible to create a single community system, structures and mechanisms for improving coordination need to be explored. Typical interagency committees or councils and services integration approaches for specific populations may not be adequate to achieve this coordination. Legislation and regulations may not be the answer. Researchers in one study, for example, found that states had difficulty trying to achieve the complex coordination required by the Handicapped Infants and Toddlers Program for this single population (Shafft, Erlanger, Rudolph, Yin, & Scott, 1987).

Option 3

How can a system ensure adequate service delivery and quality of services? Although a variety of quality assurance mechanisms exist, they have been developed independently. Options to solve this problem require cooperative work among the helping professionals, government bodies, and health insurance companies.

A move toward a national policy of support for caregiving families will require the same type of organization at the national level as in communities that are developing a comprehensive system of care. Social workers can lead the effort to integrate service systems and services for all types of caregiving families. Occupational social workers can mobilize corporations. The National Association of Social Workers can mobilize voluntary and professional organizations. Social workers in all levels of government can inform and involve political leaders. The National Center on Social Policy and Practice can work with foundations to stimulate funding for services (trust funds and other approaches) and to evaluate options and efforts to implement developmental planning. Practitioners can establish effective developmental planning approaches without national policies or support. However, practitioners can only help more families and establish more comprehensive community systems if national support exists.

REFERENCES

Alperin, D. E., & Richie, N. D. (1989). Community-based AIDS service organizations: Challenges and educational preparation. *Health and Social Work, 14,* 165–173.

Bass, D. (1986). *Planning to meet lifecare needs.* Silver Spring, MD: National Association of Social Workers.

Carlton, T. O. (1989). Education for health social work: Opportunities and constraints in schools and hospitals [Editorial]. *Health and Social Work, 14,* 147–152.

Center for Research in Ambulatory Health Care Administration, Medical Group Management Association. (1988). *A demonstration project integrating gerontology program models in medical group settings: First year's annual report, January 1, 1987 through December 31, 1987.* Denver, CO: Author.

Collins, L. (1990). Family treatment of alcohol abuse: Behavioral and systems perspectives. In R. L. Collins, K. E. Leonard, & J. S. Searles (Eds.), *Alcohol and the family* (pp. 285–308). New York: Guilford.

Gallagher, J. J., Harbin, G., Thomas, D., Wenger, M., & Clifford, R. (1988). *A survey of current status on implementation of infants and toddlers' legislation* (A Report for Cooperative Agreement No. G0087C3065 for the Office of Special Education Programs, U.S. Department of Education). Washington, DC.

Griss, B. (1988–89). Strategies for adapting the private and public health insurance systems to the health-related needs of persons with disabilities or chronic illness. In B. Griss (Ed.), *Access to health care* (vol. 1, pp. 1–38). Washington, DC: World Institute on Disability.

Johnson, J. L., & Rolf, J. E. (1990). When children change: Research perspectives on children of alcoholics. In R. L. Collins, K. E. Leonard, & J. S. Searles (Eds.), *Alcohol and the family* (pp. 162–193). New York: Guilford.

Light, E., & Lebowitz, B. D. (Eds.). (1989). *Alzheimer's disease treatment and family stress: Directions for research.* Rockville, MD: U.S. Department of Health and Human Services, Public Health Service, Alcohol, Drug Abuse, and Mental Health Administration, National Institute of Mental Health.

Roosevelt Center for American Policy Studies. (1989). *Balancing work and family: A citizens' agenda for the '90s.* Washington, DC: Author.

Schreyer, W. A. (1989). A CEO's perspective on business, aging, and the financing of long-term care. *Generations, 13,* 44–47.

Shafft, G., Erlanger, W., Rudolph, L., Yin, R. K., & Scott, A. C. (1987). *Joint study of services and funding for handicapped infants and toddlers, ages 0 through 2 years* (Final Report for Contract No. 300-85-0143, Division of Innovation and Development, Office of Special Education Programs, U.S. Department of Education). Washington, DC.

Stewart, B. (1989, April 6). Statement before the Select Education Subcommittee of the House Education and Labor Committee, U.S. House of Representatives.

Winston, W. (1984). *Marketing long-term and senior care services.* New York: Haworth.

APPENDIX A

Health Care Financing Administration Regional Offices

Office	Telephone Number
Boston	(617) 223–6871
New York	(212) 264–4488
Philadelphia	(215) 596–1351
Atlanta	(404) 221–2329
Chicago	(312) 353–8057
Dallas	(214) 767–6427
Kansas City	(816) 374–5233
Denver	(303) 837–2111
San Francisco	(415) 556–0254
Seattle	(206) 442–0425

SOURCE: Health Care Financing Administration. (1988). *Health Care Financing Program Statistics Medicare and Medicaid data book* (Pub. No. 03270). Baltimore, MD: U.S. Department of Health and Human Services.

APPENDIX B

Single State Medicaid Agencies

Alabama

Alabama Medicaid Agency
2500 Fairlane Drive
Montgomery, AL 36130
(205) 277–2710

Alaska

Alaska Department of Health and
  Social Services
P.O. Box H-01
Juneau, AK 99811-0601
(907) 465–3355

Arizona

Arizona Health Care Cost
  Containment System
  Administration
801 East Jefferson Street
Phoenix, AZ 85034
(602) 234–3655

Arkansas

Arkansas Department of Human
  Services
7th and Main Streets
P.O. Box 1437
Little Rock, AR 72201
(501) 371–1806

California

California State Department of
  Health Services
714 P Street, Room 1253
Sacramento, CA 95814
(916) 445–1248

Colorado

Colorado Department of Social
  Services
P.O. Box 181000
Denver, CO 80218-0899
(303) 294–5800

Connecticut

Connecticut Department of
  Income Maintenance
110 Bartholomew Avenue
Hartford, CT 06106
(203) 566–2008

Delaware

Delaware Department of Health
  and Social Services
Administration Building
Delaware State Hospital
P.O. Box 906
New Castle, DE 19720
(302) 421–6705

District of Columbia

Department of Human Services
801 North Capitol Street, Room
  700
Washington, DC 20002
(202) 727–0450

Florida

Florida Department of Health and
  Rehabilitative Services
1317 Winewood Boulevard
Tallahassee, FL 32303
(904) 488–7721

Georgia

Georgia Department of Medical
  Assistance
2 Martin Luther King Drive
1220 West Tower
Atlanta, GA 30334
(404) 656–4479

Guam

Department of Public Health and
  Social Services
P.O. Box 2816
Agana, GU 96910
(671) 734–2083

Hawaii

Hawaii Department of Social
  Services and Housing
P.O. Box 339
Honolulu, HI 96809
(808) 548–6260

Idaho

Idaho Department of Health and
  Welfare
State House
450 West State Street
Boise, ID 83720
(208) 334–5500

Illinois

Illinois Department of Public Aid
Jesse B. Harris Building II
2nd Floor
100 South Grand Avenue, East
Springfield, IL 62762
(217) 782–6716

Indiana

Indiana Department of Public
  Welfare
State Office Building
100 North Senate Avenue, Room
  701

Indianapolis, IN 46204
(317) 232–4705

Iowa

Iowa Department of Human
  Services
Hoover State Office Building
5th Floor
East 13th and Walnut
Des Moines, IA 50319
(515) 281–5452

Kansas

Kansas Department of Social and
  Rehabilitation Services
Docking State Office Building,
  Room 628-S
Topeka, KS 66612
(913) 296–3271

Kentucky

Kentucky Department for
  Medicaid Services
CHR Building
275 East Main Street
Frankfort, KY 40621
(502) 564–4321

Louisiana

Louisiana Department of Health
  and Human Resources
P.O. Box 3776
Baton Rouge, LA 70821
(504) 342–6711

Maine

Maine Department of Human
  Services
221 State Street
Statehouse, Station 11
Augusta, ME 04333
(207) 289–2736

Maryland

Maryland Department of Health
and Mental Hygiene
Herbert R. O'Connor Building
201 West Preston Street
Baltimore, MD 21201
(301) 225–6500

Massachusetts

Massachusetts Department of
Public Welfare
180 Tremont Street
Boston, MA 02111
(617) 574–0200

Michigan

Michigan Department of Social
Services
300 South Capitol Avenue
P.O. Box 30037
Lansing, MI 48909
(517) 373–2000

Minnesota

Minnesota Department of Human
Services
Centennial Office Building
4th Floor
658 Cedar Street
St. Paul, MN 55155
(612) 296–2701

Mississippi

Division of Medicaid
Office of the Governor
4785 1-55 North
P.O. Box 16786
Jackson, MS 39236-0786
(601) 981–4507

Missouri

Missouri Department of Social
Services
Broadway State Office Building

P.O. Box 1527
Jefferson City, MO 65102
(314) 751–4815

Montana

Montana Department of Social
and Rehabilitative Services
P.O. Box 4210
Helena, MT 59604
(406) 444–5622

Nebraska

Nebraska Department of Social
Services
301 Centennial Mall, South
P.O. Box 95026
5th Floor
Lincoln, NE 68509-5026
(402) 471–3121

Nevada

Nevada Department of Human
Resources
Kinkead Building–Capitol
Complex
505 East King Street
Carson City, NV 89710
(702) 885–4730

New Hampshire

New Hampshire Department of
Health and Human Services
6 Hazen Drive
Concord, NH 03301-6521
(603) 271–4331

New Jersey

New Jersey Department of Human
Services
Capitol Place One
222 South Warren Street
Trenton, NJ 08625
(609) 292–3717

New Mexico

New Mexico Department of
  Human Services
P.O. Box 2348
Santa Fe, NM 87501-2348
(505) 827–4315

New York

New York State Department of
  Social Services
Ten Eyck Office Building
40 North Pearl Street
Albany, NY 12243
(518) 474–9475

North Carolina

North Carolina Department of
  Human Resources
325 North Salisbury Street
Raleigh, NC 27611
(919) 733–4534

North Dakota

North Dakota Department of
  Human Services
State Capitol Building
Bismarck, ND 58505
(701) 224–2310

Ohio

Ohio Department of Human
  Services
30 East Broad Street
32nd Floor
Columbus, OH 43266-0423
(614) 466–6282

Oklahoma

Oklahoma Department of Human
  Services
P.O. Box 25352
Oklahoma City, OK 73125
(405) 521–3646

Oregon

Oregon Department of Human
  Resources
318 Public Service Building
Salem, OR 97310
(503) 378–3034

Pennsylvania

Pennsylvania State Department of
  Public Welfare
Health and Welfare Building,
  Room 333
Harrisburg, PA 17120
(717) 787–1870

Puerto Rico

Puerto Rico Department of Health
P.O. Box 70184
San Juan, PR 00936
(809) 751–8259

Rhode Island

Rhode Island Department of
  Human Services
Aime J. Forand Building
600 New London Avenue
Cranston, RI 02920
(401) 464–2121

South Carolina

South Carolina State Health and
  Human Services Finance
  Commission
P.O. Box 8206
Columbia, SC 29202-8206
(803) 253–6100

South Dakota

South Dakota Department of
  Social Services
Richard F. Kneip Building
700 Governor's Drive
Pierre, SD 57501
(605) 733–3165

Tennessee

Tennessee Department of Health
and Environment
344 Cordell Hull Building
Nashville, TN 37219
(615) 741–0213

Texas

Texas Department of Human
Services
701 West 51st Street
P.O. Box 2960
Austin, TX 78769
(512) 450–3030

Utah

Utah Department of Health
P.O. Box 16700
Salt Lake City, UT 84116-0700
(801) 538–6111

Vermont

Vermont Department of Social
Welfare
Agency on Human Services
103 South Main Street
Waterbury, VT 05676
(802) 241–2220

Virginia

Virginia Department of Medical
Assistance Services
600 East Broad Street, Suite 1300
Richmond, VA 23219
(804) 786–7933

Virgin Islands

Virgin Islands Department of
Health
P.O. Box 7309
Charlotte Amalie
St. Thomas, VI 00801

Washington

Division of Medical Assistance
Washington Department of Social
and Health Services
Mail Stop HB-41
Olympia, WA 98504
(206) 753–1777

West Virginia

West Virginia Department of
Human Services
1900 Washington Street, East
Charleston, WV 25305
(304) 348–8990

Wisconsin

Wisconsin Department of Health
and Social Services
1 West Wilson Street, Room 650
P.O. Box 7850
Madison, WI 53701
(608) 266–3681

Wyoming

Wyoming Department of Health
and Social Services
Hathaway Building
Cheyenne, WY 82002
(307) 777–7121

SOURCE: Health Care Financing Administration. (1988). *Health Care Financing Program Statistics Medicare and Medicaid data book* (Pub. No. 03270). Baltimore, MD: U.S. Department of Health and Human Services.

APPENDIX C

Social Services Block Grant Agencies

Alabama

Alabama Department of Human
  Resources
Administrative Building
64 North Union Street
Montgomery, AL 63130
(205) 261–3190

Alaska

Alaska Department of Health and
  Social Services
Box H-01
Juneau, AK 99811-0601

Arizona

Arizona Department of Economic
  Security
1717 West Jefferson Street
Phoenix, AZ 85007
(602) 255–5678

Arkansas

Arkansas Department of Human
  Services
Donaghey Building, Suite 306
7th and Main Streets
Little Rock, AR 72201
(501) 371–1001

California

Department of Social Services,
  State of California
744 P Street, Mail Station 17-11
Sacramento, CA 95814
(916) 445–2077

Colorado

Colorado Department of Human
  Services
717 17th Street
P.O. Box 181000
Denver, CO 80218-0899
(303) 294–5800

*Commonwealth of the Northern
Mariana Islands*

Department of Community and
  Cultural Affairs
Saipan, Mariana Islands 96950
(670) 322–9556

Connecticut

Connecticut Department of
  Human Resources
1049 Asylum Avenue
Hartford, CT 06105
(203) 566–3318

Delaware

Delaware Department of Health
  and Social Services
1910 North Dupont Highway
New Castle, DE 19720
(302) 421–6705

District of Columbia

D.C. Department of Human
  Services
801 North Capitol Street, NE
Washington, DC 20002
(202) 727–0310

Florida

Department of Health and
    Rehabilitative Services
1317 Winewood Boulevard
Tallahassee, FL 32399-0700
(904) 488–7721

Georgia

Georgia Department of Human
    Resources
47 Trinity Avenue, SW, Room
    522-H
Atlanta, GA 30334–1202

Guam

Department of Public Health and
    Social Services
P.O. Box 2816
Agana, GU 96910
(671) 734–2947

Hawaii

Hawaii State Department of
    Social Services and Housing
P.O. Box 339
Honolulu, HI 96809
(808) 548–6260

Idaho

Idaho Department of Health and
    Welfare
State House
450 West State Street
Boise, ID 83720
(208) 334–5500

Illinois

Illinois Department of Public Aid
Jesse B. Harris Building II
100 South Grand Avenue, East
Springfield, IL 62762
(217) 782–6716

Indiana

Indiana Department of Human
    Services
251 North Illinois Street
P.O. Box 7083
Indianapolis, IN 46207-7083
(317) 232–7000
*1-(800) 545–7763

Iowa

Iowa Department of Human
    Services
Hoover State Office Building
5th Floor
East 13th and Walnut
Des Moines, IA 50319
(515) 281–5452

Kansas

Kansas Department of Social and
    Rehabilitation Services
Docking State Office Building,
    Room 603-N
Topeka, KS 66612
(913) 296–3271

Kentucky

Kentucky Department for Social
    Services
275 East Main Street, 4th Floor
    West
Frankfort, KY 40621
(502) 564–7130

Louisiana

Louisiana Department of Health
    and Human Resources
P.O. Box 3776
Baton Rouge, LA 70821
(504) 342–6711

---

*In-state toll-free number

Maine

Maine Department of Human
  Services
221 State Street
Statehouse, Station 11
Augusta, ME 04333
(207) 289–2736

Maryland

Department of Human Resources
311 West Saratoga Street
Baltimore, MD 21201
(301) 333–0001

Massachusetts

Department of Social Services
150 Causeway Street
11th Floor
Boston, MA 02114
(617) 727–0900, extension 202

Michigan

Michigan Department of Social
  Services
300 South Capitol Avenue
P.O. Box 30037
Lansing, MI 48909
(517) 373–2000

Minnesota

Minnesota Department of Human
  Services
Centennial Office Building
4th Floor
658 Cedar Street
St. Paul, MN 55155
(612) 296–6117

Mississippi

Department of Planning and
  Policy
Governor's Office of Federal–State
  Programs

637 North President Street
Jackson, MS 39201
(601) 354–7017

Missouri

Missouri Department of Social
  Services
Broadway State Office Building
P.O. Box 1527
Jefferson City, MO 65201
(314) 751–4815

Montana

Montana Department of Social
  and Rehabilitation Services
P.O. Box 4210
Helena, MT 59604
(406) 444–5622

Nebraska

Nebraska Department of Social
  Services
301 Centennial Mall, South
P.O. Box 95026
5th Floor
Lincoln, NE 68509-5026
(402) 471–3121

Nevada

Nevada Department of Human
  Resources
Kinkead Building—Capitol
  Complex, Room 600
505 East King Street
Carson City, NV 89710
(702) 885–4400

New Hampshire

New Hampshire Department of
  Health and Human Services
6 Hazen Drive
Concord, NH 03301-6505
(603) 271–4334

New Jersey

New Jersey Department of Human
   Services
Capital Place One, CN-700
222 South Warren Street
Trenton, NJ 08625
(609) 292–3717

New Mexico

New Mexico Department of
   Human Services
P.O. Box 2348
Santa Fe, NM 87501-2348
(505) 827–4072

New York

New York State Department of
   Social Services
40 North Pearl Street
Albany, NY 12243
(518) 474–9475

North Carolina

North Carolina Department of
   Human Resources
325 North Salisbury Street
Raleigh, NC 27611
(919) 733–4534

North Dakota

Office of Human Services
North Dakota Department of
   Human Services
State Capitol Building
Bismarck, ND 58505
(701) 224–4050

Ohio

Ohio Department of Human
   Services
30 East Broad Street
32nd Floor
Columbus, OH 43266-0423
(614) 466–6282

Oklahoma

Oklahoma Department of Human
   Services
P.O. Box 25352
Oklahoma City, OK 73125
(405) 521–3646

Oregon

Oregon Department of Human
   Resources
318 Public Service Building
Salem, OR 97310
(503) 378–3033

Pennsylvania

Pennsylvania State Department of
   Public Welfare
Health and Welfare Building,
   Room 333
Harrisburg, PA 17120
(717) 787–2600

Puerto Rico

Puerto Rico Department of Social
   Services
P.O. Box 11398
Santurce, PR 00910
(809) 725–4511

Rhode Island

Rhode Island Department of
   Human Services
Aime J. Forand Building
600 New London Avenue
Cranston, RI 02920
(401) 464–2121

South Carolina

South Carolina State Health and
   Human Services Finance
   Commission
P.O. Box 8206
Columbia, SC 29202-8206
(803) 253–6100

South Dakota

South Dakota Department of
  Social Services
Richard F. Kneip Building
700 Governor's Drive
Pierre, SD 57501
(605) 773-3165

Tennessee

Tennessee Department of Human
  Services
Citizens Plaza Building
400 Deaderick Street
Nashville, TN 37219
(615) 741-3241

Texas

Texas Department of Human
  Services
701 West 51st Street
P.O. Box 2960
Austin, TX 78769
(512) 450-3011

Utah

Utah Department of Social
  Services
P.O. Box 45500
Salt Lake City, UT 84145-0500
(801) 533-5331

Vermont

Vermont Department of Social
  Welfare
Agency on Human Services
103 South Main Street
Waterbury, VT 05676
(802) 241-2705

Virginia

Virginia Department of Social
  Services

Blair Building
8007 Discovery Drive
Richmond, VA 23229-8699
(804) 281-9236

Virgin Islands

Virgin Islands Department of
  Social Welfare
P.O. Box 539
St. Thomas, VI 00801
(809) 774-0930

Washington

Washington Department of Social
  and Health Services
Mail Stop OB-44
Olympia, WA 98503
(206) 753-3395

West Virginia

West Virginia Department of
  Human Services
Building B, Room 617
1900 Washington Street, East
Charleston, WV 25305
(304) 348-2400

Wisconsin

Wisconsin Department of Health
  and Social Services
1 West Wilson Street, Room 650
P.O. Box 7850
Madison, WI 53701
(608) 266-3681

Wyoming

Wyoming Department of Health
  and Social Services
Hathaway Building
Cheyenne, WY 82002
(307) 777-7658

SOURCE: Office of Policy, Planning and Legislation, Office of Human Development
  Services, Department of Health and Human Services, 1989.

APPENDIX D

State Agencies on Aging

Alabama

Alabama Commission on Aging
136 Catoma Street
2nd Floor
Montgomery, AL 36130
(205) 261–5743

Alaska

Older Alaskans Commission
P.O. Box C, MS 0209
Juneau, AK 99811
(907) 465–3250

American Samoa

Territorial Administration on
  Aging
Government of American Samoa
Pago Pago, AS 96799
(684) 633–1251

Arizona

Aging and Adult Administration
Department of Economic Security
1400 West Washington Street
Phoenix, AZ 85007
(602) 542–4446
*1-(800) 352–3792

Arkansas

Division of Aging and Adult
  Services
Arkansas Department of Human
  Services

7th and Main Streets
Donaghey Building, Suite 142
Little Rock, AR 72201
(501) 682–2441

California

California Department of Aging
1600 K Street
Sacramento, CA 95814
(916) 322–5290

Colorado

Aging and Adult Services
Department of Social Services
1575 Sherman Street
10th Floor
Denver, CO 80203-1714
(303) 866–5905

Commonwealth of the Northern
  Mariana Islands

Office on Aging
Department of Community and
  Cultural Affairs
Civic Center
Commonwealth of the Northern
  Mariana Islands
Saipan, Mariana Islands 96950
(670) 234–6011

---

*In-state toll-free number

180

Connecticut

Connecticut Department on Aging
175 Main Street
Hartford, CT 06106
(203) 566–3238
*1-(800) 443–9946

Delaware

Delaware Division on Aging
Department of Health and Social
  Services
1901 North Dupont Highway
2nd Floor
New Castle, DE 19720
(302) 421–6791
*1-(800) 223–9074

District of Columbia

District of Columbia Office on
  Aging
Executive Office of the Mayor
1424 K Street, NW
Second Floor
Washington, DC 20005
(202) 724–5622

Federated States of Micronesia

State Agency on Aging
Office of Health Services
Department of Social Services
Kolonia, Ponape, Eastern Carolina
  Islands 96941

Florida

Aging and Adult Services
Department of Health and
  Rehabilitative Services
Building 2, Room 328

1312 Winewood Boulevard
Tallahassee, FL 32399-0700
(904) 488–8922
*1-(800) 342–0825

Georgia

Office of Aging
Department of Human Resources
6th Floor
878 Peachtree Street, NE
Atlanta, GA 30309
(404) 894–5333

Guam

Division of Senior Citizens
Department of Public Health and
  Social Services
P.O. Box 2816
Government of Guam
Agana, GU 96910
(671) 734–2942

Hawaii

Hawaii Executive Office on Aging
335 Merchant Street, Room 241
Honolulu, HI 96813
(808) 548–2593

Idaho

Idaho Office on Aging
Statehouse, Room 108
Boise, ID 83720
(208) 334–3833

Illinois

Illinois Department on Aging
421 East Capitol Avenue
Springfield, IL 62701
(217) 785–2870
*1-(800) 252–8966

---

*In-state toll-free number

Indiana

Indiana Department of Human
　Services
251 North Illinois Street
P.O. Box 7083
Indianapolis, IN 46207-7083
(317) 232–1139
*1-(800) 545–7763

Iowa

Department of Elder Affairs
Jewett Building, Suite 236
914 Grand Avenue
Des Moines, IA 50319
(515) 281–5187
*1-(800) 532–3213

Kansas

Kansas Department on Aging
Docking State Office Building,
　Room 122-S
915 Southwest Harrison
Topeka, KS 66612-1500
(913) 296–4986
*1-(800) 432–3535

Kentucky

Division for Aging Services
Cabinet for Human Resources
Department for Social Services
275 East Main Street
Frankfort, KY 40621
(502) 564–6930

Louisiana

Governor's Office of Elderly
　Affairs
P.O. Box 80374
Baton Rouge, LA 70898-0374
(504) 925–1700

Maine

Bureau of Maine's Elderly
Department of Human Services
221 State Street
Statehouse, Station 11
Augusta, ME 04333
(207) 289–2561

Maryland

Maryland Office on Aging
301 West Preston Street
Baltimore, MD 21201
(301) 225–1102
*1-(800) 338–0153

Massachusetts

Massachusetts Executive Office of
　Elder Affairs
38 Chauncy Street
Boston, MA 02111
(617) 727–7750
*1-(800) 882–2003

Michigan

Office of Services to the Aging
P.O. Box 30026
Lansing, MI 48909
(517) 373–8230

Minnesota

Minnesota Board on Aging
Human Services Building
4th Floor
444 Lafayette Road
St. Paul, MN 55155-3843
(612) 296–2770
*1-(800) 652–9747

---

*In-state toll-free number

Mississippi

Mississippi Council on Aging
301 West Pearl Street
Jackson, MS 39203-3092
(601) 949–2070
*1-(800) 222–7622

Missouri

Division of Aging
Missouri Department of Social
  Services
2701 West Main Street
P.O. Box 1337
Jefferson City, MO 65102
(314) 751–3082
*1-(800) 235–5503

Montana

Department of Family Services
P.O. Box 8005
Helena, MT 59604
(406) 444–5900
*1-(800) 332–2272

Nebraska

Department on Aging
301 Centennial Mall, South
P.O. Box 95044
Lincoln, NE 68509-5044
(402) 471–2306

Nevada

Division for Aging Services
State Mail Room
Las Vegas, NV 89158
(702) 486–3545

New Hampshire

Division of Elderly and Adult
  Services
New Hampshire Department of
  Health and Human Services

6 Hazen Drive
Concord, NH 03301
(603) 271–4390
*1-(800) 852–3311

New Jersey

New Jersey Division on Aging
Department of Community Affairs
101 South Broad Street, CN 807
Trenton, NJ 08625-0807
(609) 292–0920
*1-(800) 792–8820

New Mexico

New Mexico State Agency on
  Aging
La Villa Rivera Building
4th Floor
224 East Palace Avenue
Santa Fe, NM 87501
(505) 827–7640
*1-(800) 432–2080

New York

New York State Office for the
  Aging
Agency Building No. 2
Empire State Plaza
Albany, NY 12223-0001
(518) 474–5731
*1-(800) 342–9871

North Carolina

North Carolina Division on Aging
Department of Human Resources
Kirby Building
1985 Umstead Drive
Raleigh, NC 27603
(919) 733–3983
*1-(800) 662–7030

---

*In-state toll-free number

North Dakota

Aging Services Division
North Dakota Department of
Human Services
State Capitol Building
Bismarck, ND 58505
(701) 224–2577
*1-(800) 472–2622

Ohio

Ohio Department of Aging
50 West Broad Street
9th Floor
Columbus, OH 43215
(614) 466–5500

Oklahoma

Aging Services Division
Oklahoma Department of Human
    Services
P.O. Box 25352
Oklahoma City, OK 73125
(405) 521–2327

Oregon

Senior Services Division
Oregon Department of Human
    Resources
313 Public Service Building
Salem, OR 97310
(503) 378–4728

Pennsylvania

Pennsylvania Department of
    Aging
231 State Street (Barto Building)
Harrisburg, PA 17101
(717) 783–1550

Puerto Rico

Puerto Rico Office of Elderly
    Affairs

Call Box 50063
Old San Juan Station, PR 00902
(809) 721–0753

Republic of the Marshall Islands

State Agency on Aging
Department of Social Services
Republic of the Marshall Islands
Marjuro, Marshall Islands 96960

Republic of Palau

State Agency on Aging
Department on Aging
Department of Social Services
Republic of Palau
Koror, Palau 96940

Rhode Island

Department of Elderly Affairs
79 Washington Street
Providence, RI 02903
(401) 277–2858
*1-(800) 752–8088

South Carolina

South Carolina Commission on
    Aging
400 Arbor Lake Drive, Suite B-
    500
Columbia, SC 29223
(803) 735–0210
*1-(800) 922–1107

South Dakota

Office of Adult Services and
    Aging
Richard F. Kneip Building
700 Governor's Drive
Pierre, SD 57501-2291
(605) 773–3656

---

*In-state toll-free number

Tennessee

Tennessee Commission on Aging
706 Church Street, Suite 201
Nashville, TN 37219-5573
(615) 741–2056

Texas

Texas Department on Aging
P.O. Box 12786
Capitol Station
Austin, TX 78711
(512) 444–2727
*1-(800) 252–9240

Utah

Utah Division of Aging and Adult
  Services
120 North, 200 West, Room 4A
P.O. Box 45500
Salt Lake City, UT 84145-0500
(801) 538–3910

Vermont

Vermont Office on Aging
Waterbury Complex
103 South Main Street
Waterbury, UT 05676
(802) 241–2400
*1-(800) 642–5119

Virginia

Virginia Department for the Aging
700 East Franklin Street
10th Floor
Richmond, VA 23219-2327

Virgin Islands

Virgin Islands Department of
  Human Services

Barbel Plaza South
Charlotte Amalie
St. Thomas, VI 00802
(809) 774–0930

Washington

Aging and Adult Services
  Administration
Washington Department of Social
  and Health Services
Mail Stop OB-44-A
Olympia, WA 98504
(206) 586–3768
*1-(800) 422–3263

West Virginia

West Virginia Commission on
  Aging
State Capitol Complex–Holly
  Grove
1710 Kanawha Boulevard
Charleston, WV 25305
(304) 348–3317
*1-(800) 642–3671

Wisconsin

Bureau on Aging
Wisconsin Department of Health
  and Social Services
1 West Wilson Street, Room 480
P.O. Box 7851
Madison, WI 53701
(608) 266–2536

Wyoming

Commission on Aging
Hathaway Building, 1st Floor
Cheyenne, WY 82002
(307) 777–7986

---

*In-state toll-free number

Source: Administration on Aging, Department of Health and Human Services, 1989.

APPENDIX E

VA Medical Centers and Clinics

Alabama

Birmingham
Montgomery
Tuscaloosa

Alaska

Anchorage

Arizona

Phoenix
Prescott
Tucson

Arkansas

Fayetteville
Little Rock

California

Fresno
Livermore
Loma Linda
Long Beach
Los Angeles
Martinez
Palo Alto
San Diego
San Francisco
Sepulveda
West Los
   Angeles

Colorado

Denver
Fort Lyon
Grand Junction

Connecticut

Newington
West Haven

Delaware

Wilmington

**District of
   Columbia**

Florida

Bay Pines
Gainesville
Lake City
Miami
Pensacola
Tampa

Georgia

Atlanta
Augusta
Dublin

Hawaii

Honolulu

Idaho

Boise

Illinois

Chicago
   (Lakeside)
Chicago
   (Westside)

Danville
Hines
Marion
North Chicago

Indiana

Evansville
Fort Wayne
Indianapolis
Marion

Iowa

Des Moines
Iowa City
Knoxville

Kansas

Leavenworth
Topeka
Wichita

Kentucky

Lexington
Louisville

Louisiana

Alexandria
New Orleans
Shreveport

Maine

Togus

Maryland

Baltimore
Fort Howard
Perry Point

Massachusetts

Bedford
Boston
Brockton/West
   Roxbury
Northampton

Michigan

Allen Park
Ann Arbor
Battle Creek
Iron Mountain
Saginaw

Minnesota

Minneapolis
St. Cloud

Mississippi

Biloxi
Jackson

Missouri

Columbia
Kansas City
Poplar Bluff
St. Louis

Montana

Fort Harrison
Miles City

Nebraska

Grand Island
Lincoln
Omaha

Nevada

Las Vegas
Reno

*New
Hampshire*

Manchester

New Jersey

East Orange
Lyons

New Mexico

Albuquerque

New York

Albany
Batavia
Bath
Bronx
Brooklyn/St.
 Albans
Buffalo
Canandaigua
Castle Point
Montrose
New York
 (Manhattan)

Northport
Syracuse

North Carolina

Asheville
Durham
Fayetteville
Salisbury

North Dakota

Fargo

Ohio

Chillicothe
Cincinnati
Cleveland
Columbus
Dayton

Oklahoma

Muskogee
Oklahoma City

Oregon

Portland
Roseburg
White City

Pennsylvania

Allentown
Altoona
Butler
Coatesville
Erie
Harrisburg
Lebanon
Philadelphia

Pittsburgh
 (High)
Pittsburgh
 (University)
Wilkes Barre

Puerto Rico

San Juan

Rhode Island

Providence

South Carolina

Charleston
Columbia

South Dakota

Fort Meade
Hot Springs
Sioux Falls

Tennessee

Memphis
Mountain Home
Murfreesboro
Nashville

Texas

Amarillo
Big Spring
Bonham
Dallas
El Paso
Houston
Kerrville
Lubbock
Marlin

San Antonio
Temple
Waco

Utah

Salt Lake City

Vermont

White River
 Junction

Virginia

Hampton
Richmond
Salem

Washington

Seattle
Spokane
Tacoma
Vancouver
Walla Walla

West Virginia

Beckley
Clarksburg
Huntington
Martinsburg

Wisconsin

Madison
Tomah
Wood

Wyoming

Cheyenne
Sheridan

SOURCE: Department of Veterans Affairs.

APPENDIX F

State Maternal and Child Health Programs

Alabama

Alabama Division of Family
Health Services
State Department of Public Health
434 Monroe Street
Montgomery, AL 36130-1701
(205) 261–5052

Alaska

Family Health Section
State Department of Health and
Social Services
1231 Gamble Street, Room 314
Anchorage, AL 99501-4627
(907) 274–7626

American Samoa

Department of Health
Pago Pago, American Samoa
96799
(684) 633–5743

Arizona

State of Arizona Department of
Health
1740 West Adams
Phoenix, AZ 85007
(602) 255–1870

Arkansas

Division of Maternal and Child
Health
State Health Department of
Arkansas
4815 West Markham

Little Rock, AR 72201
(501) 661–2762

California

California State Department of
Health
Maternal and Child Health
Branch
714 P Street, Room 740
Sacramento, CA 95814
(916) 322–3096

Colorado

Colorado Department of Health
4210 East 11th Avenue
Denver, CO 80220
(303) 331–8359

*Commonwealth of the Northern
Mariana Islands*

Department of Public Health and
Environment Service
Commonwealth of the Northern
Mariana Islands
Saipan, Mariana Islands 96950
(670) 234–8950

Connecticut

Connecticut State Department of
Health
150 Washington Street
Hartford, CT 06106
(203) 566–4282

Delaware

Maternal and Child Health
  Services
Division of Public Health
P.O. Box 637
Dover, DE 19903
(202) 736–4785

District of Columbia

Office of Maternal and Child
  Health
Commission of Public Health
1660 L Street, NW, Suite 907
Washington, DC 20036
(202) 673–4551

Florida

Florida Department of Health and
  Rehabilitative Services
Building 1, Room 204
1323 Winewood Boulevard
Tallahassee, FL 32301
(904) 487–1321

Georgia

Division of Public Health
Georgia Department of Human
  Resources
878 Peachtree Street, NE
Suite 271
Atlanta, GA 30309
(404) 894–6622

Guam

Department of Public Health and
  Social Services
Government of Guam
P.O. Box 2816
Agana, Guam 96910
(671) 734–9910

Hawaii

Maternal and Child Health
  Branch
Hawaii Department of Health
741-A Sunset Avenue
Honolulu, HI 96816
(808) 548–6554

Idaho

Bureau of Child Health and Child
  Care Services
Idaho Department of Health and
  Welfare
450 West State
Boise, ID 83720
(208) 334–5968

Illinois

Division of Family Health
Illinois Department of Public
  Health
535 West Jefferson Street
Springfield, IL 62716
(217) 782–2736

Indiana

Indiana State Board of Health
1330 West Michigan
P.O. Box 1964
Indianapolis, IN 46206
(316) 633–0170

Iowa

Division of Family and
  Community Health
Iowa State Department of Health
Lucas State Office Building
Des Moines, IA 50319-0075
(515) 281–4910

Kansas

Division of Public Health
Kansas State Department of
    Health and Environment
State Office Building
Topeka, KS 66620
(913) 296–1205

Kentucky

Division of Maternal and Child
    Health
Kentucky State Department of
    Human Resources
275 East Main Street
Frankfort, KY 40621
(502) 564–4830

Louisiana

Office of Preventive and Public
    Health Services
P.O. Box 60630
New Orleans, LA 70160
(504) 565–6874

Maine

Division of Child Health and
    Child Care Services
Maine Department of Human
    Services
150 Capital Street
Statehouse, Station 11
Augusta, ME 04333
(207) 289–3311

Maryland

Division of Infant, Child and
    Adolescent Health
Maryland State Department of
    Health and Hygiene
201 West Preston Street
Baltimore, MD 20201
(301) 225–6749

Massachusetts

Maternal and Child Health
    Section
Massachusetts Department of
    Public Health
150 Tremont Street
Boston, MA 02111
(617) 727–0940

Michigan

Bureau of Community Service
Michigan Department of Public
    Health
3500 North Logan Street
P.O. Box 30035
Lansing, MI 48909
(517) 335–8955

Minnesota

Division of Maternal and Child
    Health
Minnesota Department of Health
17 Delaware Street, SE
P.O. Box 9441
Minneapolis, MN 55440
(612) 623–5166

Mississippi

Bureau of Personal Health
    Services
P.O. Box 1700
Jackson, MS 39205-1700
(601) 960–7463

Missouri

Division of Personal Health
    Services
Missouri Department of Health
1738 E. Elm
P.O. Box 570
Jefferson City, MO 65102
(314) 751–6174

Montana

Bureau of Maternal and Child
  Health
Cogswell Building
Helena, MT 59620
(406) 444–4740

Nebraska

Bureau of Medical Services and
  Grants
301 Centennial Mall, South
3rd Floor
P.O. Box 95007
Lincoln, NE 68509
(402) 471–3890

Nevada

Nevada Health Division
Department of Human Resources,
  Room 200
Kinkead Building
505 E. King Street
Carson City, NV 98710
(702) 885–4885

New Hampshire

New Hampshire Division of
  Public Health Services
Hazen Drive
Concord, NH 03301
(603) 271–4726

New Jersey

Maternal and Child Health
  Services
New Jersey Department of Health,
  CN 364
Trenton, NJ 08625
(609) 292–5656

New Mexico

Maternal and Child Care Section
New Mexico Health and
  Environment Department
1190 St. Francis Drive
P.O. Box 968
Santa Fe, NM 87504
(505) 827–2350

New York

Division of Family Health
  Services
New York State Department of
  Health
Towe Building, Room 890
Albany, NY 12237
(518) 473–7922

North Carolina

Maternal and Child Care Section
North Carolina Division of Health
  Services
P.O. Box 2091
Raleigh, NC 27602-2091
(919) 733–3816

North Dakota

Division of Maternal and Child
  Health
North Dakota State Department of
  Health
State Capitol Building
Bismarck, ND 58505
(701) 224–2493

Ohio

Division of Maternal and Child
  Health
Ohio State Department of Health
246 North High Street
Columbus, OH 43266-0118
(614) 466–3263

Oklahoma

Maternal and Child Health
  Services
Oklahoma State Department of
  Health
1000 Northeast 10th Street, Room
  703
Oklahoma City, OK 73152
(405) 271–4470

Oregon

Office of Health Services
Oregon State Health Division
P.O. Box 231, Room 508
Portland, OR 97207
(503) 229–6380

Pennsylvania

Division of Maternal and Child
  Health
Pennsylvania State Department of
  Health, Room 725
Health and Welfare Building
P.O. Box 90
Harrisburg, PA 17108
(717) 787–7440

Puerto Rico

Maternal and Child Health, and
  Child Care Programs
Commonwealth of Puerto Rico
Department of Health
Call Box 70184
San Juan, PR 00936
(809) 763–7104

Rhode Island

Division of Family Health
Rhode Island Department of
  Health
75 Davis Street, Room 302
Providence, RI 02908
(401) 277–2312

South Carolina

Bureau of Maternal and Child
  Care
South Carolina Department of
  Health and Environmental
  Control
2600 Bull Street
Columbia, SC 29201
(803) 734–4670

South Dakota

Division of Health Services and
  CCHS Program
South Dakota State Department of
  Health
313 Joe Foss Building
523 E. Capitol Street
Pierre, SD 57501
(605) 773–3737

Tennessee

Tennessee Maternal and Child
  Health Bureau of Health
  Services
100 9th Avenue North, 2nd Floor
Nashville, TN 37219-5405
(615) 741–7353

Texas

Division of Maternal and Child
  Health
Texas Department of Health
1100 West 49th Street
Austin, TX 78756
(512) 458–7321

Utah

Division of Family Health
  Services
Utah Department of Health
44 Medical Drive
Salt Lake City, UT 84113
(801) 533–4084

Vermont

Medical Services Division
Vermont Department of Health
1193 North Avenue
P.O. Box 70
Burlington, VT 05402
(802) 863–7347

Virginia

Division of Maternal and Child
  Health
Virginia State Department of
  Health
109 Governor Street
Richmond, VA 23219
(804) 786–7367

Virgin Islands

Maternal and Child Health
  Ambulatory Services
Cristiansted
P.O. Box 520
St. Croix, VI 00802
(809) 778–6567

Washington

Bureau of Parent-Child Health
  Services
Industrial Park Building 3, MS,
  LC 11A
Washington Department of Social
  and Health Services

Olympia, WA 98504
(809) 753–7021

West Virginia

Division of Maternal and Child
  Health
West Virginia Department of
  Health
State Office Building 1
1143 Dunbar Avenue
Charleston, WV 25064
(304) 768–6295

Wisconsin

Maternal and Child Health Unit
Family and Community Health
  Section
Wisconsin Division of Health
P.O. Box 309
One West Wilson Street
Madison, WI 53701
(608) 266–2670

Wyoming

Division of Health and Medical
  Services
Wyoming Department of Health
  and Social Services
Hathaway Office Building
Cheyenne, WY 82002
(307) 777–6296

SOURCE: American Association of University Affiliated Programs for Persons with Developmental Disabilities. (1989). *Resource guide to organizations concerned with developmental handicaps.* Silver Spring, MD. Supported in part by Grant No. MCH-917 from the Bureau of Maternal and Child Health and Resources Development, U.S. Department of Health and Human Services.

APPENDIX G

Developmental Disabilities State Administering Agencies

Alabama

Alabama Department of Health/
Mental Retardation
200 Interstate Park Drive
P.O. Box 3710-5403
Montgomery, AL 36193-5001
(205) 271–9209

Alaska

Alaska Department of Health and
Social Services
Pouch H-p4
Juneau, AK 99811-0001
(907) 465–3370

American Samoa

Office of Vocational
Rehabilitation
American Samoa Government
P.O. Box 3492
Pago Pago, American Samoa
96799-0320

Arizona

Arizona Department of Economic
Security
1717 West Jefferson Street
P.O. Box 6123
Phoenix, AZ 85007-6123
(602) 542–5678

Arkansas

Arkansas Health Services and
Development Agency

4815 West Markham
Little Rock, AR 72205-3867
(501) 661–2509

California

California Department of
Developmental Services
1600 9th Street, NW
2nd Floor
Sacramento, CA 95814-6404
(916) 445–6951

Colorado

Colorado Department of
Institutions
3550 West Oxford Avenue
Denver, CO 80236-3108
(303) 762–4410

*Commonwealth of the Northern
Mariana Islands*

Department of Education
Office of the Superintendent
Commonwealth of the Northern
Mariana Islands
Saipan, Mariana Islands 96950-
9999

Connecticut

Connecticut Department of
Mental Retardation
90 Pitkin Street
East Hartford, CT 06108-3318
(203) 528–7141

Delaware

Delaware Department of
Community Affairs
156 South State Street
P.O. Box 1401
Dover, DE 19901-7329
(302) 736–4456

District of Columbia

D.C. Department of Human
Services
801 North Capitol Street, NE
Washington, DC 20002-1557
(202) 724–5696

Florida

Florida Department of Health and
Rehabilitative Services
1317 Winewood Boulevard
Building 1, Room 216
Tallahassee, FL 32399-0001
(904) 487–2705

Georgia

Georgia Department of Human
Resources
878 Peachtree Street, NE
Room 304
Atlanta, GA 30334-3917
(404) 894–6300

Guam

Vocational Rehabilitation
Department
East Hospital Loop, Building 284
Pale Son Vitore Road
Tamuning, Guam 96911-3618
(671) 472–8808

Hawaii

Hawaii State Department of
Health
1250 Punchbowl Street
P.O. Box 3378

Honolulu, HI 96801-3378
(808) 548–6505

Idaho

Idaho Department of Health and
Welfare
Towers Building, 10th Floor
Statehouse Mail
Boise, ID 83720-0001
(208) 334–4181

Illinois

Division of Developmental
Disabilities
Illinois Department of Mental
Health and Developmental
Disabilities
401 South Spring Street
402 William Stratton Building
Springfield, IL 62706-0002
(217) 782–7393

Indiana

Governor's Planning Council for
People with Disabilities
Harrison Building, Suite 404
143 West Market Street
Indianapolis, IN 46204
(317) 232–7770

Iowa

Iowa Department of Human
Services
Hoover State Office Building
Des Moines, IA 50319-0001
(515) 281–5452

Kansas

Kansas Department of Mental
Health and Mental Retardation
Services
State Office Building, 5th Floor
Topeka, KS 66612-9999
(913) 296–3774

Kentucky

Mental Retardation Services
Kentucky Department for Mental
    Health
275 East Main Street
Frankfort, KY 40621-0001
(502) 564–3970

Louisiana

Office of the Secretary
Louisiana Department of Health
    and Hospitals
1201 Capitol Access Drive
P.O. Box 629
Baton Rouge, LA 70821-4215
(504) 342–9500

Maine

Maine Department of Mental
    Health and Mental Retardation
State Office Building, Station 40
Augusta, ME 04333
(207) 289–4223

Maryland

Governor's Office for
    Handicapped Individuals
One Market Center, Box 10
300 West Lexington Street
Baltimore, MD 21201-3418
(301) 333–3688

Massachusetts

Massachusetts Administering
    Agency for Developmental
    Disabilities
600 Washington Street, Room 670
Boston, MA 02111-1704
(617) 727–4178

Michigan

Michigan Department of Mental
    Health

Lewis-Cass Building, 6th Floor
Lansing, MI 48913-9999
(517) 373–3500

Minnesota

State Planning Agency
300 Centennial Office Building
658 Cedar Street
St. Paul, MN 55145-0002
(612) 297–2325

Mississippi

Mississippi Department of Mental
    Health
1101 Robert E. Lee Building
239 North Larmor Street
Jackson, MS 39201-1311
(601) 359–1293

Missouri

Missouri Department of Mental
    Health
1915 Southridge Drive
P.O. Box 687
Jefferson City, MO 65102
(314) 751–4122

Montana

Developmental Disabilities
    Division
Montana Department of Social
    and Rehabilitation Services
P.O. Box 4210
111 Sanders
Helena, MT 59604-4210
(406) 444–5622

Nebraska

Nebraska Department of Health
P.O. Box 95007
Lincoln, NE 68509-5007
(402) 471–2133

Nevada

Rehabilitation Division
Nevada Department of Human
  Resources
505 East King Street, Room 502
Carson City, NV 89710-0001
(702) 885–4440

New Hampshire

New Hampshire Department of
  Health and Human Services
6 Hazen Drive
Concord, NH 03301-6505
(603) 271–4331

New Jersey

Department of Human Services
Division of Developmental
  Disabilities
Capital Place One
222 South Warren Street
Trenton, NJ 08625-0001
(609) 292–3742

New Mexico

Health and Environment
  Department, Office of Planning
  and Evaluation
1190 St. Francis Drive
Harold Runnels Building, 4th
  Floor
Santa Fe, NM 87503-0968
(505) 827–2721

New York

Office of Mental Retardation and
  Developmental Disabilities
44 Holland Avenue
Albany, NY 12229-0001
(518) 473–1997

North Carolina

North Carolina Department of
  Human Resources

Adams Building
101 Blair Drive
Albemarle Building
Raleigh, NC 27603
(919) 733–4534

North Dakota

North Dakota Department of
  Human Services
Bismarck, ND 58505-9999
(701) 224–2970

Ohio

Ohio Department of Mental
  Retardation and Developmental
  Disabilities
30 East Broad Street, Room 1280
Columbus, OH 43215-3414
(614) 466–5214

Oklahoma

Oklahoma Department of Human
  Services
Developmental Disabilities
  Services
P.O. Box 25352
Oklahoma City, OK 73125-0352
(405) 521–3571

Oregon

Mental Retardation Services and
  Mental Health Division
2575 Bittern Street, NE
Salem, OR 97310-0001
(503) 378–2429

Pennsylvania

Pennsylvania State Department of
  Public Welfare
333 Health and Welfare Building
Harrisburg, PA 17105
(717) 787–2600

Puerto Rico

Department of Health
Commonwealth of Puerto Rico
P.O. Box 70184
San Juan, PR 00936

Rhode Island

Rhode Island Department of
  Mental Health, Retardation and
  Hospitals
Aime Forland Building
600 New London Avenue
Cranston, RI 02920
(401) 464–3201

South Carolina

Governor Division
South Carolina Health and
  Human Services Division
1205 Pendleton Street, Room 366
Columbia, SC 29201-3731
(803) 734–0467

South Dakota

South Dakota Department of
  Human Services
Division of Developmental
  Disabilities and Mental Health
Richard F. Kneip Building
700 Governor's Drive
Pierre, SD 57501-2237
(605) 773–3438

Tennessee

Tennessee Department of Mental
  Health/Mental Retardation
Doctors Building, 6th Floor
706 Church Street
Nashville, TN 37203-3510
(615) 741–3107

Texas

Texas Rehabilitation Commission
118 East Riverside Drive

Austin, TX 78704-1297
(512) 445–8108

Utah

Division of Mental Health
Utah Department of Social
  Services
3rd Floor, Section 317
150 West North Temple, Room
  310
P.O. Box 4550
Salt Lake City, UT 84103-1507
(801) 533–4940

Vermont

Agency for Human Services
103 South Main Street
Waterbury, VT 05676-1534
(802) 241–2220

Virginia

Department of Mental Health,
  Mental Retardation and
  Substance Abuse Services
P.O. Box 1797
Richmond, VA 23214
(804) 786–5313

Virgin Islands

Commission on the Handicapped
P.O. Box 11179
St. Thomas, VI 00801-8102
(809) 776–2043

Washington

Department of Community
  Development
Social and Health Services
9th & Columbia Building, MS/
  GH-51
Olympia, WA 98504-0001
(206) 586–8966

West Virginia

West Virginia Department of
Health
1800 Washington Street, East
Charleston, WV 25305-0001
(304) 348–2971

Wisconsin

Department of Health and Social
Services

1 West Wilson Street, Room 650
Madison, WI 53702-0001
(608) 255–3681

Wyoming

State Planning Coordinator's
Office
Office of the Governor
Cheyenne, WY 82002-0001
(307) 777–7230

SOURCE: The Administration on Developmental Disabilities, Office of Human
Development Services, Department of Health and Human Services. (1989).

APPENDIX H

Developmental Disabilities State Planning Councils

Alabama

Alabama Developmental
Disabilities Planning Council
200 Interstate Park Drive
P.O. Box 3710
Montgomery, AL 36193-5001

Alaska

Developmental Disabilities
Planning Council
600 University Avenue, Suite B
Fairbanks, AK 99709-3651

American Samoa

Developmental Disabilities
Planning Council
American Samoa Government
P.O. Box 3823
Pago Pago, American Samoa
96799-0320

Arizona

Governor's Council on
Developmental Disabilities
1717 West Jefferson Street, MS
0742
Phoenix, AZ 85007-3202

Arkansas

Governor's Developmental
Disabilities Planning Council
4815 West Markham
Little Rock, AR 72205-3867

California

State Council on Developmental
Disabilities
2000 O Street, Room 100
Sacramento, CA 95814-5220

Colorado

Colorado Developmental
Disabilities Council
777 Grant Street, Suite 410
Denver, CO 80203

*Commonwealth of the Northern
Mariana Islands*

Department of Education
Office of the Superintendent
Commonwealth of the Northern
Mariana Islands
Saipan, Mariana Islands 96956-
9999

Connecticut

Planning Council on
Developmental Disabilities
Department of Mental Retardation
90 Pitkin Street
East Hartford, CT 06108-3318

Delaware

Developmental Disabilities
Planning Council
Department of Community
Affairs, Box 1401
156 South State Street
Dover, DE 19901-7329

200

District of Columbia

Developmental Disabilities
Planning Council
605 G Street, NW, Suite 1108
Washington, DC 20001-3754

Florida

Florida Developmental
Disabilities Planning Council
1317 Winewood Boulevard,
Building 1, Room 309
Tallahassee, FL 32399-0700

Georgia

Governor's Council on
Developmental Disabilities
878 Peachtree Street, NE, Room
620
Atlanta, GA 30309-3917

Guam

The State Planning Council for
Developmental Disabilities
c/o Life Skills Center
284 East Hospital Loop
Tamuning, Guam 96911-9999

Hawaii

Hawaii State Planning Council on
Developmental Disabilities
P.O. Box 3378
Honolulu, HI 96801-3378

Idaho

Idaho State Council on
Developmental Disabilities
450 West State Street
Boise, ID 83720-0001

Illinois

Illinois Developmental
Disabilities Council

840 South Spring Street
Springfield, IL 62706

Indiana

Governor's Planning Council for
People with Disabilities
Harrison Building, Suite 404
143 West Market Street
Indianapolis, IN 46204

Iowa

Governor's Planning Council for
Developmental Disabilities
Iowa Department of Human
Services
Hoover State Office Building
5th Floor
Des Moines, IA 50319-0114

Kansas

Kansas Planning Council on
Developmental Disabilities
Services
Department of Social and
Rehabilitation Services
Docking State Office Building
5th Floor North
Topeka, KS 66612-9999

Kentucky

Kentucky Developmental
Disabilities Planning Council
Department for Mental Health/
Mental Retardation
Retardation Services
275 East Main Street
Frankfort, KY 40621-0001

Louisiana

Louisiana State Planning Council
on Developmental Disabilities
P.O. Box 3455
Baton Rouge, LA 70821-3455

Maine

Maine Developmental Disabilities
    Council
Nash Building
Capitol and State Streets, Station
    139
Augusta, ME 04333-9999

Maryland

Maryland State Planning Council
    on Developmental Disabilities
One Market Center, Box 10
300 West Lexington Street
Baltimore, MD 21201-2323

Massachusetts

Massachusetts Developmental
    Disabilities Planning Council
600 Washington Street
Boston, MA 02111-1704

Michigan

Michigan Developmental
    Disabilities Council
Lewis-Class Building, 6th Floor
Lansing, MI 48913

Minnesota

Minnesota Developmental
    Disabilities Planning Council,
    Room 300
658 Cedar Street
St. Paul, MN 55155

Mississippi

Mississippi Developmental
    Planning Council
1101 Robert E. Lee Building
Jackson, MS 39201

Missouri

Missouri Planning Council for
    Developmental Disabilities

P.O. Box 687
1915 Southridge Drive
Jefferson City, MO 65102

Montana

Developmental Planning and
    Advisory Council
25 South Ewing, Room 506
P.O. Box 4210
Helena, MT 59620

Nebraska

Governor's Planning Council on
    Developmental Disabilities
P.O. Box 95007
Lincoln, NE 68509-5007

Nevada

Nevada Planning Council for
    Developmental Disabilities
Rehabilitation Division,
    Department of Human
    Resources
505 East King Street, Room 502
Carson City, NV 89710-0001

New Hampshire

New Hampshire Council on
    Developmental Disabilities
Concord Center, 10 Ferry Street
P.O. Box 315
Concord, NH 03301-5022

New Jersey

Developmental Disabilities
    Planning Council
108-110 North Broad Street, CN
    700
Trenton, NJ 08625-0001

New Mexico

Developmental Disabilities
  Planning Council
State of New Mexico
Ark Plaza, Suite B-200
2025 South Pachco Street
Santa Fe, NM 87505

New York

New York State Developmental
  Disabilities Planning Council
155 Washington Avenue
2nd Floor
Albany, NY 12210-0001

North Carolina

North Carolina Council on
  Developmental Disabilities
1508 Western Boulevard
Raleigh, NC 27606-1359

North Dakota

Developmental Disabilities
  Council
North Dakota Department of
  Human Services
State Capitol
Bismarck, ND 58505-9999

Ohio

Ohio Developmental Disabilities
  Planning Council
Department of Mental
  Retardation/Developmental
  Disabilities
8 East Long Street, 6th Floor
Columbus, OH 43215-3414

Oklahoma

Developmental Disabilities
  Planning Council
Department of Human Services
P.O. Box 25352
Oklahoma City, OK 73125-0352

Oregon

Oregon Developmental
  Disabilities Planning Council
Mental Retardation/
  Developmental Disabilities
  Program Office
Mental Health Division
2575 Bittern Street, NE
Salem, OR 97310-0520

Pennsylvania

Developmental Planning Council
Room 569, Forum Building
Commonwealth Avenue
Harrisburg, PA 17120-0001

Puerto Rico

Puerto Rico Developmental
  Disabilities Council
P.O. Box 9543
Santurce, PR 00908-0543

Rhode Island

Rhode Island Developmental
  Disabilities Council
600 New London Avenue
Cranston, RI 02920-3028

South Carolina

South Carolina Developmental
  Disabilities Planning Council
Edgar Brown Building, Room 372
1205 Pendleton Street
Columbia, SC 29201-3731

South Dakota

South Dakota Department of
  Human Services
Division of Developmental
  Disabilities
Richard F. Kneip Building
700 Governor's Drive
Pierre, SD 57501-2237

Tennessee

Developmental Disabilities
   Planning Council
Tennessee Department of Mental
   Health and Mental Retardation
Doctor's Building, 3rd Floor
706 Church Street
Nashville, TN 37219-5393

Texas

Texas Planning Council for
   Developmental Disabilities
4900 North Lamar Boulevard
Austin, TX 78751-2316

Utah

Utah Council for Handicapped
   and Developmentally Disabled
   Persons
P.O. Box 1958
Salt Lake City, UT 84110-1958

Vermont

Vermont Developmental
   Disabilities Council
Waterbury Office Complex
103 South Main Street
Waterbury, VT 05676-1534

Virginia

Virginia Board for Rights of the
   Disabled
James Monroe Building
17th Floor
101 North 14th Street
Richmond, VA 23219-3641

Virgin Islands

Virgin Islands Developmental
   Disabilities Council
P.O. Box 2671 Kings Hill
St. Croix, VI 00850-9999

Washington

Developmental Disabilities
   Planning Council
Washington Department of
   Community Development,
   Room 360
9th Columbia Building,
   Mailstop-GH-51
Olympia, WA 98504-4151

West Virginia

Developmental Planning Council
c/o West Virginia Department of
   Health
625 D Street
South Charleston, WV 25303-
   3111

Wisconsin

Council on Developmental
   Disabilities
State of Wisconsin
P.O. Box 7851
Madison, WI 53707-7851

Wyoming

Governor's Planning Council on
   Developmental Disabilities
Herschler Building, 1 East
122 West 25th
Cheyenne, WY 82001

SOURCE: The Administration on Developmental Disabilities, Office of Human Development Services, Department of Health and Human Services. (1989).

APPENDIX I

State Directors of Special Education

Alabama

Anne Ramsey
Exceptional Children and Youth
State Department of Education
1020 Monticello Court
Montgomery, AL 36117
(205) 261–5099

Alaska

William S. Mulnix
Office of Special Education
Department of Education
Pouch F
Juneau, AK 99811
(907) 465–2970

American Samoa

Jane French
Special Education
Department of Education
Pago Pago, American Samoa
96799
(684) 633–4789

Arizona

Kathryn Lund
Deputy Associate Superintendent
Special Education

1535 West Jefferson
Phoenix, AZ 85007
(601) 542–3183

Arkansas

Diane Sydoriak
Special Education Section
State Education Building C
Room 105-C
Little Rock, AR 72201
(501) 682–4221

California

Patrick Campbell
California Department of
    Education
Special Education Division
721 Capitol Mall, Room 610
Sacramento, CA 95814
(916) 323–4753

Colorado

Brian A. McNulty
Colorado Department of
    Education
201 East Colfax
Denver, CO 80203
(303) 866–6695

NOTE: The information in this appendix was correct as of December 1989.

Commonwealth of the Northern Mariana Islands

Margaret De LaCruz
Special Education Coordinator
Special Education Programs
Department of Education
Mariana Lower Base
Saipan, Northern Mariana Islands 96950
(670) 322–9956

Connecticut

Tom B. Gillung
Bureau of Student Services
Connecticut State Department of Education
P.O. Box 2219
Hartford, CT 06145
(203) 566–3561

Delaware

Carl M. Haltom
Exceptional Children and Special Programs Division
Department of Public Instruction
P.O. Box 1402
Townsend Building
Dover, DE 19903
(302) 736–5471

District of Columbia

Keener Cobb
Division of Exceptional Children
Office of Indian Education Programs
Bureau of Indian Affairs
Department of Interior
Washington, DC 20245
(202) 343–6675

Doris A. Woodson
D.C. Public Schools
Division of Public Education

Department of Education
Webster Administration Building
10th and H Streets, NW
Washington, DC 20001
(202) 724–4018

East Carolina Islands

Yosiro Suta
Federal Education Program Coordinator
Federated States of Micronesia National Government, Office of Education
Kolonia, Panape
East Carolina Islands 96941

Florida

Elinor Elfner
Bureau of Education for Exceptional Students
Florida Department of Education
Knott Building
Tallahassee, FL 32399
(904) 488–1570

Georgia

Joan A. Jordan
Georgia Department of Education
Program for Exceptional Children
Twin Towers East, Suite 1970
Atlanta, GA 30334
(404) 656–2425

Guam

Steven L. Spencer
Associate Superintendent of Special Education
Department of Education
P.O. Box DE
Agana, Guam 96910
Overseas Operator-472–8703

Hawaii

Margaret Donovan
Special Needs Branch
State Department of Education
3430 Leahi Avenue
Honolulu, HI 96815
(808) 737-3720

Idaho

Vickie Simmons
Special Education Section
State Department of Education
Len B. Jordan Building
650 West State Street
Boise, ID 83720
(208) 334-3940

Illinois

[To be announced]
Specialized Educational Services
Illinois State Board of Education
100 North First Street
Springfield, IL 62777
(217) 782-6601

Indiana

Paul Ash
Indiana Division of Special
    Education
229 State House
Indianapolis, IN 46204
(317) 369-9462

Iowa

Frank Vance
Special Education Division
Iowa Department of Public
    Instruction
Grimes State Office Building
Des Moines, IA 50319-0146
(515) 281-3176

Kansas

James E. Marshall
Kansas Department of Education
120 East 10th Street
Topeka, KS 66612
(913) 296-4947

Kentucky

Linda Hargan
Department of Education
Office of Education for
    Exceptional Children
Capitol Plaza Tower, 8th Floor
Frankfort, KY 40601
(502) 564-4970

Louisiana

Walter Gatlin
Louisiana Department of
    Education
P.O. Box 94064
Baton Rouge, LA 70804
(504) 342-3633

Maine

David Noble Stockford
Division of Special Education
State Department of Educational
    and Cultural Services
State House, Station 23
Augusta, ME 04333
(207) 289-5953

Maryland

Joseph Shilling
Division of Special Education
State Department of Education
200 West Baltimore Street
Baltimore, MD 21201
(301) 333-2200

Marshall Islands

Jobidrik Ittu
Director of Special Education
Education Department
Majuro, Marshall Islands 96960
692-9-3359

Massachusetts

Mary-Beth Fafard
Massachusetts State Department
    of Education
Quincy Center Plaza
1385 Hancock Street
Quincy, MA 02169
(617) 770-7468

Michigan

Teressa Staten
Michigan Department of
    Education
Special Education Services
P.O. Box 30008
Lansing, MI 48909
(517) 373-9433

Minnesota

Norena Hale
Minnesota Department of
    Education
Capitol Square Building,
    Room 813
550 Cedar Street
St. Paul, MN 55101
(612) 296-1793

Mississippi

Carolyn Black
State Department of Education
P.O. Box 771
Jackson, MS 39205
(601) 359-3498

Missouri

John Allan
Division of Special Education
Department of Elementary and
    Secondary Education
P.O. Box 480
Jefferson City, MO 65102
(314) 751-2965

Montana

Bob Runkel
Office of Public Instruction
State Capitol
Helena, MT 59620
(406) 444-4429

Nebraska

Gary M. Sherman
Special Education Branch
Nebraska Department of
    Education
Box 94987
301 Centennial Mall, South
Lincoln, NE 68509
(402) 471-2471

Nevada

Jane Early
Special Education Branch
Division of Special Education
Nevada Department of Education
400 West King Street
Capitol Complex
Carson City, NV 89710
(702) 885-3140

New Hampshire

Robert Kennedy
Division of Special Education
State Department of Education
101 Pleasant Street
Concord, NH 03301
(603) 271-3741

New Jersey

Jeffrey V. Osowski
Division of Special Education
State Department of Education
CN 500
Trenton, NJ 08625
(609) 292–0147

New Mexico

Jim Newby
Special Education Unit
State Department of Education
Educational Building
Santa Fe, NM 87501-2786
(505) 827–6541

New York

Thomas Neveldine
Office for Education of Children
  with Handicapping Conditions
New York State Department of
  Education
Education Building Annex
Albany, NY 12234
(518) 474–5548

North Carolina

Lowell Harris
Division for Exceptional Children
State Department of Public
  Instruction
Raleigh, NC 27603
(919) 733–3921

North Dakota

Gary Gronberg
Department of Public Instruction
State Capitol
Bismarck, ND 58505-0164
(701) 224–2277

Ohio

Frank New
Division of Special Education
933 High Street
Worthington, OH 43085-4087
(614) 466–2650

Oklahoma

Connie Siler
Special Education Section
State Department of Education
2500 North Lincoln
Oklahoma City, OK 73105
(405) 521–3352

Oregon

Karen Brazeau
Special Education and Student
  Services
State Department of Education
700 Pringle Parkway, SE
Salem, OR 97310
(503) 378–3591

Palau

Peter Elechuus
Special Education Coordinator
Department of Education
Koror, Palau 96940
(011) 568

Pennsylvania

James Tucker
Pennsylvania Department of
  Education
333 Market Street
P.O. Box 911
Harrisburg, PA 17126-0333
(717) 783–6913

Puerto Rico

Lucila Torres Martinez
Department of Education
G.P.O. Box 759
Hato Rey, PR 00919
(809) 764–8059

Rhode Island

Robert M. Pryhoda
Rhode Island Department of
    Education
Roger Williams Building,
    Room 209
22 Hayes Street
Providence, RI 02908
(401) 277–3505

South Carolina

Robert S. Black
Office of Programs for the
    Handicapped
South Carolina Department of
    Education
Kroger Executive Center
Santee Building, A-24
100 Executive Center Drive
Columbia, SC 29210
(803) 737–8710

South Dakota

Dean Myer
Section for Special Education
Richard F. Kneip Building
700 North Illinois
Pierre, SD 57501
(605) 773–4689

Tennessee

Joleta Reynolds
Division of Special Programs
Department of Education
132 Cordell Hull Building
Nashville, TN 37219
(615) 741–2851

Texas

Jill Gray
Department of Special Education
Texas Education Agency
1701 North Congress
Austin, TX 78701
(512) 463–9277

Utah

Stevan J. Kukic
Utah State Office of Education
Special Education Department
250 East 500 South
Salt Lake City, UT 84111
(801) 538–7700

Vermont

Marc Hull
Division of Special and
    Compensatory Education
Department of Education
State Capitol Office Building
120 State Street
Montpelier, VT 05602
(802) 828–3141

Virginia

William Helton
Administrative Director
Office of Special and
    Compensatory Education
Department of Education
P.O. Box 6Q
Richmond, VA 23216
(804) 225–2402

Virgin Islands

Priscilla Stridiron
Division of Special Education
Department of Education
P.O. Box 6640
St. Thomas, VI 00801
(809) 776–5802

Washington

Robert LaGarde
Office of Superintendent of
 Public Instruction
Old Capitol Building, FG-11
Olympia, WA 98504
(206) 753–6733

West Virginia

Nancy Thabet
Office of Special Education
 Administration
West Virginia Department of
 Education
Capitol Complex, Building 6,
 Room B, 304
Charleston, WV 25305
(304) 348–2696

Wisconsin

Victor J. Contrucci
Wisconsin Department of Public
 Instruction
125 South Webster Street
P.O. Box 7841
Madison, WI 53707
(608) 266–1649

Wyoming

Maggie Simeno
Special Programs Unit
2nd Floor
Hathaway Building
Cheyenne, WY 82882
(307) 777–7417

SOURCE: Office of Special Education and Rehabilitative Services, Department of Education. (1989).

APPENDIX J

Temporary Child Care for Handicapped Children and Crisis Nurseries

FISCAL YEAR 1988, SECTION 203

Alabama

Portis Cunningham, Project
  Director
Alabama Department of Mental
  Health and Mental Retardation
Division of Mental Retardation/
  Region V
P.O. Box 3710
Montgomery, AL 36193-5001
(205) 271–9291

Arkansas

C. Ray Tribble, Project Director
Arkansas Department of Human
  Services
Division of Economic and
  Medical Services
P.O. Box 1437—Slot 526
Little Rock, AR 72203
(501) 682–8374

California

Lee Stolmack, Project Director
California Department of Social
  Services
744 P Street
Sacramento, CA 95814
(916) 322–1194

Colorado

Janet Motz, Project Director
Colorado Department of Social
  Services
Division of Child Welfare
  Services
1575 Sherman Street, 2nd Floor
Denver, CO 80203-1714
(303) 866–5947

Florida

J. Paul Rollings, Project Director
Florida Department of Health/
  Rehabilitative Services
Alcohol, Drug Abuse and Mental
  Health Program
1317 Winewood Boulevard
Tallahassee, FL 32399-0700
(904) 444–8843

Illinois

Bobby Hall, Project Director
Illinois Department of Children
  and Family Services
Program Development and
  Support
406 East Monroe, Floor 7
Springfield, IL 62707
(217) 785–8843

Kansas

Azzie Young, Project Director
Kansas Department of Health and
Environment Services for
Children with Special Health
Care Needs, Bureau of Maternal
and Child Health
900 SW Jackson Street
Topeka, KS 66612-1290
(913) 296–1313

Massachusetts

Jane Stolleroff, Project Director
Massachusetts Department of
Social Services
Central Office—Special Projects
150 Causeway Street, 11th Floor
Boston, MA 02114
(617) 727–0900

Michigan

Jan Bocskay, Project Director
Michigan Department of Social
Services
300 South Capitol Street
P.O. Box 30037
Lansing, MI 48909
(517) 373–3558

Nebraska

Mona L. Way, Project Director
Nebraska Department of Social
Services
Division of Human Services
P.O. Box 95026
Lincoln, NE 68509-5026
(402) 471–9328

North Carolina

Barbara Harris, Project Director
North Carolina Department of
Human Resources

Division of Mental Health, Mental
Retardation, and Substance
Abuse Services
325 North Salisbury Street
Raleigh, NC 27611
(919) 733–7013

New Hampshire

Richard Lepore, Project Director
New Hampshire Division of
Mental Health and
Developmental Services
105 Pleasant Street
Concord, NH 03301
(603) 271–5013

New York

William Phillips, Project Director
New York State Department of
Social Services
Division of Family and Children's
Services
40 North Pearl Street, 11th Floor
Albany, NY 12243
(518) 443–2536

Tennessee

Mary Rolando, Project Director
Tennessee Department of Mental
Health and Mental Retardation
Doctor's Building
706 Church Street
Nashville, TN 37219
(615) 741–3708

Vermont

John E. Pierce, Project Director
Vermont Department of Mental
Health
Division of Mental Health
103 South Main Street
Waterbury, VT 05676
(802) 241–2621

Virginia

Irene Carney, Project Director
Virginia Commonwealth
    University

School of Education
Box 568—MCV Station
Richmond, VA 23298-0568
(804) 225–3876

FISCAL YEAR 1988, SECTION 204

Arizona

Beth Rosenberg, Project Director
Arizona Department of Economic
    Security
Administration for Children,
    Youth and Families
P.O. Box 6123
Phoenix, AZ 85005
(602) 542–3981

California

Robert L. Garcia, Project Director
California Department of Social
    Services
744 P Street
Sacramento, CA 95814
(916) 322–1194

Florida

Shirley Hammond, Project
    Director
Florida Department of Health and
    Rehabilitative Services
Children, Youth and Families
    Services
1317 Winewood Boulevard
Tallahassee, FL 32399-0700
(904) 444–8843

Hawaii

Alan Taniguchi, Project Director
Hawaii Department of Health
FHSD/Children with Special
    Health Needs Branch

741 Sunset Avenue
Honolulu, HI 96816
(808) 735–0434

Idaho

Anne McNevin, Project Director
Idaho Department of Health and
    Welfare
Division of Family and Children's
    Services
450 West State Street
Boise, ID 83720
(208) 734–4000

Illinois

Bobby J. Hall, Project Director
Illinois Department of Children
    and Family Services
Office of Program Development
    and Support
406 East Monroe Street
Springfield, IL 62701-1498
(217) 785–2655

Maryland

Laura Skaff, Project Director
Maryland Department of Human
    Resources
Social Services Administration
Child Protective Services
Baltimore, MD 21201
(301) 669–9702

New Jersey

Ertha Drayton, Project Director
New Jersey Department of Human
    Services
Division of Youth and Family
    Services
One South Montgomery Street
Trenton, NJ 08625
(609) 633–2116

North Carolina

Lenore Behar, Project Director
North Carolina Division of Mental
    Health, Mental Retardation, and
    Substance Abuse Services
325 North Salisbury Street
Raleigh, NC 27611
(919) 733–0398

North Dakota

Hansine Fisher, Project Director
Families First—The Child Welfare
    Reform Initiative
Office of the Lieutenant Governor
State Capitol
Bismarck, ND 58505
(701) 777–3442

Ohio

Ann Louise Maxwell, Project
    Director
Ohio Department of Human
    Services
Office of Program Enhancement
30 East Broad Street, 32nd Floor
Columbus, OH 43266-0423
(614) 466–8510

Oregon

Robin Karr-Morse, Project
    Director
Oregon Children's Services
    Division

Family Services
198 Commercial Street, SE
Salem, OR 97304
(503) 378–3016

Pennsylvania

Julia Danzy, Project Director
Pennsylvania Department of
    Public Welfare
Office of Children, Youth and
    Families
P.O. Box 2675
Harrisburg, PA 17105
(717) 787–4756

Puerto Rico

Carlos Ivan Palacios, Project
    Director
Puerto Rico Department of Social
    Services
Bureau for Residential Facilities
Box 11398
San Juan, PR 00910
(809) 722–7045

Utah

Sherry Olson Reese, Project
    Director
Utah State Division of Family
    Services
P.O. Box 45500
Salt Lake City, UT 84145-0500
(801) 538–4100

Washington

Joyce Hopson, Project Director
Washington Department of Social
    and Health Services
Division of Children and Family
    Services
Mailstop OB 41
Olympia, WA 98504
(206) 586–6066

FISCAL YEAR 1989, SECTION 5117A

Connecticut

Annette M. Lawning
Connecticut Department of
Human Resources
Bureau of Grants Management
1049 Asylum Avenue
Hartford, CT 06105
(203) 566–4972

Delaware

Kathy Goldsmith
Delaware Department of Services
for Children, Youth and Their
Families
Division of Child Protective
Services
1825 Faulkland Road
Wilmington, DE 19802
(302) 633–2665

Florida

Nickolas C. Anthony
Florida Department of Health and
Rehabilitative Services
Alcohol, Drug Abuse, and Mental
Health Program
1317 Winewood Boulevard
Tallahassee, FL 32399-0700
(813) 936–2211, extension 274

Georgia

Charles Kimber
Georgia Department of Human
Resources
Division of Mental Health, Mental
Retardation and Substance
Abuse

878 Peachtree Street, SE
Atlanta, GA 30309
(404) 894–6313

Hawaii

Jean Stewart
Hawaii Department of Health
Family Health Services
3627 Kilauea Avenue, #106
Honolulu, HI 96816
(808) 735–0434

Massachusetts

Grace G. Healey
Massachusetts Department of
Mental Retardation
160 North Washington Street
Boston, MA 02114
(617) 727–5608

Mississippi

Tillie Rosen
Mississippi Department of Public
Welfare
P.O. Box 352
Jackson, MS 39205
(601) 354–0341

Missouri

John G. Solomon
Missouri Department of Mental
Health
Mental Retardation/
Developmental Disabilities
P.O. Box 687
Jefferson City, MO 65102
(314) 751–4054

New Jersey

Anne E. Brody
New Jersey Department of Human
   Services
Division of Developmental
   Disabilities
222 S. Warren Street, CN-700
Trenton, NJ 08625
(608) 633-7407

North Carolina

Susan Robinson
North Carolina Department of
   Human Resources
DMH/MR/SAS
Albermarle Building
325 North Salisbury Street
Raleigh, NC 27611
(919) 733-0598

North Dakota

Hansine Fisher
North Dakota Children Services
   Coordinating Committee
State Capital
Bismarck, ND 58505
(701) 224-3586

Oklahoma

Marilyn Knott
Oklahoma Department of Human
   Services
P.O. Box 25352
Oklahoma City, OK 73125
(405) 521-2907

Pennsylvania

Ann Zenzinger (717) 787-0823
Kay Arnold (717) 787-3438
Pennsylvania Department of
   Public Welfare
Office of Social Programs
P.O. Box 2675
Harrisburg, PA 17105

Rhode Island

Edward Hutchins
Rhode Island Department for
   Children and Their Families
Community Resources
610 Mt. Pleasant Avenue
Providence, RI 02908
(401) 457-4748

Tennessee

Louise Barnes
Tennessee Department of Mental
   Health and Mental Retardation
Doctor's Building
706 Church Street
Nashville, TN 37219
(615) 741-3708

Texas

Mary Elder
Texas Department of Health
Inter-Agency Council/ECI
1100 West 49th Street
Austin, TX 78756
(512) 458-7673

FISCAL YEAR 1989, SECTION 5117B

Arkansas

Jimmy Fields
Arkansas Department of Human
   Services

Division of Child and Family
   Services
P.O. Box 1437
Little Rock, AR 72203
(501) 682-8757

California

Judy Osteri
California Department of Social
  Services
744 P Street
Sacramento, CA 95814
(209) 464–4524

Colorado

Janet Motz
Colorado Department of Social
  Services
1575 Sherman Street, 6th Floor
Denver, CO 80203
(303) 866–5947

Connecticut

Laurie Hart Docknevick
Connecticut Department of
  Children and Youth Services
170 Sigourney Street
Hartford, CT 06103
(203) 566–8090

Idaho

Donna Francis
Idaho Department of Health and
  Welfare
Division of Community
  Rehabilitation
P.O. Drawer B
Lewiston, ID 83501
(208) 799–3310

Indiana

Deborah Wolf
Indiana Department of Human
  Services
Family Services Unit/SSD
251 North Illinois Street
P.O. Box 7083
Indianapolis, IN 46207
(317) 232–1750

Iowa

John Holtkamp
Iowa Department of Human
  Services
Adult Children and Family
  Services
Hoover State Office Building,
  5th Floor
Des Moines, IA 50319
(515) 281–5583

Louisiana

Lorroine R. Dunkley
Louisiana Department of Social
  Services
Office of Community Services
P.O. Box 3318
Baton Rouge, LA 70821
(504) 342–4049

Michigan

Jan Bocskay
Michigan Department of Social
  Services
Office of Planning, Budget and
  Evaluation
300 South Capitol Avenue
Lansing, MI 48909
(517) 373–3558

Missouri

John Solomon
Missouri Department of Mental
  Health
Division of Mental Retardation/
  Developmental Disabilities
P.O. Box 687
Jefferson City, MO 65102
(314) 751–4054

Nevada

Christa Peterson
Nevada Department of Human
    Resources
Kinkaid Building
505 East King Street, Room 600
Carson City, NV 89716
(702) 486–6100

New Mexico

Phyllis Nye
New Mexico Department of
    Health and Social Services
P.O. Box 2348
Oera Building, Room 519
Santa Fe, NM 87501
(505) 827–4370

North Carolina

Lenore Behar
North Carolina Department of
    Human Resources
Division of Mental Health/
    MR/SAS
325 North Salisbury Street
Raleigh, NC 27611
(919) 733–0598/0599

Oklahoma

Martha Scales
Oklahoma Department of Human
    Services
P.O. Box 25352
Oklahoma City, OK 73125
(405) 521–3777

Puerto Rico

Luisa Pacheco
Puerto Rico Department of Social
    Services

Bureau for Residential Facilities
P.O. Box 11398
San Juan, PR 00910
(904) 722–7432

Rhode Island

Andrew Lindk
Rhode Island Department for
    Children and Their Families
610 Mt. Pleasant Avenue
Providence, RI 02908
(401) 457–4740

South Carolina

Ira Barbell
South Carolina Department of
    Social Services
Office of Children, Family and
    Adult Services
P.O. Box 1520
Columbia, SC 29202-1520
(803) 734–5670

Texas

Kathy Kramer
Texas Department of Human
    Services
P.O. Box 149030
M.C. 234-E
Austin, TX 78714
(512) 450–3653

Wisconsin

Kay Kroll
Wisconsin Department of Health
    and Social Services
Division of Community Services
P.O. Box 7851-1 West Wilson
    Street
Madison, WI 53703
(414) 227–4243

Source: Administration on Children, Youth and Families, Office of Human Development
    Services, Department of Health and Human Services. (1989).

APPENDIX K

Department of Defense Family Support Programs

DIRECTORY FOR ARMY COMMUNITY SERVICE CENTERS INSIDE THE CONTINENTAL UNITED STATES

Address	U.S. Command	Military Telephone (AUTOVON)	Commercial Telephone
Alabama			
Commander Anniston Army Depot ATTN: SDSAN-DPCA-CFA Anniston, AL 36201-5042		571–7155	(205) 235–7155
Army Community Service ATTN: ATZN-DP-FFA Bldg. 2203 Fort McClellan, AL 36205	TRADOC	865–5546 865–4525	(205) 238–5546 238–4525

Commander, U.S. Army
   Missile Command
ATTN: AMSMI-RA-CF
Bldg. 118
Redstone Arsenal, AL
   35898-5355
	AMC	746–2859
		
		746–2073
		
		(Director)
			(205) 876–2859
			
			876–2073
			
			(Director)

CDR, USAAVNC Army Community Service ATTN: ATZQ-PAC-FS-ACS Bldg. 3907 Fort Rucker, AL 36362-5000	TRADOC	558–3643 558–3817 558–3815	(205) 255–3643 255–3817 255–3815

Address	U.S. Command	Military Telephone (AUTOVON)	Commercial Telephone
Arizona			
Army Community Service ATTN: ASH-PCA-CFA Bldg. 50010 Fort Huachuca, AZ 85613-6000	USAISC	879–2330 879–5972 879–5719 879–3234 879–2437 879–5312	(602) 538–2330 538–5972 538–5719 538–3234 538–2437 538–5312
Army Community Service ATTN: STEYP-CA-AD Bldg. 1000 Yuma Proving Ground Yuma, AZ 85365-9102	AMC	899–2852	(602) 328–2513
Arkansas			
Army Community Service (Point of Contact) ATTN: SARPB-AD Pine Bluff Arsenal Pine Bluff, AR 71601	AMC	966–3026 966–3027	
California			
Army Community Service ATTN: AFZJ-PAP-A (ACS) National Training Center & Ft. Irwin Fort Irwin, CA 92310-5000	FORSCOM	470–3690 470–5051	(619) 386–3690 386–5051
Army Community Service ATTN: AFZW-CA-FSCS Bldg. 3010 Fort Ord, CA 93941-5600	FORSCOM	929–3903 929–6687 929–5713	(408) 242–3903 242–6687 242–5713
Family Support Branch ATTN: SDSSI-FSB Sierra Army Depot Herlong, CA 96113-5166	AMC	830–9425	(916) 827–4663

Address	U.S. Command	Military Telephone (AUTOVON)	Commercial Telephone
Army Community Service Sharpe Army Depot ATTN: SDSSH-AMW-ACS Lathrop, CA 95331-5214	AMC	462–2142 462–2419	(209) 982–2142 982–2419
Army Community Service ATTN: MTW-GC-S Bldg. 780 Oakland Army Base, CA 94626-5000	MTMC	859–3457 859–2508	(415) 466–3457 466–2508
Army Community Service Bldg. 566 Presidio of San Francisco, CA 94129-5065	FORSCOM	586–5057 586–5256 586–5155	(415) 561–5057 561–5256 561–5155
Army Community Service Sacramento Army Depot ATTN: SDSSA-AMW-1 Sacramento, CA 95813-5080	AMC	839–2059 839–2019	(916) 388–2059 388–2019

Colorado

Address	U.S. Command	Military Telephone (AUTOVON)	Commercial Telephone
Commander Fitzsimmons Army Medical Center ATTN: HSHG-PNF-S Bldg. 133, Ground Floor Aurora, CO 80045-5000	HSC	943–8101 943–8856 943–8659	(303) 341–8101 341–8856 341–8659
Army Community Service ATTN: DFZC-PA-FAM Bldg. 1526 Fort Carson, CO 80913-5000	FORSCOM	691–4590 691–4357 691–4591	(303) 579–4590 579–4357 579–4591
Commander Rocky Mountain Arsenal ATTN: SMCRM-AD Commerce City, CO 80022-2180	AMC	556–2140	(303) 288–2140

Address	U.S. Command	Military Telephone (AUTOVON)	Commercial Telephone
Army Community Service Pueblo Army Depot Activity ATTN: SDSTE-PUI-C Bldg. 2 Pueblo, CO 81001-5000	AMC	877–4432	(719) 549–4432

District of Columbia

Address	U.S. Command	Military Telephone (AUTOVON)	Commercial Telephone
Army Community Service ATTN: HSHL-PEH-A Bldg. I, Room 312 Walter Reed Army Medical Center Washington, DC 20307-5000	HSC	291–3412 291–3414 291–3415	(202) 576–3412 576–3414 576–3415

Georgia

Address	U.S. Command	Military Telephone (AUTOVON)	Commercial Telephone
Army Community Service ATTN: ATZB-PA-FS-CS Bldg. 2640 Fort Benning, GA 31905-5223	TRADOC	835–4043 784–4969	(404) 545–4043 544–4969
HQ, 2d Army ATTN: AFRD-PRH Fort Gillem, GA 30050-7000		979–7762 979–7764	(404) 362–7762 362–7764
Army Community Service ATTN: ATZH-PAC-FC Fort Gordon, GA 30905-5020	TRADOC	780–2147 780–4718	(404) 791–2147 791–4718
Army Community Service ATTN: AFZP-PAA-A Bldg. 401 Hunter Army Airfield, GA 31409	FORSCOM	971–5301	(912) 352–5301
Army Community Service ATTN: AFZK-PA-FAS Bldg. 65, Room 30 Fort McPherson, GA 30330-5000	FORSCOM	572–3879 572–3612	(404) 752–3879 752–3612

Address	U.S. Command	Military Telephone (AUTOVON)	Commercial Telephone
Commander Army Community Service ATTN: AFZP-PAA-A Bldg. 251 Fort Stewart, GA 31313	FORSCOM	870–5059 870–2707 870–3434	(912) 767–5059 767–2707 767–3434
Illinois			
Army Community Service ATTN: AFZO-PA-FSD Fort Sheridan, IL 60037-5000	FORSCOM	459–2272 459–3135	(312) 926–2272 926–3135
Army Community Service U.S. Army St. Louis Area Support Center (SLASC) ATTN: SAVAS-CMA Bldg. 185 Granite City, IL 62040-1801	AMC	892–4260 892–4550	(618) 452–4260 452–4550
Army Community Service Rock Island Arsenal ATTN: SMCRI-ADW-S Rock Island, IL 61299-5000	AMC	793–3908	(309) 794–3908
Army Community Service (Point of Contact) Savanna Army Depot Savanna, IL 61074	AMC	585–8821 585–8822	(815) 273–2211 Ext. 8821/8822
Indiana			
Army Community Service ATTN: ATZI-PAC-SA Bldg. 32 Fort Benjamin Harrison, IN 46216-5130	TRADOC	699–4360 699–4357	(317) 542–4360 542–4357
Kansas			
Army Community Service ATTN: ATZL-GPC-FA Bldg. 55, Dickenson Hall Fort Leavenworth, KS 66027-5091	TRADOC	552–4357 552–4895	(913) 684–4357 684–4895

Address	U.S. Command	Military Telephone (AUTOVON)	Commercial Telephone
Army Community Service ATTN: AFZN-PA-CFF Bldg. 37 Fort Riley, KS 66442-6421	FORSCOM	856–3091	(913) 239–3091
Kentucky			
Army Community Service ATTN: AFZB-PA-F-AC Bldg. T-74 Fort Campbell, KY 42223-1399	FORSCOM	635–5080 635–2727	(502) 798–5080 798–2727
HQ U.S. Army Armor Center and Fort Knox Army Community Service ATTN: ATZK-PA-CF-ACS Bldg. 1384, Vine Grove Road Fort Knox, KY 40121-5000	TRADOC	464–6291 464–1996 464–8291	(502) 624–6291 624–1996 624–8291
Army Community Service Lexington-Blue Grass Army Depot ATTN: SDSLB-ASA-ACS Lexington, KY 40511-5010	AMC	745–3649	(606) 293–3649
Louisiana			
HQ 9th Infantry Division (Mech.) and Ft. Polk ATTN: AFZX-PA-FSS ACS Bldg. 420 Fort Polk, LA 71459-5000	FORSCOM	863–2823 863–2840	(318) 535–2823 535–2840
Maryland			
Commander U.S. Army Aberdeen Proving Ground Installation Support Activity ATTN: STEAP-PA-CF-S Bldg. 2485 Aberdeen Proving Ground, MD 21005-5001	AMC	298–7570 298–4372	(301) 278–7570 278–4372

Address	U.S. Command	Military Telephone (AUTOVON)	Commercial Telephone
Army Community Service U.S. Army Garrison, Bldg. 501 ATTN: HSHD-PCA-ACS Fort Detrick Frederick, MD 21701-5000	HSC	343–2452 343–2552	(301) 677–2452 677–2552
Army Community Service ATTN: AFZI-PAF-FSD(ACS) Bldg. 4483 Fort Meade, MD 20755-5078	FORSCOM	923–5590 923–3418	(301) 677–5590 677–3418
Army Community Service ATTN: ASNJ-P-CF-FA Bldg. 351 Fort Ritchie, MD 21719-5010	USAISC	277–5034 277–5100	(301) 878–5034 878–5100
Commander U.S. Army Laboratory Command ATTN: AMSLC-PE-WC (Wellness Center) 2800 Powder Mill Road Adelphi, MD 20783-1145	AMC	290–1037	(202) 394–1037
Massachusetts			
Army Community Service ATTN: AFZD-PCF-FSA Bldg. T-2013 Fort Devens, MA 01433-5000	FORSCOM	256–3023 256–2582 256–3642	(617) 796–3023 796–3528 796–2582
Michigan			
Commander U.S. Army Tank Automotive Command Support Activity ATTN: AMSTA-XYAF Bldg. 945 Selfridge Air National Guard Base, MI 48045-5016	AMC	273–5903 273–5949	(313) 466–5903 466–5949

Address	U.S. Command	Military Telephone (AUTOVON)	Commercial Telephone
Missouri			
Army Community Service Bldg. 315 ATTN: ATZT-PA-CFS-A Fort Leonard Wood, MO 65473-5000	TRADOC	581–1126 581–7613	(314) 368–1126 368–7613
New Jersey			
Army Community Service ATTN: MTE-BY-IOC-F Bldg. 72 Military Ocean Terminal Bayonne, NJ 07002-5301	MTMC	247–5669	(201) 823–5669
Army Community Service USAARDC, Bldg. 3124 ATTN: SMCAR-ISQ-F Dover, NJ 07801-5001	AMC	880–2145 880–4939	(201) 724–2145 724–4939
Army Community Service ATTN: ATZD-GAC-FA Bldg. 6049 Fort Dix, NJ 08640-5130	TRADOC	944–2767 944–2962	(609) 562–2767 562–2962
Army Community Service Bldg. 812, Murphy Drive ATTN: SELHI-CS-FS-ACS Fort Monmouth, NJ 07703-5000	AMC	992–2076	(201) 532–2076
New Mexico			
Army Community Service ATTN: STEWS-DP-AS 105 Twin Cities White Sands Missile Range, NM 88002-5040	AMC	258–6789	(505) 678–6789
New York			
Army Community Service Fort Hamilton, Bldg. 111 ATTN: ATZD-FHB-ACS Brooklyn, NY 11252-5260	TRADOC	232–4332 232–4754	(718) 630–4332 630–4754

Address	U.S. Command	Military Telephone (AUTOVON)	Commercial Telephone
Army Community Service Seneca Army Depot ATTN: SDSSE-PEF Romulus, NY 14541-5001	AMC	489–0388 489–0424	(607) 869–0388 869–0424
Headquarters 10th Mountain Division (Light Infantry) and Fort Drum ATTN: AFZS-PA-FSS Bldg. T-147 Fort Drum, NY 13602-5099	FORSCOM	341–6566	(315) 772–6566
Commander Watervliet Arsenal ATTN: SMCWV-PCC-A Watervliet, NY 12189-4050	AMC	974–5920	(518) 266–5920
North Carolina			
Commander XVIII Airborne Corps & Ft. Bragg ATTN: AFZA-PA-FC-(ACS) Bldg. 4T-1367 Fort Bragg, NC 28307-5000	FORSCOM	236–5521 236–6316 236–8682 236–8410	(919) 396–5521 396–6316 396–8682 396–8401
Oklahoma			
Army Community Service Post Office Box 33097 ATTN: ATZR-PCA Bldg. 922 Fort Sill, OK 73503-0097	TRADOC	639–5018 639–6818 639–6816 639–4916	(405) 351–5018 351–6818 351–6816 351–4916
Commander McAlester Army Ammunition Plant ATTN: SMCMC-ASM McAlester, OK 74501-5000	AMC	956–6780	(918) 421–6780

Address	U.S. Command	Military Telephone (AUTOVON)	Commercial Telephone
Oregon			
Commander U.S. Army Depot Activity Umatilla ATTN: SDSTE-UAI-MS ACS Bldg. 33 Hermiston, OR 97838		790–5295	(503) 567–6421 Ext. 295
Pennsylvania			
Army Community Service Bldg. T-O-1, Room 27 Fort Indiantown Gap Annville, PA 17003-5011	FORSCOM	235–2610	(717) 865–5444 Ext. 2610
Army Community Service ATTN: ATZE-PA-ACS Bldg. 842 Carlisle Barracks, PA 17013-5002	TRADOC	242–4357	(717) 245–4357
Army Community Service Letterkenny Army Depot ATTN: SDSLE-BAF Bldg. 664 Chambersburg, PA 17201-4150	AMC	570–9051	(717) 267–9051
Army Community Service New Cumberland Army Depot ATTN: SDSNC-AA-S New Cumberland, PA 17070-5001	AMC	977–6203 977–7737	(717) 770–6203 770–7737
Army Community Service Tobyhanna Army Depot ATTN: SDSTO-AW-S Tobyhanna, PA 18466-5099	AMC	795–7584	(717) 894–7584
South Carolina			
Army Community Service ATTN: ATZJ-PCA-CFS (ACS) Bldg. 5418 Fort Jackson, SC 29207-5140	TRADOC	734–5256 734–5258	(803) 751–5256 751–5258

Address	U.S. Command	Military Telephone (AUTOVON)	Commercial Telephone
Texas			
Army Community Service ATTN: ATZC-PAC-FA Bldg. 50 Fort Bliss, TX 79916-5116	TRADOC	978–1132 978–3503 978–4614	(915) 568–1132 568–3503 568–4614
Commander Corpus Christi Army Depot Bldg. 1727 Corpus Christi, TX 78419		861–2004 861–2304 861–2259	(512) 939–2004 939–2304 939–2259
Commander III Corps and Fort Hood ATTN: AFZF-PA-FSD-ACS Fort Hood, TX 76544-5056	FORSCOM	737–4936 737–3726	(817) 287–4936 287–3726
Army Community Service ATTN: AFZG-PA-FFCS Bldg. 2797, Stanley Rd. Fort Sam Houston, TX 78234-5000	FORSCOM	471–2418 471–5705 471–4357	(512) 221–2418 221–5705 221–4357
Army Community Service Red River Army Depot ATTN: SDSRR-AN Texarkana, TX 75507-5000	AMC	829–2466	(214) 838–2466
Utah			
Army Community Service ATTN: STEDP-F-S Dugway Proving Ground Dugway, UT 84022-5000	AMC	831–2278	(801) 522–2278
Tooele Army Depot Family Support Branch ATTN: SDSTE-PCCF-F Bldg. 1004 Tooele, UT 84074-5008	AMC	790–7435	(801) 882–7435

Address	U.S. Command	Military Telephone (AUTOVON)	Commercial Telephone
Virginia			
Army Community Service 1169 Middleton Road Fort Belvoir, VA 22060-5023	MDW	354–3965 354–6664 354–6665	(703) 664–3965 664–6664 664–6665
Army Community Service Bldg. 661 Fort Eustis, VA 23604-5114	TRADOC	927–3638 927–5601	(804) 878–3638 878–5601
Army Community Service Bldg. T-12001 Fort Lee, VA 23801-5141	TRADOC	687–5137 687–5165	(804) 734–5137 734–5165
Army Community Service ATTN: ATZG-PAA-FS Bldg. 96 Fort Monroe, VA 23651-6130	TRADOC	680–3878	(804) 727–3878
Army Community Service ATTN: ANPE-CFS-F Bldg. 202 Fort Myer, VA 22211-5050	MDW	222–3510 222–3511	(202) 696–3510 696–3511
Army Community Service ATTN: ATZF-FS-ACS Bldg. 564 Fort Story, VA 23459-5042	TRADOC	438–7311	(804) 422–7311
Army Community Service Vint Hill Farms Station ATTN: IAZP-S Bldg. 200 Warrenton, VA 22186-5070	INSCOM	249–6489 249–6474	(703) 347–6489 347–6474
Washington			
Army Community Service ATTN: AFZH-PAW-C Bldg. 5219 Fort Lewis, WA 98433-5000	FORSCOM	357–7166	(206) 967–7166

Address	U.S. Command	Military Telephone (AUTOVON)	Commercial Telephone
Wisconsin			
Army Community Service Fort McCoy ATTN: AFZR-PAF-ACS Bldg. 1747 Sparta, WI 54656-5000	FORSCOM	280–3505 280–2412	(608) 388–3505 388–2412

DIRECTORY FOR ARMY COMMUNITY SERVICE CENTERS OUTSIDE THE CONTINENTAL UNITED STATES

Address	U.S. Command	Military Telephone (AUTOVON)	Commercial Telephone
Alaska			
Army Community Service (Fort Greely, HQ, 6th Infantry Division AK) ATTN: AFVR-FG-PAH APO Seattle, WA 98733	FORSCOM	317-872-3197	(907) 872–3197
Army Community Service HQ, 6th Infantry Division (Light) ATTN: AFVR-PA-CFA Fort Richardson, AK 99505-5100	FORSCOM	317-862-6218 317-864-1199 317-863-1122	(907) 862–6218 864–1199 863–1122
Army Community Service ATTN: AFZT-FW-PA-ACS Bldg. 4061 Fort Wainwright, AK 99703	FORSCOM	317-353-6369 353-7298	(907) 353–6369 353–7298
Belgium			
Commander NATO/SHAPE (US) USMCA-Belgium ATTN: AERSH-AA APO New York 09088-0015	21 SUPCOM	Mons, Belgium Bldg. 318, Room 222 423–5324 423–4896	

Address	U.S. Command	Military Telephone (AUTOVON)
Commander NATO SUPACT (US) ATTN: ACS APO New York 09667	NATO SUPACT (US)	Brussels, Belgium NATO SUPACT (US) Civ. (02720–) 9015
Commander 294th USA Arty Grp. ATTN: ACS APO New York 09345	294th Arty Grp.	Flensburg, Belgium Apt 14 Flensburg Gov't Hsg Civ. (04761–) 93960

England

| Commander
47th Area Spt. Grp.
ATTN: ACS Center
APO New York 09075-0015 | 21 SUPCOM | Warrington, UK
Buttonwood Army Depot
Headquarters Bldg.
AV 243–1203
243–1354 |

Germany

Commander, Military Subcommunity Amberg ATTN: ACS Center APO New York 09452-0015	7th ATC	Pond Barracks Bldg. 6, Room 107 476–5790
Commander, Military Community Ansbach ATTN: ACS Center APO New York 09177-0015	VII Corps	Bleidorn Housing Center 468–7844 468–7674
Commander, Military Community Aschaffenburg ATTN: ACS Center APO New York 09162-0015	VII Corps	Jaeger Kaserne Bldg. 26, Room 212 323–7165 323–8840
Commander, Military Community Augsburg ATTN: ACS Center APO New York 09178-0015	VII Corps	Sheridan Kaserne Bldg. 102, Room 204/206 434–6300 434–7306

Address	U.S. Command	Military Telephone (AUTOVON)
Commander, Military Subcommunity Babenhausen ATTN: ACS Center APO New York 09455-0015	V Corps	Babenhausen Kaserne Bldg. 4501 348–3–847 348–3–647
Commander, Military Subcommunity Bad Hersfeld ATTN: ACS Center APO New York 09141-0015	V Corps	Sub Post Bldg. 6449, Basement 321–5–882
Commander, Military Subcommunity Bad Kissingen ATTN: ACS Center APO New York 09330-0015	VII Corps	Daley Barracks Bldg. 82 354–2–670 354–2–725
Commander, Military Community 53d ASG, Bad Kreuznach ATTN: ACS Center APO New York 09252	V Corps	Family Housing Area Bldg. 5610 (Basement) "C Stairwell" 490–6482 490–7107
Commander, Military Community Bad Toelz ATTN: ACS Center APO New York 09050-0015	VII Corps	Flint Kaserne Bldg. 1 441–4866 441–4705
Commander, Military Community Bamberg ATTN: ACS Center APO New York 09139-0015	VII Corps	Warner Barracks Bldg. 17029, Room 117 469–8795 469–7793
Commander, Military Community Baumholder ATTN: ACS Center APO New York 09034-0015	V Corps	HD Smith Barracks Bldg. 8746, 2nd Floor 485–6604 485–7196

Address	U.S. Command	Military Telephone (AUTOVON)
Commander, Military Community US Army Berlin ATTN: AEBA-GA-ACS APO New York 09742	Berlin	Berlin, W-Germany Truman Plaza 332–6585 332–6500
Commander, Military Subcommunity Bindlach/Bayreuth ATTN: ACS Center APO New York 09411-0015	7th ATC	Christiansen Kaserne Bldg. 9246 462–3606
Commander, Military Subcommunity Boeblingen-Sindelfingen ATTN: ACS Center APO New York 09046-0015	VII Corps	Panzer Barracks Bldg. 2468 431–2–695 431–2–524
Commander, Military Subcommunity Buedingen ATTN: ACS Center APO New York 09076-0015	V Corps	Armstrong Barracks Bldg. 2309 321–4–786 321–4–804
Commander, Military Subcommunity Butzbach ATTN: ACS Center APO New York 09077-0015	V Corps	Schloss Kaserne Bldg. 4129 343–2–759
Commander, Military Subcommunity Crailsheim ATTN: ACS Center APO New York 09751-0015	VII Corps	McKee Barracks Bldg. 54 420–3–534
Commander, Military Community Darmstadt ATTN: ACS Center APO New York 09175-0015	V Corps	Cambrai-Fritsch Kaserne Bldg. 4501, Room 223 348–6472 348–8411

Address	U.S. Command	Military Telephone (AUTOVON)
Commander, Military Subcommunity Dexheim ATTN: ACS Center APO New York 09111-0015	V Corps	Dexheim Housing Area Bldg. 6449 (Basement) 334–852
Commander, Military Subcommunity Erlangen ATTN: ACS Center APO New York 09066-0015	VII Corps	Ferris Barracks Bldg. 4022, Room 1 464–3–800
Commander, Military Community Frankfurt ATTN: ACS Center APO New York 09710-0015	V Corps	132 Hansa Allee Main Building 320–7443 320–7428
Commander, Military Subcommunity Friedberg ATTN: ACS Center APO New York 09074-0015	V Corps	Bad Nauheim Housing Bldg. 5618, Upstairs 324–8065
Commander, Military Community Fulda ATTN: ACS Center APO New York 09146-0015	V Corps	27 Haimbachstrasse Karmann House 321–3–687 321–3–838
Commander, Military Community Garmish ATTN: ACS Center APO New York 09053-0015	VII Corps	Breitenau Hsg Area Bldg. 723 440–2–777 440–2–477
Commander, Military Subcommunity Gelnhausen ATTN: ACS Center APO New York 09091-0015	V Corps	Coleman Village Bldg. 1824 A 321–2–790

Address	U.S. Command	Military Telephone (AUTOVON)
Commander, Military Subcommunity Germersheim ATTN: ACS Center APO New York 09095-0015	21 SUPCOM	Germersheim Army Depot Bldg. 7859 378–546 378–700
Commander, Military Community Giessen ATTN: ACS Center APO New York 09169-0015	V Corps	Pendleton Bks. Bldg. 503 (2nd floor over mess hall) 343–7135 343–6647
Commander, Military Community Goeppingen ATTN: ACS Center APO New York 09454-0015	VII Corps	Cooke Barracks Bldg. 150 425–3832
Commander, Military Subcommunity Grafenwoehr ATTN: ACS Center APO New York 09114-0015	7th ATC	Grafenwoehr Bldg. 215 475–8371 475–7115
Commander, Military Community Hanau ATTN: ACS Center APO New York 09165-0015	V Corps	Pioneer Kaserne Bldg. 4, 1st Floor, Room 133 322–8093 322–8828
Commander, Military Community Heidelberg ATTN: AEUSG-PE-SA APO New York 09102-0015	26th SUPGP	Heidelberg Shopping Center Bldg. 2860 370–6975 370–8141
Commander, Military Community Heilbronn ATTN: ACS Center APO New York 09176-0015	VII Corps	Wharton Barracks Bldg. 12 426–2454 426–2666

Address	U.S. Command	Military Telephone (AUTOVON)
Commander, Military Subcommunity Herbornseelbach ATTN: ACS Center APO New York 09169-0015	V Corps	22 Leipziger Strasse Herborn Installation Complex Phone through Giessen ACS
Commander, Military Subcommunity Herzo Base ATTN: ACS Center APO New York 09352-0015	VII Corps	Herzo Base Bldg. 1616 465–3–871 465–3–614
Commander, Military Subcommunity Hohenfels ATTN: ACS Center APO New York 09173-0015	7th ATC	Hohenfels Bldg. 83 466–286 466–208
Commander, Military Subcommunity Illesheim ATTN: ACS Center APO New York 09140-0015	VII Corps	Stork Barracks Bldg. 6508 467–547
Commander, 29th Area Support Group Kaiserslautern ATTN: AERAS-CS-V APO New York 09054-0015	21 SUPCOM	Vogelweh Kaserne Bldg. 1044 489–7521 489–6476
Commander, Military Community Karlsruhe ATTN: AERQ-AC APO New York 09164-0015	21 SUPCOM	Smiley Barracks Bldg. 9261, Room 315 376–6542 376–7142
Commander, Military Subcommunity Kitzingen ATTN: ACS Center APO New York 09031-0015	VII Corps	Harvey Barracks Bldg. 141, Room 3 355–8513

Address	U.S. Command	Military Telephone (AUTOVON)
Commander, LARMC Landstuhl ATTN: ACS Center, Box 51 APO New York 09180-0015	21 SUPCOM	Landstuhl Army Medical Center Bldg. 3705, Room 213 486–8221 486–7162
Commander, Military Subcommunity Ludwigsburg-Kornwestheim ATTN: ACS Center APO New York 09107-0015	VII Corps	Pattonville Hsg Area Bldg. 942, Room 222 428–2–681
Commander, Military Community Mainz ATTN: ACS Center APO New York 09185-0015	V Corps	Dragonner Kaserne Headquarters Bldg. 6653 334–7144 334–8552
Commander, Military Community Mannheim ATTN: AERM-AC APO New York 09086-0015	21 SUPCOM	Benjamin Franklin Village Bldg. 255 380–6240 380–8180
Commander, USA SPT GRP Norddeutschland ATTN: AERAN-D-B APO New York 09069-0015	21 SUPCOM	U.S. Army Hospital Bldg. 662 342–7640 342–7701
Commander, Military Subcommunity Nuernburg ATTN: ACS Center APO New York 09093-0015	VII Corps	Merrell Barracks Bldg. 5256 2625–746 2625–897
Commander, Military Subcommunity Miesau ATTN: AERZM-ACS APO New York 09059-0015	21 SUPCOM	Miesau Army Depot Bldg. 1354 486–3–753 486–3–877

Address	U.S. Command	Military Telephone (AUTOVON)
Commander, Military Subcommunity Moehringen/Degerloch ATTN: ACS Center APO New York 09107-0015	VII Corps	Kelley Barracks Bldg. 3312 4212–600
Commander, Military Subcommunity Muenster ATTN: ACS Center APO New York 09078-0015	V Corps	Handorf Community Center Civ 0251–394255 Civ 0251–324572
Commander, Military Community Munich ATTN: ACS Center APO New York 09407-0015	VII Corps	McGraw Kaserne Bldg. 397A, Room 121 440–6343 440–7268
Commander, Military Subcommunity Nellingen/Esslingen ATTN: ACS Center APO New York 09061-0015	VII Corps	Nellingen Barracks Bldg. 3500 421–6415 421–7216
Commander, Military Community Nuernberg-Fuerth ATTN: ACS Center APO New York 09696-0015	VII Corps	W.O. Darby Kaserne Balbeiberstr. 17 Bldg. 90 460–7052
Commander, Military Community Neu Ulm ATTN: ACS Center APO New York 09035-0015	VII Corps	Wiley Kaserne Bldg. 208 427–6106
Commander Neubruecke Subcommunity ATTN: ACS Center APO New York 09305-0015	V Corps	Neubruecke Kaserne Bldg. 9920, Room 100B 493–7119

Address	U.S. Command	Military Telephone (AUTOVON)
Commander, Military Subcommunity Osterholz-Scharmbeck ATTN: ACS Center APO New York 09355-0015	21 SUPCOM	Community Center Am Pumleberg, 2860 O/S Civ (04791–)8881
Commander, Military Community Pirmasens ATTN: AERP-PS APO New York 09189-0015	21 SUPCOM	Husterhoeh Kaserne Bldg. 4624 495–7202
Commander, Military Subcommunity Regensburg ATTN: ACS Center APO New York 09173-0015	7th ATC	Pioneer Kaserne Bldg. 5 471–3
Commander USMCA Rheinberg ATTN: AERV-PG APO New York 09712		Reichel Bldg. 5th Floor Civ (02843–)70685/ 70686/70687
Commander, Military Subcommunity Schwabach ATTN: ACS Center APO New York 09142-0015	VII Corps	O'Brien Barracks Bldg. 1036 (Basement) 463–3–727
Commander, Military Subcommunity Schwaebisch-Gmuend ATTN: ACS Center APO New York 09281-0015	VII Corps	Bismark Kaserne Bldg. 526 427–733
Commander, Military Subcommunity Schwaebisch Hall ATTN: ACS Center APO New York 09025-0015	VII Corps	Dolan Barracks Bldg. 306, Room 106 426–560

Address	U.S. Command	Military Telephone (AUTOVON)
Commander, Military Community Schweinfurt ATTN: ACS Center APO New York 09033-0015	VII Corps	Ledward Barracks Bldg. 242 354–7186
Commander Strassburg Subcommunity ATTN: ACS Center APO New York 09322-0015	V Corps	Strassburg Kaserne Bldg. 9034 492–6919
Commander, Military Subcommunity Vaihingen ATTN: ACS Center APO New York 09131-0015	VII Corps	Patch Barracks Bldg. 2307, Room 116 430–7270 430–5674
Commander, Military Subcommunity Vilseck ATTN: ACS Center APO New York 09112-0015	7th ATC	Vilseck ACS Center 476–2650 476–2733
Commander Weirhof Military Subcommunity APO New York 09058-0015	21 SUPCOM	Weirhof Family Housing Bldg. 3989 491–2–801
Commander, Military Subcommunity Wertheim ATTN: ACS Center APO New York 09047-0015	VII Corps	Peden Barracks Bldg. 3 355–5–667
Commander USMCA Wiesbaden ATTN: AETV-WSB-ACS APO New York 09457-0015	V Corps	Hainerberg Hsg Area Bldg. 07790 337–5611 337–5754 337–5034

Address	U.S. Command	Military Telephone (AUTOVON)
Commander, Military Community Wildflecken ATTN: AETV-WFL-CS APO New York 09026-0015	V Corps	Wildflecken Garrison Bldg. 143 (DPCA) E Street, Room 105 326–3–558 326–3–951
Commander, Military Community Worms ATTN: AERWP-CS APO New York 09058-0015	21 SUPCOM	Takkunen Barracks Bldg. 5829 383–7546 383–7790
Commander, Military Community Wuerzburg ATTN: Chief FSD APO New York 09801-0015	VII Corps	Faulenburg Kaserne Bldg. 258, Room 102 350–6337 350–2321
Commander, Military Community Zweibruecken ATTN: AERZP-DS APO New York 09052-0015	21 SUPCOM	Kreuzberg Kaserne Bldg. 4011 494–7224 494–6586 Ext. 62
Commander, Military Subcommunity Zuffenhausen/Bad Cannstatt ATTN: ACS Center APO New York 09154-0015		Robinson Barracks Bldg. 132, Room 356 422–2–6046 422–2–7110

Hawaii				*Commercial Telephone*
Army Community Service, SB ATTN: APZV-PAF-FA Schofield Barracks, HI 96857-5000	USARPAC	455–4663	(808) 655–4663	
Army Community Service, USASCH ATTN: APZV-PAF-FA Bldg. 513-F Schofield Barracks, HI 96857-5000	USARPAC	455–4861	(808) 655–4861	

Address	U.S. Command	Military Telephone (AUTOVON)	Commercial Telephone
Army Community Service, FS ATTN: APZV-PAF-FA Bldg. 330 Fort Shafter, HI 96858-5000	USARPAC	438–9285	(808) 438–9285
Army Community Service Aliamanu Military Reservation ATTN: APZV-PAF-FA Fort Shafter, HI 96858-5000	USARPAC		(808) 833–2342

Italy

Commander, 22nd Area Spt. Grp. (PROV) ATTN: AESE-KVPF-A APO New York 09221-0015	SETAF	Vicenza, Italy Caserma Ederle, Bldg. 108 633–7500	
Commander, 8th Support Group ATTN: AESE-LI-PAC APO New York 09019-0015	SETAF	Livorno, Italy Camp Darby, Bldg. 730 633–7814 633–7620	

Japan

Headquarters 9th Area Spt. Grp. (Prov) Army Community Service ATTN: AJGH-PA-CFAC APO San Francisco 96343-0064	USARJ	Camp Zama 0462–51–1520 Ext. 223–4357 Ext. 223–3557	
Army Community Service 10th ASG (Prov) (USAGO) Bldg. 236 Torii Station ATTN: DPCA-AJGO-A-FS APO San Francisco 96331-0008	USARJ	1–011–8198938–112 Ext. 631–4378 Ext. 631–4385 Ext. 631–4743 Torii Station	

Korea

Army Community Service 2nd Infantry Division ATTN: EAIDDC-ACS (Camp Casey) APO San Francisco 96224-0289		733–3846 733–3866	299–3846 299–3866

Address	U.S. Command	Military Telephone (AUTOVON)	Commercial Telephone
Army Community Service 34th Support Group (Camp Hialeah) ATTN: EANC-P-DPCA (Pusan; Hialeah Compound) APO San Francisco 96259-0260		754–3846 754–3577	263–3224 263–3577
Army Community Service 20th Support Group ATTN: EANC-T-DPCA (Camp Henry) APO San Francisco 96218-0171		753–7112 753–7951	268–7112 268–7951
Army Community Service 501st Support Group, Yongsan ATTN: EAGY-DPCA-ACS APO San Francisco 96301-0076		738–3007 738–4655	298–3007 298–4655
Army Community Service 23rd Support Group ATTN: EANC-HG-PAACS APO San Francisco 96271-0164		756–8402 756–8401 (Camp Humphreys)	253–8402 253–8401
Commander Combined Field Army ATTN: CFAR-ST (Camp Red Cloud) APO San Francisco 96358		299–6034 299–6046	

The Netherlands

Address	U.S. Command	Military Telephone (AUTOVON)	Commercial Telephone
Commander, Military Subcommunity USMCA The Netherlands ATTN: AERAN-AA APO New York 09011-0015	21 SUPCOM	Brunssum, NL Schinnen Mine Complex Bldg. T-8 360–3–4141–153 360–3–4141–231	
Commander, CEBNW ATTN: ACS APO New York 09292	21 SUPCOM	Coevorden The Netherlands	
Commander, MTMC/TTCE Rotterdam ATTN: ACS APO New York 09292	21 SUPCOM	Capelle a/d ljffel The Netherlands Civ (010–) 581911 Ext. 458	

Address	U.S. Command	Military Telephone (AUTOVON)	Commercial Telephone
Commander, 8th USAFAD Steenwijk ATTN: ACS APO New York 09292	21 SUPCOM	Steenwijk The Netherlands Civ (05210–) 15422 Ext. 4	
Commander, 23d USAFAD t'Harde ATTN: ACS APO New York 09292	21 SUPCOM	t'Harde The Netherlands CQ Bldg. Civ (05255–) 27272440	

Panama

Address	U.S. Command	Military Telephone (AUTOVON)	Commercial Telephone
Army Community Service 193d Inf Bde (Panama) (Pacific) ATTN: AFZU-PCS APO Miami 34004-5000	FORSCOM	313–287–6169 313–287–3804	
Army Community Service 193d Inf Bde (Panama) (Atlantic) ATTN: SOGA-PCF-FA Bldg. 8348 APO Miami 34005-5000	FORSCOM	313–289–4206	

Puerto Rico

Address	U.S. Command	Military Telephone (AUTOVON)	Commercial Telephone
Commander HQ Fort Buchanan ATTN: AFZK-B-PA-FS-CS Fort Buchanan, PR 00934-5007	FORSCOM	740–8285 740–2218	(809) 783–8285 783–2218

DIRECTORY FOR AIR FORCE FAMILY SUPPORT AND SERVICE CENTERS INSIDE THE CONTINENTAL UNITED STATES

Address	Military Telephone (AUTOVON)	Commercial Telephone
Family Service Center 443 ABG/FS Altus AFB, OK 73523-5065	866–6761	(405) 481–6761

Address	Military Telephone (AUTOVON)	Commercial Telephone
Family Service Center 76 ABG/DPE Andrews AFB Washington, DC 20331-5000	858–7581	(301) 981–7581
Family Service Center 2 CSG/DPE Barksdale AFB, LA 71110-5000	781–3331	(318) 456–3331
Family Service Center 100 CSG/DPE Beale AFB, CA 95903-5000	368–2294	(916) 634–2294
Family Service Center 67 CSG/FS Bergstrom AFB, TX 78743-5000	685–2244 685–2252	(512) 479–2244
Family Service Center 97 CSG/DPE Blytheville AFB, AR 72315-5000	637–7522	(501) 762–7522
Family Service Center 1100 ABG/FSS Bolling AFB Washington, DC 20332-5000	297–6280 297–6281	(202) 767–6280 767–6281
Family Service Center 6670 ABG/DPE Brooks AFB, TX 78235-5000	240–2533	(512) 536–2533
Family Service Center 27 CSG/FS Cannon AFB, NM 88103-4428	681–4228	(505) 784–4228
Family Service Center 7 CSG/DPMA Carswell AFB, TX 76127-5065	739–7877	(817) 735–7877
Family Service Center 93 CSG/DPE Castle AFB, CA 95342-5000	347–2131	(209) 726–2131

Address	Military Telephone (AUTOVON)	Commercial Telephone
Family Support Center 3345 ABG/FS Chanute AFB, IL 61868-5000	862–3204	
Family Service Center 437 ABG/MAP Charleston AFB, SC 29404-5000	553–3146	(803) 544–3146
Family Service Center 14 ABG/DPE Columbus AFB, MS 39701-5000	742–4595	(601) 434–4595
Family Service Center 836 CSG/FS Davis-Monthan AFB, AZ 85707-5000	361–4024	(602) 748–4024
Family Support Center 436 ABG/FS Dover AFB, DE 19902-5000	455–6178	
Family Service Center 355 CSG/DPE Duluth, MN 55814-5000	825–2490	(218) 727–8211
Family Service Center 96 CSG/DPE Dyess AFB, TX 79607-5000	461–2409	(915) 696–2409
Family Service Center 6510 ABG/FS Edwards AFB, CA 93523-5000	527–0723	(805) 277–0723
Family Service Center 3201 ABG/DPE Eglin AFB, FL 32542-5000	872–2893	(904) 882–2893
Family Service Center 44 CSG/FS Ellsworth AFB, SD 57706-5000	747–2830	(605) 399–2830
Family Service Center 23 CSG/FS England AFB, LA 71311-5000	683–2359 683–2360	(318) 448–2359 448–2360

Address	Military Telephone (AUTOVON)	Commercial Telephone
Family Service Center 92 CSG/FS Fairchild AFB, WA 99011-5000	352–2246	(509) 247–2246
Family Service Center 35 CSG/DPE George AFB, CA 92392-5000	353–3375 353–2618	(619) 269–3375 269–2618
Family Service Center 3480 ABG/DPE/FS Goodfellow AFB, TX 76903-5000	477–3425	(915) 653–3425
Family Service Center 321 CSG/DPE Grand Forks AFB, ND 58205-5000	362–6221	(701) 594–6221
Family Service Center 416 CSG/DPE Griffiss AFB, NY 13441-5000	587–2031	(315) 330–2031
Family Service Center 305 CSG/DPE Grissom AFB, IN 46971-5000	928–2476	(317) 689–2476
Family Service Center Bldg. 823 Gunter AFB, AL 36114-5000	446–3222	(205) 279–3222
Family Support Center 3245 ABG/FS Hanscom AFB, MA 01731-5000	478–3436	(617) 861–3436
Family Support Center 2849 ABG/FS Hill AFB, UT 84056-5000	458–4681 458–4682	
Family Service Center 49 CSG/DPE Holloman AFB, NM 88330-5000	867–3944 867–3454	(505) 479–3944

Address	Military Telephone (AUTOVON)	Commercial Telephone
Family Service Center 31 CSG/DPE Homestead AFB, FL 33039-5000	791–8878	(305) 257–8878
Family Service Center 834 CSG/DPE Hurlburt Field, FL 32544-5000	872–6201	(904) 884–6201
Family Service Center 3380 MSSQ/FS Keesler AFB, MS 39534-5000	868–3063	(601) 377–3063
Family Support Center 2851 ABG/FSS Kelly AFB, TX 78241-5000	945–6419 945–3546	
Family Service Center 1606 ABW/FS Kirtland AFB, NM 87117-5000	246–0741 246–0751	(505) 844–0741 844–0751
Family Service Center (707) 482-2411 Klamath AFB Requa, CA 95561-5000		
Family Service Center 3700 ABG/FS Bldg. 2110 Lackland AFB, TX 78236-5000	473–2593	(512) 671–4858 671–4875
1st Combat Spt. Apt/DPMAPF Family Services 4500 ABG/DPE Langley AFB, VA 23665-5065	574–4858 574–4875	(703) 764–7526
Family Support Center 47 ABG/FS Laughlin AFB, TX 78843-5000	732–5222	
Family Service Center 314 CSG/FS Little Rock AFB, AR 72076-5000	731–6801	(501) 988–1252

Address	Military Telephone (AUTOVON)	Commercial Telephone
Family Service Center 42 CSG/DPE Loring AFB, ME 04750-5000	920–6100	(207) 999–6100
Family Service Center 6592 ABG/FS Los Angeles, CA 90009-2960	833–1121 833–1122 833–1123	
Family Support Center 3415 ABG/FS Lowry AFB, CO 80230-5000	926–2207 926–2208	(303) 370–2207
Family Support Center 832 ABG/FS Luke AFB, AZ 85309-5000	853–6362 853–6841 853–6378	
Family Service Center 56 CSG/HC MacDill AFB, FL 33608-5000	968–3621	(813) 830–3621
Family Service Center 341 CSG/DPE Malmstrom AFB, MT 59402-5000	632–3686	(406) 731–3686
Family Service Center 22 CSG/DPE March AFB, CA 92518-5000	947–3686	(714) 655–3686
Family Support Center 323 ABG/FS Mather AFB, CA 95655-5000	828–4357	
Family Support Center 3800 ABW/FS Maxwell AFB, AL 36112-5000	875–2353 875–6469 875–6425 875–5015	
Family Service Center 62 ABG/DPE McChord AFB, WA 98438-5000	976–2813	(206) 984–2813

Address	Military Telephone (AUTOVON)	Commercial Telephone
Family Service Center 2852 ABG/FSS McClellan AFB, CA 95652-5000	633–3815	(916) 643–3815
Family Service Center 381 CSG/DPE McConnell AFB, KS 67221-5000	743–5027	(316) 681–5027
Family Support Center 438 ABG/FS McGuire AFB, NJ 08641-5000	440–3086 440–2258	
Family Service Center (701) 727–2471 91 CSG/DPE Minot AFB, ND 58701-5000		
Family Support Center 347 MSS/FS Moody AFB, GA 31699-5000	460–3333	(912) 333–3068
Family Service Center 366 CSG/FSS Mountain Home AFB, ID 83648-5000	857–2458	(208) 828–2458
Family Service Center 364 CSG/DPE Myrtle Beach AFB, SC 29577-5000	748–7857	(803) 448–7857
Family Support Center 554 CSG/FSS Nellis AFB, NV 89191-5000	682–3327	
Family Service Center 63 ABG/DPE Norton AFB, CA 92409-5000	876–7137	(714) 382–7137
Family Support Center 3902 ABW/FSS Offutt AFB, NE 68113-5000	271–4329	

Address	Military Telephone (AUTOVON)	Commercial Telephone
Family Service Center 6550 ABG/DPMAP-FSS Patrick AFB, FL 32925-5000	854–4907	(305) 494–4907
Family Service Center CSG/DPMAP-FSS Pease AFB, NH 03801-5000	852–3330	(603) 436–3330
Family Support Center 380 MSS/MFS Plattsburgh AFB, NY 12903-5000	689–7512 689–7389	
Family Service Center 317 CSG/FS Pope AFB, NC 28308-5000	486–2147	(919) 394–2147
Family Service Center 12 ABG/DPMAPF Randolph AFB, TX 78148-5000	487–3060 487–2908	(512) 652–3060 652–2908
Family Service Center 64 FTW/DPMAPF Stop 33 Reese AFB, TX 79489-5000	838–3305 838–3306	(806) 885–3305 885–3333
Family Service Center 2853 ABG/DPE Robins AFB, GA 31098-5000	468–3454 468–6648	(912) 926–3454 926–3466
Family Service Center 410 CSG/DPE K.I. Sawyer AFB, MI 49843-5000	472–2366	(906) 346–2366
Family Support Center HQ AFCC/MPPFR Scott AFB, IL 62225-5000	638–6632 638–6633	
Family Service Center 4 CSG/DPE Seymour Johnson AFB, NC 27530-5000	488–5484	(919) 736–5484

Address	Military Telephone (AUTOVON)	Commercial Telephone
Family Service Center 363 CSG/DPE Shaw AFB, SC 29152-5000	965–3533	(806) 668–3533
Family Support Center 3750 ABG/FSS Sheppard AFB, TX 73145-5000	736–4257	
Family Support Center 46 AERODW/FSS 1033 Space Spt. Grp/FS Peterson AFB, CO 80914-5000	692–3585 692–5378	
Family Service Center 2854 ABG/FS Tinker AFB, OK 73145-5000	339–2747 339–2417	(405) 339–2747 339–2417
Family Support Center 60 ABG/FSS Travis AFB, CA 94535-5000	837–2486	
Family Service Center Bldg. 6556 USAF Academy, CO 80840-5000	259–3595	(303) 472–3595
Family Service Center 71 ABG/DMMAP/FS Vance AFB, OK 73705-5000	962–7322	(405) 249–7322
Family Service Center 4392 AEROSG/FS Vandenberg AFB, CA 93437-5000	276–0037 276–0039	(805) 866–0037
Family Service Center 90 CSG/DPE F.E. Warren AFB, WY 82001-5000	481–3739	(307) 775–3739
Family Service Center 351 CSG/DPMAP-FS Whiteman AFB, MO 65305-5000	975–3498	(816) 687–3498
Family Service Center 82 ABG/DPE Williams AFB, AZ 85224-5000	474–5284	(602) 988–5284

Address	Military Telephone (AUTOVON)	Commercial Telephone
Family Service Center 2750 ABW/DPMAPF Wright-Patterson AFB, OH 45433-5000	787–3592	(513) 257–3592
Family Service Center 379 CSG/DPE Wurtsmith AFB, MI 48753-5000	623–2054	(517) 747–2054

DIRECTORY FOR AIR FORCE FAMILY SUPPORT AND SERVICE CENTERS OUTSIDE THE CONTINENTAL UNITED STATES

Address	Military Telephone (AUTOVON)
Alaska	
Family Support Center 343 CSG/FSS Eielson AFB, AK APO Seattle 99702-5000	377–3103 377–2178
Family Support Center 21 ABG/FSS Elmendorf AFB, AK 99508-5000	812–522–4133
Crete	
Family Service Center Iraklion Air Station APO New York 09291-5000	314–668–3561
England	
Family Support Center 10 CSG/FSS RAF Alconbury, UK APO New York 09238-5000	223–2280

Address	Military Telephone (AUTOVON)
Family Service Center CSG/DPE RAF Bentwaters, UK APO New York 09755-5000	225–2191
Family Service Center 7274 ABG/DPE RAF Chicksands, UK APO New York 09193-5000	314–234–1110
Family Service Center Bldg. 68 RAF Greenham Common, UK APO New York 09150-5000	
Family Service Center Bldg. 201 High Wycombe Air Station, UK APO New York 09241-5000	232–2238 232–2138
Family Support Center 48 CSG/FSS RAF Lakenheath, UK APO New York 09179-5000	226–7491 226–7013
Family Service Center 513 CSG/DPE RAF Mildenhall, UK APO New York 09127-5000	222–2105
Family Support Center 20 CSG/FSS RAF Upper Heyford, UK APO New York 09194-5000	263–4894
Family Service Center RAF Wethersfield, UK APO New York 09120-5000	231–2299

Germany

Family Service Center Det. 3 81st TFW Ahlhorn AB, GE APO New York 09069	771–8700

Address	Military Telephone (AUTOVON)
Family Support Center 36 CSG/FS Bitburg AB, GE APO New York 09132-5000	453–7491
Family Service Center 50 CSG/DPE Hahn AB, GE APO New York 09109-5000	06543–5–7036
Family Service Center Lindsey AS, GE APO New York 09633-5000	472–6285
Family Service Center Neubrucke, GE APO New York 09305-5000	
Family Service Center 86 CSG/DPE Ramstein AB, GE APO New York 09012-5000	480–7287
Family Service Center 51st Combat Spt. Grp. (PACAF) Bldg. 782 APO San Francisco 96570	284–5440 284–5226 284–5344 284–6496
Family Support Center 435 CSG/FSS Rhein-Main AB, GE APO New York 09057-5000	330–6379 330–7992
Family Service Center 601 CSG/DPE Sembach AB, GE APO New York 09130-5000	427–7191
Family Service Center 52 CSG/DPE Spangdahlem AB, GE APO New York 09123-5000	454–6143

Address	Military Telephone (AUTOVON)
Family Support Center 7350 ABG/DPMAP-FS APO New York 09611-5000	442–5191
Family Support Center 26 CSG/FSS Zweibrucken AB, GE APO New York 09860-5000	498–2567
Greece	
Family Service Center 7206 ABG/DPE Hellenikon AB, GR APO New York 09223-5000	662–5464
Hawaii	
Family Support Center 15 ABW/FS Hickam AFB, HI 96853-5000	449–2494
Italy	
Family Service Center 40 CSS/DPE Aviano AB, IT APO New York 09293-5000	632–2598
Family Service Center 7275 ABG/FS San Vito Dei Normanni AS, IT APO New York 09240-5000	622–3563
Family Support Center 487 CSG/FS Comiso AS (Sicily) APO New York 09694	628–7999
Japan	
Family Support Center 18 CSW/FSS Kadena AB, Japan APO San Francisco 96239-5000	315–630–110 Ext. 42171 Ext. 42172

Address	Military Telephone (AUTOVON)
Family Service Center 6112 ABG/FSS Misawa AB, Japan APO San Francisco 96519-5000	266–4735 266–4569
Family Support Center 475 ABW/FSS Yokota AB, Japan APO San Francisco 96328-5000	248–1101 Ext. 8725 Ext. 8749

The Netherlands

Family Service Center
Cp New Amsterdam
APO New York 09292-5000

Norway

Family Service Center
AF Complex Oslo
APO New York 09085-5000

Panama

Family Service Center   313–84–3968
24 CSG/DPMAPFS
Howard AFB
APO Miami 34001-5000

Philippines

Family Support Center   822–1101
3 CSG/FSS   Ext. 46283
Clark AB, Philippines
APO San Francisco 96274-5000

Portugal

Family Support Center   723–1410
1605 ABG/FS   Ext. 4138
Lajes Field, Azores, Portugal   Ext. 2312
APO New York 09406-5000

Address	Military Telephone (AUTOVON)
Spain	
Family Service Center 401 CSG/DPE Torrejon AB, SP APO New York 09283-5000	723–7234
Family Service Center 406 CSG/DPE Zaragoza AB, SP APO New York 09286-5000	742–2169
Turkey	
Family Service Center Bldg.-Downtown Ankara, TK APO New York 09254-5000	672–3124
Family Support Center 39th CSS/FSS (USAFE) Incirlik, TK APO New York 09289-5000	676–6755 676–6516
Family Service Center Bldg. 12 Izmir, TK APO New York 09224-5000	

DIRECTORY FOR COAST GUARD COMMUNITY SUPPORT CENTERS

Address	Commercial Telephone
Community Support Center U.S. Coast Guard Airstation Cape Cod(p) Otis ANGB, MA 02542	(617) 968–5342
Community Support Center Building 866 Governors Island New York, NY 10004-5097	(212) 668–6444

Address	Commercial Telephone
Community Support Center U.S. Coast Guard Training Center Cape May, NJ 08204	(609) 884–6925
Community Support Center Greater Antilles Section c/o Coast Guard Base San Juan, PR 00903	(809) 722–5500 Ext. 241
Community Support Center Aviation Training Center Mobile, AL 36608	(205) 476–4690
Community Support Center U.S. Coast Guard Training Center Petaluma, CA 94952	(707) 778–2318
Community Support Center U.S. Coast Guard Support Center P.O. Box 14 Kodiak, AK 99619	(907) 487–5542

DIRECTORY FOR NAVY FAMILY SERVICE CENTERS INSIDE THE CONTINENTAL UNITED STATES

Address	Military Telephone (AUTOVON)	Commercial Telephone
Family Service Center U.S. Naval Air Station Alameda, CA 94501	686–4111 686–4112	(415) 869–4111 869–4112
Family Service Center U.S. Naval Air Station, Code 13 Lemoore, CA 93246-5001	949–3456 949–3457	(209) 998–3456 998–3457
Family Service Center U.S. Naval Station, Code 11 Long Beach, CA 90822	360–6126	(213) 547–6126 547–8220

Address	Military Telephone (AUTOVON)	Commercial Telephone
Family Service Center Naval Post Graduate School, Code 008 Monterey, CA 93943-5100	878–3211 878–2524	(408) 646–3211 646–2524
Family Service Center Naval Air Station Miramar, Code 230 San Diego, CA 92145	959–2746	(619) 271–2746
Family Service Center Naval Air Station Moffett Field, CA 94035	462–4912	(415) 966–4912
Family Service Center U.S. Naval Construction Battalion Center Port Hueneme, CA 93043	360–4885	(805) 982–4885
Family Service Center Naval Air Station, Code 6800 Point Mugu, CA 93042	351–8351	(805) 982–8351
Taylor-Leavor Family Service Center U.S. Naval Station Norman Scott Rd. San Diego, CA 92136	958–4706 958–4707	(619) 235–4706 235–4707
Family Service Center U.S. Naval Station North Island San Diego, CA 92135-5000	951–6693	(619) 437–6693
Family Service Center Naval Submarine Base 140 Sylvester Rd., Bldg. 212 San Diego, CA 92106	933–1434	(619) 221–1434

Address	Military Telephone (AUTOVON)	Commercial Telephone
Family Service Center Area Coordinator COMNAVBASE, Code 017 937 North Harbor Dr. San Diego, CA 92132	958–3111	(619) 235–3111
Family Service Center Naval Station Treasure Island San Francisco, CA 94130-5003	869–5789	(415) 765–5789
Family Service Center Naval Support Activity Mare Island, Code 70 Vallejo, CA 94592-5000	253–2527	(707) 646–2527
Family Service Center U.S. Naval Submarine Base New London Groton, CT 06349-5000	241–3383	(203) 449–3383
Family Service Center Enterprise Hall, Bldg. 72 Anacostia Naval Station Washington, DC 20374	288–6150	(202) 433–6150
Family Service Center U.S. Naval Air Station Cecil Field, FL 32215	860–5194 860–5239	(904) 778–5194 778–5239
Family Service Center U.S. Naval Air Station Jacksonville, FL 32212-5000	942–5706 942–2766	(904) 772–5706 772–2766
Family Service Center U.S. Naval Air Station Key West, FL 33040	483–4200/1/2	(305) 294–5760
Family Service Center U.S. Naval Station Mayport, FL 32228-5000	960–6600	(904) 241–6600

Address	Military Telephone (AUTOVON)	Commercial Telephone
Family Service Center Human Resource Management Department U.S. Naval Air Station Whiting Field Milton, FL 32570	868–7177	(904) 623–7177 623–7622
Family Service Center Naval Training Center Bldg. 2010 Orlando, FL 32813	791–4144	(305) 646–4144
Family Service Center U.S. Naval Air Station Bldg. 25 Pensacola, FL 32508-5000	922–3393	(904) 452–3393
Family Service Center U.S. Naval Training Center Bldg. 42 Great Lakes, IL 60088-5125	792–3603	(312) 688–3603
Family Service Center NAVSUBBASE (N13) King's Bay, GA 31547	860–4512	(912) 673–4512
Family Service Center U.S. Naval Academy Annapolis, MD 21402-5073	281–2602	(301) 267–2602
Family Service Center Naval Air Station Patuxent River, MD 20670	356–4911	(301) 863–4911
Family Service Center U.S. Naval Air Station Box 66 Brunswick, ME 04011	476–2273	(207) 921–2273
Family Service Center Naval Security Group Activity Box 4093 ATTN: 17 Fort Meade, MD 20755-6845	923–6848	(301) 677–6848

Address	Military Telephone (AUTOVON)	Commercial Telephone
Family Service Center Naval Air Station, Bldg. 41 South Weymouth, MA 02190	955–2581 955–2583	(617) 786–2581 786–2583
Family Service Center U.S. Naval Construction Battalion Center Code 13, Bldg. 29 Gulfport, MS 39501	363–2581	(601) 865–2581
Family Service Center Naval Air Station Box 1 Meridian, MS 39309	446–2360	(601) 679–2360
Family Service Center Naval Support Activity, Code N8 New Orleans, LA 70142	485–2558	(504) 361–2558 361–2648
Family Service Center Chaplain's Office Naval Air Engineering Center Lakehurst, NJ 08733	624–2539	(201) 323–2539
Family Service Center (516) 486–1922 Naval Station New York Bldg. 82-B, Mitchel Manor E. Meadow, NY 11554		
Family Service Center U.S. Naval Station, Code 6 Bldg. 888 Philadelphia, PA 19112	443–5126 443–5127	(215) 897–5126 897–5127
Family Service Center U.S. Naval Education & Training Center Bldg. 71, Code 013 Newport, RI 02840	948–2283 948–2284	(401) 841–2283 841–2284

Address	Military Telephone (AUTOVON)	Commercial Telephone
Family Service Center U.S. Naval Base Charleston, SC 29408-5100	794–6289 794–6250	(803) 743–6289 743–6250
Family Service Center Naval Weapons Station Bldg. 786 Charleston, SC 29408-5100	794–7294	(803) 743–7294
Family Service Center U.S. Naval Air Station (S-770) Millington, TN 38054	966–5075	(901) 872–5075
Family Service Center U.S. Naval Air Station Chase Field Beeville, TX 78103-5000	861–5304	(512) 354–5304
Family Service Center U.S. Naval Air Station Corpus Christi, TX 78419	861–2372 861–3722	(512) 939–2372 939–3722
Family Service Center Naval Air Station, Bldg. 12 Dallas, TX 75211	874–6137	(214) 266–6137
Family Service Center Naval Air Station Kingsville, TX 78363-5000	861–6333	(512) 595–6333 595–6325
Family Service Center 8910 Hampton Blvd. Norfolk, VA 23505-1299	564–2102	(804) 444–2102
Family Service Center U.S. Naval Air Station Oceana, Bldg. 320 Virginia Beach, VA 23460	433–2912	(804) 433–2912
Family Service Center Naval Regional Medical Center Bldg. 206 Portsmouth, VA 23708	FTS 939–5403 Ext. 612/607	(804) 398–5403 Ext. 612/607

Address	Military Telephone (AUTOVON)	Commercial Telephone
Family Service Center Puget Sound Naval Shipyard, Code 810 Bremerton, WA 98314	439–5113	(206) 476–5113
Family Service Center Naval Submarine Base Bangor Bremerton, WA 98315	744–4115 744–4023	(206) 396–4115 396–4023
Family Service Center U.S. Naval Air Station Bldg. 108 Whidbey Island Oak Harbor, WA 98278	820–2903	(206) 257–2903
Family Service Center Naval Amphibious Base Little Creek, Bldg. 3005 Norfolk, VA 23521	680–7213	(804) 464–7213

DIRECTORY FOR NAVY FAMILY SERVICE CENTERS OUTSIDE THE CONTINENTAL UNITED STATES

Family Service Center U.S. Naval Station Box 75 Adak, Alaska FPO Seattle, WA 98791-1275	317–592–8357	(907) 592–8357
Family Service Center U.S. Naval Air Station Public Affairs Bermuda FPO New York 09560	938–6308 938–6627	(809) 293–6308 293–6627
Family Service Center Commander, U.S. Naval Base Box 16 Guam FPO San Francisco 96630	343–2981	

Address	Military Telephone (AUTOVON)	Commercial Telephone
Personal Assistance Development Department U.S. Naval Air Station, Bldg. 1890 Barbers Point, HI 96862	684–7198/7290	(808) 684–7198 684–7290
Personal Assistance Center U.S. Naval Station Box 9, Code 60 Pearl Harbor, HI 96860	474–1256 474–1257	(808) 474–1256
Family Service Center NAVCAMSEASTPAC Wahiawa, HI 96786	453–5539	(808) 653–5539
Family Service Center U.S. Naval Station Keflavik, Iceland FPO New York 09571	450–4401	(011) 354–25 Ext. 4401
Family Service Center U.S. Naval Support Activity Detachment FPO New York 09522-1003	625–0111 Ext. 4797/8/9	Gaeta, Italy (0771) 465715/ 465842
Family Service Center NAVSUPPO FPO New York 09533	726–1110 Ext. 205/6	La Maddalena, Italy
Family Service Center U.S. Naval Support Activity Box 53 FPO New York 09521	625–0111 Ext. 4808/30	Naples, Italy (081) 724–4808 724–4830
Family Service Center Commander, Fleet Activities Box 1 FPO Seattle, WA 98762	234–6716	Yokosuka, Japan (468) 234–6716
Family Service Center Naval Air Facility Box 32 FPO Seattle, WA 98767	228–3241	Atsugi, Japan

Address	Military Telephone (AUTOVON)	Commercial Telephone
Joint Marine Corps/ Navy Family Service Center Marine Corps Base Camp S.D. Butler FPO Seattle, WA 98773	634–3554 634–3506	Okinawa
Family Service Center U.S. Naval Station Guantanamo Bay, Cuba Box 25 FBPO Norfolk, VA 23593	723–3960 Ext. 4141/4153	011–53–99–4141 011–53–99–4153
Family Service Center U.S. Naval Station, Box 2 FPO San Francisco 96651-1000	884–3458 3700	Subic Bay, PR
Family Service Center U.S. Naval Station FPO Miami, FL 34061	282–4106	Panama
Family Service Center U.S. Naval Station, Box 3591 Roosevelt Roads, Puerto Rico 00635	831–5377 5420	(809) 865–2000
Family Service Center U.S. Naval Station Box 2 FPO New York 09540-1075	727–1110 Ext. 7231	Rota, Spain (345) 686–2440 Ext. 7231
Family Service Center U.S. Naval Support Activity Holy Loch FPO New York 09514-1008	221–8634	United Kingdom (011) 44–369–4273 (011) 44–369–4284
Family Service Center U.S. Naval Air Station FPO NY 09523	624–4291 624–4292 624–4293	Sigonella, Italy (399) 556–4291 556–4292 556–4293
Family Support Center 487th CSG/FSC APO NY 09694		

Address	Military Telephone (AUTOVON)	Commercial Telephone

DIRECTORY FOR MARINE CORPS FAMILY SERVICE CENTERS INSIDE AND OUTSIDE THE CONTINENTAL UNITED STATES

Address	Military Telephone (AUTOVON)	Commercial Telephone
Commanding General ATTN: Family Service Center Marine Corps Base Camp Lejeune, NC 28542-5023	484–1362	(919) 451–1362
Commanding General ATTN: Family Service Center Marine Corps Base Camp Pendleton, CA 92055-5023	365–5361	(619) 725–5361
Commanding General ATTN: Family Service Center Marine Corps Air Ground Combat Center Twentynine Palms, CA 92278-5023	952–6344	(619) 368–6344
Commanding General ATTN: Family Service Center Marine Corps Development and Education Command Quantico, VA 22134-5023	278–2659	(703) 640–2659
Commanding General ATTN: Family Service Center Marine Corps Air Station Cherry Point, NC 28533-5023	582–5856	(919) 466–5856
Commanding General ATTN: Family Service Center Marine Corps Air Station, El Toro Santa Ana, CA 92709-5023	997–2771	(714) 651–2771
Commanding General ATTN: Family Service Center Marine Corps Recruit Depot/WRR San Diego, CA 92140-5023	957–4357	(619) 225–4357

Address	Military Telephone (AUTOVON)	Commercial Telephone
Commanding General ATTN: Family Service Center Marine Corps Air Station Iwakuni, Japan FPO Seattle, WA 98764-5023	236–3070	Base Operator (0827) 21-4171 Ext. 3070
Commanding General ATTN: Family Service Center Marine Corps Recruit Depot/ERR Parris Island, SC 29905-5023	832–3791	(803) 525–3791
Commanding General ATTN: Family Service Center Marine Corps Logistics Base Barstow, CA 92311-5023	282–6533	(619) 577–6533 577–6853
Commanding General ATTN: Family Service Center Marine Corps Logistics Base Albany, GA 31704-5023	460–5276/7	(912) 439–5276 439–5277
Commanding Officer ATTN: Family Service Center Marine Corps Air Station Kaneohe Bay, HI 96863-5023		(808) 257–2128 257–2129 257–3168
Commanding Officer ATTN: Family Service Center Marine Corps Air Station Beaufort, SC 29902-5023	832–7351	(803) 846–7351
Commanding Officer ATTN: Family Service Center Marine Corps Air Station Yuma, AZ 85369-5023	951–3421	(602) 726–3421
Commanding Officer ATTN: Family Service Center HQ Battalion, HQMC, Henderson Hall Arlington, VA 22124-5023	224–5064	(202) 694–5064 694–5065 694–4876

Address	Military Telephone (AUTOVON)	Commercial Telephone
Commanding Officer ATTN: Family Service Center Marine Corps Base Camp Smedley D. Butler FPO Seattle, WA 98773-5023		634-3506
Commanding Officer ATTN: Family Service Center Marine Corps Finance Center Kansas City, MO 64197-5023	465–7210 465–7106 465–7107 465–7155	(816) 926–7210 926–7106 926–7107 926–7155
Commanding Officer ATTN: Family Service Center Marine Corps Air Station Tustin, CA 92710-5023	997–7266	(714) 651–7266
Commanding Officer ATTN: Family Service Center Marine Corps Air Station, New River Jacksonville, NC 28542-5023	484–6110 484–6185 484–6069	(919) 451–6110 451–6185 451–6069
Military Family Support Center 6501 Loisdale Court, Suite 1107 Springfield, VA 22150		(703) 922–7671 Toll Free 1–800–336–4592 (except Virginia)

Index

About the Author

Deborah S. Bass, MSW, is a professional consultant to government and private organizations on the design, implementation, management, and evaluation of health and human services. Until January 1990, when she became a consultant, she had worked 16 years in government. Her government experience included planning, policy development, administration, research, and management for the Department of Health and Human Services. She also served as the Director of the Executive Secretariat for the Assistant Secretary for Human Development Services. In that capacity, she was responsible for workload management and policy and program review of final products for the Assistant Secretary.

Ms. Bass has done voluntary professional work with committees and management of professional and voluntary organizations. She currently serves on the National Program Committee of the National Association of Social Workers. She organized, and led, from 1986 to 1990, the Federal Social Workers Consortium, a network for social workers employed by the federal government. She is particularly interested in the development of integrated social policy and programs to ensure that individuals and families achieve their maximum level of functioning. She has written several articles and occasional papers on care-related topics.